Library of
Davidson College

VOID

SEVEN ROMAN STATESMEN

BUST OF JULIUS CÆSAR.
From the Museum at Naples.

SEVEN ROMAN STATESMEN OF THE LATER REPUBLIC

THE GRACCHI. SULLA. CRASSUS
CATO. POMPEY. CÆSAR.

BY

Sir CHARLES OMAN

*WITH PORTRAITS AND
ILLUSTRATIONS*

Essay Index Reprint Series

 BOOKS FOR LIBRARIES PRESS
FREEPORT, NEW YORK

First Published 1902
Reprinted 1971

937.05
O54s
1971

INTERNATIONAL STANDARD BOOK NUMBER:
0-8369-2288-3

Replacement
LIBRARY OF CONGRESS CATALOG CARD NUMBER:
75-156699

PRINTED IN THE UNITED STATES OF AMERICA

PREFACE

THERE are several general histories of the decline and fall of the Roman Republic, dealing with its political and constitutional aspects. This little book is not a history, but a series of studies of the leading men of the century, intended to show the importance of the personal element in those miserable days of storm and stress. It is thus, I think, that their true meaning is best brought out.

It is a pleasant duty to express the gratitude which I owe to my friend Mr. J. Wells, of Wadham College, for having been good enough to read through my proofs, and to make a great number of valuable suggestions, which I have done my best to carry out.

I have also to thank the Authorities of the British Museum Coin-Room (and especially Mr. G. F. Hill) for the kindness with which they aided me in selecting the Roman coins for my three plates of illustrations.

C. OMAN.

NAPLES, *April* 11, 1902.

SEVEN ROMAN STATESMEN

CHAPTER I

THE LATER DAYS OF THE ROMAN REPUBLIC

THERE was a time, not so very long ago, when the taunt was true that history was written as if it were a mere string of anecdotal biographies of great men. But for the last forty years the pendulum has been swinging so much in the other direction, that it has become necessary to enforce the lesson that the biographies of great men are, after all, a most important part of history. It is well to have conceptions of the streams of tendency and the typical developments of every age, but the blessed word "evolution" will not account for everything, and it is absurd to neglect the influence of the great personalities.

Roman history in particular has been so much treated of late years as a mere example of constitutional growth and degeneration, or as a bundle of interesting administrative and legal details, that it seems not out of place to recall that other aspect of it which was more familiar to elder generations, and to look at it for a moment from the personal and biographical point of view, with Plutarch before us as well as Mommsen and Marquardt's *Staatsrecht* and *Staatsverwaltung*.

This is all the more rational because in the last century of the Roman Republic we find ourselves in a time of dominating personalities. In Rome's earlier days this

2 LATER DAYS OF THE ROMAN REPUBLIC

was conspicuously not the case, and her history was (as has been truly said) the history of great achievements done by men who were themselves not great. But from the Gracchi onward we come to a period in which individuals make and mar the course of the times, when the doings of a Sulla and a Cæsar, or even of a Marius and a Pompey, form the main determining element in the history of the day.

From the end of the Second Punic War down to the time of the Gracchi, Roman history is very monotonous and uninteresting to the reader. It is little more than the record of the haphazard building up of an empire, by the unintentional and unsystematic conquest of various disconnected districts round the Mediterranean. The wars are uninteresting, because they are waged by men who are little more than names to us; the commander, be he a Flamininus or a Mummius, disappears from the historical stage when his consulship is over, and is lost to view once more in the ranks of an impersonal senate. Even the younger Scipio Africanus, who has to serve as a hero in these times for want of a better, soon palls upon us; he stays in our mind only as a vague impersonation of civic virtue and somewhat cold-blooded moderation.

After B.C. 133 all is different; at last we have living, interesting, individual men to deal with; the names of Tiberius Gracchus, or Sulla, or Cæsar are not remembered merely as connected with files of laws or lists of battles. At the same time both the internal and the external history of Rome becomes of absorbing interest. Externally the question arises whether the sporadic and ill-compacted empire built up in the last hundred years shall endure, or whether it shall be swept away by the brute force of the Cimbri and Teutons, or carved in two by Mithradates. Looking at the growing imbecility of Roman generals in that day, and the growing deterioration of Roman armies, it is not too much to say that, but for the intervention of two great personalities, the Roman Empire might have been swept away. If Marius had not appeared, a few more generals like Mallius and Caepio would have let the Cimbri and Teutons into Central Italy, and the exploits of Alaric in A.D. 410 might have been perpetrated by his remote ancestors. Similarly, but for Sulla the Nearer East might perchance have passed back, seven hundred years before the appointed time, into the hands of Oriental rulers, and have shared the fate which overtook Hellenistic Babylon and Bactria, by losing its touch with Western civilisation under a dynasty almost as thinly veneered with Greek culture as the Parthian Arsacidæ or the Bactrian Scyths.

Internally the problems of Roman history during this period are quite as interesting. While the imperial city was fighting abroad, to maintain her existence and her suzerainty over the whole Mediterranean basin, she was being torn at home by a great constitutional struggle which pierced to the very roots of her being. This was the problem of determining with whom should reside for the future sovereignty, in the technical sense of the word, *i.e.* the actual supreme voice in the administration and law-making of the City and the Empire.

For the last two centuries there had existed a practical compromise between the theoretical omnipotence of the Public Assembly and the actual conduct of affairs by the Senate. This compromise was no longer possible, because Rome had developed from a city-state into an imperial state. Neither the Comitia nor the Senate was really competent to rule the new empire which they had acquired. If there was anything more preposterous than the theory of the Optimates (I mean that the government of the Roman world should be conducted by a small ring of narrow-minded noble families), it was certainly the

4 LATER DAYS OF THE ROMAN REPUBLIC

opposite theory of the Democrats—that the mixed multitude of paupers and aliens into which the Comitia was fast degenerating, should supersede the senatorial oligarchy as administrators of the Empire. Complicated with this great constitutional question, as to where sovereignty should reside at Rome, were a number of social and economic questions, arising from the fact that the new commercial conditions of the Mediterranean world, which followed from the Roman conquests, were bringing about the ruin of the old farmer class which had for so many centuries formed the backbone of the state.

The details of the sporadic and never-ending wars in Spain, Macedonia, and the Hellenic East, which cover the period B.C. 200-140, hide the unwritten history of the most important changes in the social and economic conditions of Italy. In B.C. 200 Rome was still in the main a city-state of the old type, though she had already begun to acquire important transmarine domains. She was still a self-supporting agricultural community, feeding herself on home-grown corn. Moreover, she might still be described as a narrow-minded purely Italian town, little affected as yet, either in blood or in thought, by external influences. The elder Cato, with all his hard practical common sense, his stolidity, his passion for the life of the farm, and his contempt for the foreigner, was the typical Roman of that generation. By the last years of his old age he had seen a new world grow up, and complained that he was living in a city which he no longer understood.

For by B.C. 140 Rome was transformed. She was indubitably an imperial state, though she tried to shirk as long as possible the responsibilities of empire. Her population was no longer mainly a race of farmers dwelling on their own narrow acres; it was rapidly becoming divorced from the soil, and degenerating into a city-bred proletariate fed from abroad. Above all, Rome had to a large extent become cosmopolitan, having absorbed much Greek, or rather Græco-Asiatic, culture and philosophy, and still more of Hellenistic luxury and demoralisation. The very blood of the people was getting largely diluted with a foreign strain, owing to the wholesale manumission of slaves.

While Rome had been transformed, her constitution remained perfectly unchanged, and the rude administrative machinery which had sufficed to manage a small community of farmers living close around the walls of the city, was being applied with a rigid and stupid formalism to the government of a widely extended empire.

Down to the Second Punic War, Rome had not acquired any provinces that tried very seriously her power to govern. Sicily and Sardinia were close at hand, in ready and constant communication with the city. They were actually visible from the headlands of Italy—mere broken-off fragments of the peninsula. An order could without much difficulty reach them in a few days: the Senate and People could make their will felt by governors and generals in districts so close to themselves.

The serious trial of the old municipal system of government, as applicable to the administration of distant dependencies, came after the acquisition of the Carthaginian dominions in Spain at the end of the Second Punic War. Separated from Italy by the still unsubdued coast-land of Southern Gaul, Spain could only be reached by a long sea voyage, which the Roman never loved, and which he rigidly eschewed at certain seasons of the year. The proconsuls in Spain got from the first a free hand such as no previous Roman governor had possessed.

It was a long time before any other provinces were added to the over-seas empire of the Senate and People. But at last they came, Macedonia and Africa both in 146,

Asia in 133. It was the acquisition of these distant possessions that broke down the ancient power of the Senate to control the doings of the provincial magistrates. It was impossible to maintain a constant supervision over a governor at Gades, or Thessalonica, or Ephesus, or to get at him within any reasonable space of time. He had to be left very much to his own inspirations. It was but natural that the more ambitious proconsuls came to take advantage of this fact, and began to make or break treaties, to enter into wars, and to make conquests at their good pleasure. The Senate was sometimes provoked into disowning and annulling their doings, but not very often: when it did, the reason was not always creditable—as witness the case of Mancinus at Numantia.

Roughly, then, it may be said that by the third quarter of the second century before Christ, Rome had acquired an empire, but refused to take up any of the responsibilities of empire. The Senate still wished to control everything, but they could no more do so efficiently, owing to the mere difficulties of geographical distance, than in the eighteenth century the East India Company's directors could control Clive or Warren Hastings. The proconsuls, on the other hand, could govern, but each only for his short year of office, and the work of each successor generally (and often deliberately) undid the work of his predecessor.

The responsibilities of empire, of which we have made mention were, in the main, threefold. The first was to provide good government within the provinces; this the Roman Republic notoriously failed to secure. The constitution imposed on each conquered region, by the senatorial commission which drew up the *lex provinciæ* after its annexation, was often wisely designed and reasonable. But when once it was formulated, there was no proper machinery for modifying it in accordance with the neces-

MISGOVERNMENT OF THE PROCONSULS 7

sities of the times, or even for seeing that the proconsul did not violate its spirit by arbitrary tampering with the *edictum tralaticium*, the supplementary code which he could issue and vary at his own pleasure. All through the second century the control of the Senate was growing weaker, and it seemed that the wish as well as the power to check misgovernment was disappearing. The natural result was that the type of proconsul steadily deteriorated, as the probability of impunity for abuse of authority grew greater. Expedients like the establishment of the special court *De Repetundis* for the repression of financial maladministration were practically useless. To be effective, it would have required an active public prosecutor, ready to investigate every returning magistrate's record, and a bench of judges absolutely beyond the breath of suspicion. But Roman usage entrusted all prosecutions to private initiative, and the court which tried the accused was so much swayed by personal and party bias that from the first there were scandals in its working. When a condemnation did occur, it was generally whispered that the convicted magistrate was suffering for some old political escapade at home, rather than for mere maladministration abroad.

The second of the responsibilities of empire, which Rome seemed unable to discharge, was the duty of keeping the police of the high seas and suppressing piracy. This task had in earlier centuries been to some extent discharged by the old naval powers—Carthage in the west, Macedon and Egypt in the east. Rome had now destroyed Carthage and Macedon, and the Ptolemies had sunk into hopeless imbecility and decay. The Romans would not keep up a permanent national fleet, both because it was expensive, and because they themselves disliked the sea. Hence the Mediterranean swarmed with pirates in a way that had never before been seen. The poorer and wilder maritime races took to piracy *en masse*, and almost strangled commerce. The Balearic Islanders swept the western seas; the unsubdued Dalmatians, the Adriatic; the Cretans, the Ægean; the Pamphylians and Cilicians—the most numerous and reckless of all these bands—had almost taken possession of the waters of the Levant. Their pirate squadrons went out a hundred vessels strong, levied blackmail on whole regions, and often made descents on cities within the boundaries of the Roman empire. The Senate only resented their outrages by fits and starts. If they grew too insolent, a squadron was sometimes sent against them, but it was seldom composed of vessels equipped and manned from Italy. The ordinary method was to requisition a fleet from the maritime allies of the state, who rendered unwilling and inefficient service. Hence it came to pass that though many Roman expeditions had been sent against the pirates, and several commanders had celebrated triumphs over them, the evil was not removed, and the Mediterranean did not become really safe for imperial commerce till the great naval campaign of Pompey in B.C. 67.

The third great responsibility which the Romans assumed, when they annexed great and remote provinces, was that of protecting the civilised world from the outer barbarian. The conquests of Spain and Macedonia made them the neighbours of scores of wild tribes, whom the Carthaginians in the one and the kings of the house of Antigonus in the other peninsula had been wont to drive back and to keep in check. The Roman, their heir by right of conquest, discharged this duty very spasmodically and inefficiently. The main reason for this was the deep-rooted dislike of distant and prolonged foreign service among the inhabitants of Italy. The people had comprehended, fifty years before, the need for universal conscription and long service in such crises as the Second

Punic War. They could not see things in the same light when there was a call for troops to keep back Pæonian or Illyrian raids on Upper Macedon, or Lusitanian raids on Baetica. They grumbled and rioted every time that a new legion had to be raised. This made the Senate chary of calling out conscripts, or keeping them long on foreign service. But finally, the crisis always grew so dangerous that the hated levy had at last to be raised. Nothing can better illustrate the dislike of the Roman populace for the lingering and bloody wars of Spain, than the fact that twice in the middle years of the century (in 151 and in 138 B.C.) tribunes actually arrested and imprisoned consuls who persisted in enforcing the conscription, when public opinion was adverse to a new Spanish campaign. Yet the condition of the Roman borders in the Iberian peninsula was undoubtedly such that these levies were necessary. The Celtiberian and Lusitanian tribes were so warlike and turbulent that the frontier could never stand still. Raids had to be punished by retaliatory expeditions. The tribe that had been chastised would not remain quiet till it had been actually annexed; and so the process went on, for beyond each marauding clan lay another and a fiercer robber tribe. The whole peninsula was like the Afridi and Waziri frontier of North-Western India at the present day, and by advancing their boundary-marks the Romans only changed the names of their enemies. There was no finality till the Atlantic was reached, and the last Galician and Cantabrian mountaineers maintained their ferocious independence till the days of Julius Cæsar and Augustus. In the Balkan peninsula the state of affairs was much the same under the later Republic, though the Triballi and Scordisci and Pæonians were not such formidable foes as the Spaniards. Macedon was never really free from northern inroads till the days of the empire. And in the East, when annexations had once begun in Asia, similar troubles, first with Galatians and Isaurians, and later with the formidable horse-bowmen of Parthia, came pouring in upon the perplexed senatorial oligarchy, which tried to govern an empire without an imperial outfit of army, navy, and civil service.

The Roman world, in short, was badly governed and badly defended : the provinces were steadily decreasing in wealth and resources from the moment that they were annexed. And since Italy and Rome herself were—as we shall see—tending to internal decay, though certain individual Romans and Italians were drawing huge profits from the newly acquired empire, the whole Mediterranean world seemed doomed to retrogression and collapse. It is possible that the Republic might have been demolished, if there had arisen against it any really formidable and well-equipped enemy. But the outer world was singularly destitute of strong men at this period. Jugurtha and Mithradates, in spite of all the trouble that they gave, were very third-rate personalities. And the one truly dangerous foe that marched against Rome during the last century of the Republic—the Cimbri and Teutons—represented mere brute force unguided by brains and strategy. At the last moment, when they had actually passed the Alps, they were annihilated by a general who possessed the art of improvising and handling a great army. It is curious to speculate what might have happened if not Marius, but some imbecile Optimate of the type of his predecessors Mallius and Caepio, had been in command at Aquae Sextiae or on the Raudian Plain. But Europe escaped the premature coming of the Dark Ages, and the black cloud of barbarism from the north having passed away, the men of the later Republic were left free to work out their own problems in their own unhappy way, in sedition, conspiracy, civil war, and proscription, till the

THE SUCCESSION OF STATESMEN

coming of that great personality who showed the way—a bad way at the best—out of the hopeless deadlock into which Rome had fallen.

But ere Julius Cæsar appeared there were not one but many Romans who saw well enough that the Roman world was out of joint, and tried, each in his more or less futile fashion, to set it right. With some of these statesmen it is our task to deal. Their successive biographies show well enough the course of the whole history of the later Republic; there is no gap between man and man; Sulla as a boy may have witnessed the violent end of Caius Gracchus: Julius Cæsar as a boy did certainly witness and well-nigh suffer in the proscriptions of Sulla. The seven lives between them completely cover the last century of Rome's *ancien régime*.

CHAPTER II

TIBERIUS GRACCHUS

By the third quarter of the second century before Christ, the contradiction between the new conditions of Roman life and the old forms of Roman government had grown so glaring, that even the conservative Roman mind saw that the present state of things could not endure much longer. The two problems which had forced themselves to the front needed solution. What was to be done to adapt the constitution to the new needs of empire?—Was the Senate or the Public Assembly to rule the world, and by what machinery? And, secondly, how was the state to deal with the unfortunate fact that the new commercial conditions of the Mediterranean countries, brought about by the Roman conquests, were beginning to ruin Italian agriculture and to thin out the farmers who formed the backbone of the old Roman race.

A single man was fated to bring forward both these questions, to formulate them in the most contentious shapes possible, to confuse their issues in the most inextricable fashion, and to leave a heritage of strife behind him for the next three generations of Romans.

Tiberius Gracchus is one of the most striking instances in history of the amount of evil that can be brought about by a thoroughly honest and well-meaning man, who is so entirely convinced of the righteousness of his own intentions and the wisdom of his own measures, that he is driven to regard any one who strives to hinder him as not only foolish but morally wicked. The type of exalted

THE YOUTH OF TIBERIUS

doctrinaire who exclaims that any constitutional check that hinders his plans must be swept away without further inquiry, that every political opponent is a bad man who must be crushed, has been known in many lands and many ages, from ancient Greece down to the France of the Revolution. But in Rome such a figure was an exception; the stolid conservatism, the reverence for *mos majorum*, the dislike for abstract political speculation which marked the race, were against the development of such a frame of mind. The reformers of the past had been content to work slowly, to introduce changes by adding small rags and patches to the constitution, or by inventing transparent legal fictions, which gained the practical point, while leaving the theory of the law that they were attacking apparently untouched. The earnest doctrinaire, all in a hurry and perfectly regardless of ancestral landmarks, was as incomprehensible as he was distasteful to the average Roman mind. It is well to remember the delightful comment of the elder Cato, who having been induced in his old age to read some of Plato's political dialogues, gravely remarked "that this Socrates seems to have been a prating seditious fellow, who suffered, rightly enough, for having tried to undermine the ancient customs of the state, and to teach young men to hold opinions at variance with the laws."

Tiberius Gracchus was one of those unfortunate persons who are from their earliest years held up as models, and serve to point the moral and adorn the tale for their young contemporaries, till they are led on to entertain the strongest views as to their own impeccability and infallibility. The cluster of stories which Plutarch gives us to illustrate the youth of the Gracchi are almost enough by themselves to explain Tiberius's after career. He was born with every advantage of rank and wealth; he had a quick intelligence and a handsome face. But he was cursed with a mother (a very superior woman, said every voice in Rome), who was always reminding him that he was the grandson of Scipio the elder, and asking, "How long am I to be called the daughter of Africanus and not the mother of the Gracchi?" All the domestic circle marked him off from early youth as one from whom something great was expected. His very tutor made him his moral touchstone. "If Tiberius said that a thing was right," observed this good man, "right of course it must be." When he grew up, the world conspired to do him honour. He was made an augur far below the usual age. The most respected member of the Senate, chancing to lie next him at a dinner-party, offered him his daughter's hand in marriage without waiting to be asked. When Appius came home that night, he called out to his wife, as soon as he was inside the door, that he had betrothed their daughter. "Why in such a hurry," asked the lady, "unless indeed you chance to have got Tiberius Gracchus for her?" Clearly public opinion, among the matrons of Rome who were blessed with marriageable daughters, looked upon the young man as the most eligible *parti* in the city.

Tiberius saw his first military service in Africa during the Third Punic War. He was taken out under the best possible auspices, as one of the aides-de-camp of his brother-in-law, the younger Scipio Africanus. The general's kinsman was offered and took every opportunity for distinction. He returned with the decoration of a mural crown, and the esteem, as we are told, of the whole army. When he first obtained a magistracy and went to Spain as quaestor to the Consul Mancinus, chance gave him an utterly unexpected opportunity of saving a Roman army from destruction (B.C. 137). The Numantines having defeated and surrounded the consul, offered to treat for a definitive peace, not with Mancinus, but with Gracchus,

TIBERIUS AT NUMANTIA

the reason being that the young quaestor's father had enjoyed a great name for good faith and justice among the Spaniards. Tiberius drew up an equitable treaty, which was sworn to by both sides, and the army was allowed to depart. It was no fault of his if the Senate afterwards refused to ratify the agreement, and sent Mancinus in chains to Numantia. He was only remembered as the saviour of the lives of the defeated legions, and all the ignominy of the defeat was laid upon the consul.

If Tiberius had been merely fortunate and virtuous, he might have gone through life with honour and success, have gained his consulship, celebrated his triumph, and have been buried in peace in the tomb of his ancestors. Unhappily for himself and for Rome, he had enough brains to see that the times were out of joint, enough heart to feel for the misfortunes of his countrymen, enough conscience to refuse to leave things alone and take the easy path to success that lay before him, and enough self-confidence to think that he was foreordained by the gods to set all to rights. Such was the genius of the first of Rome's many self-constituted saviours of society.

The particular evil which had struck the eye of Tiberius, and which started him upon his crusade, was the terrible and rapid decline in the numbers of the free agricultural population which had been setting in for the last thirty years. He had at first no constitutional reforms in his head, but merely economic ones. Passing through Etruria on his way to Spain, as we are told, he saw no one working in the fields but slaves; tillage seemed to be dying out and the free farmer to have disappeared. The sight shocked him, and he pondered deeply over it during the leisure hours of his Spanish campaign. He learnt by inquiry that the same thing was to be seen in many other parts of Italy. Doubtless the discontented conscripts whom he had to command, told him all the woes of the poor freeholder in the days when farming had ceased to pay. At any rate, when he settled down once more in Rome, he imagined that he had probed to the bottom the existing distress and its causes, and that he had hit upon the necessary remedies.

The evils from which Italy, or rather Roman Italy, was suffering in B.C. 134 were much the same as those through which rural England has been passing during the last twenty years—the phenomenon that is vaguely called "agricultural depression." It was marked by a permanent decrease in the selling value of corn, a widespread turning of arable land into pasture, so that tillage seemed almost to have ceased in certain districts, and a slow but sure shrinkage in the numbers of the free farming population who "lived by the land."

It is usual for historians to trace the decline of Italian agriculture to various causes which began to operate as far back as the Second Punic War—to the ravages of Hannibal, the awful drain of life during his continuance in the peninsula, and after his departure to the tribute of blood levied for the never-ending and disastrous Spanish campaigns.

On the whole, too much is made of these causes. If farming is really paying, it suffers less than might be expected from a protracted war, unless indeed that war is waged within the country-side itself. Hannibal had departed seventy years before, and in a healthy state of agriculture the traces of his sojourn would long have disappeared. The Spanish and other wars of the next generation, waged far away, would not have sufficed to ruin rural Italy. As a matter of fact, the drain of life did not, for two generations after Zama, even affect the natural increase of population. The number of land-holding Roman citizens fit to bear arms went rapidly up from the end of the Punic Wars down to B.C. 159. Attaining its maximum in that year, it began very slowly but steadily to decrease. In 159 there were 338,000 *assidui*; in 154 there were 324,000; in 147, 322,000. If Hannibal did not succeed in permanently bringing down the number of Roman freeholders, we shall not be persuaded that Viriathus and the Numantines succeeded in doing so. It was really economic changes, in a time of comparative peace, that were doing the mischief. Otherwise the Roman farmer, like the British farmer in the golden days of the struggle with Napoleon, might have prayed for "a bloody war and a wet harvest," as the things most likely to send up wheat to 120s. the quarter.

Again, it is often said that the free farming class was beginning to decline because of the growth in Italy of great landed estates—the *latifundia*, worked by chain-gangs of Eastern slaves, of which we hear so many complaints. We are assured that the freeholders decayed because of the perverse wickedness of the great capitalists, who insisted on buying out their smaller neighbours, or on ousting them by means of litigation, or even by that rougher sort of process which Ahab of old applied to Naboth. All this, we are told, they did in order that they might supplant the freeholder by their gangs of Asiatic slaves. Any theory based on the hypothesis that rich men are gratuitously and perversely wicked has found eager acceptance in certain quarters ever since history began. When the land is suffering from poverty and depression, it is always popular to lay the blame on the backs of tangible and obvious individuals, rather than to search for obscure economic causes.

To us it seems that the growth of the *latifundia* and the slave-gangs was the effect, and not the cause, of the decay of the free population in the Italy of B.C. 155–135.

B

The fact simply was that under the stress of foreign competition corn-growing was ceasing to pay in many parts of the peninsula. There is a point at which the freeholder, even if he be as frugal as the old Roman farmer, and even if he lives mainly by the consumption of his own produce, will refuse to stop any longer on the soil, more especially when the alternative is not emigration to the Far West, but removal to the capital, with all its urban pleasures, its cheap food, and its opportunities of living without the back-breaking toil of plough and mattock.

Those who wish to persuade us that the *latifundia* drove out the freeholder have always neglected to explain one well-known economic fact. Cultivation by slave labour is notoriously wasteful and dear. The yeoman and his family, working for themselves, will get much more out of a farm than will a gang of slaves. The compulsory labourer, even under the lash, always succeeds in putting in much less rapid, willing, and thorough work than the freeman. Why then should the capitalist be so eager to buy out the farmer, if immediately on purchase the productive value of the purchased land went down? Surely he would have found better use for his money.

The truth seems to be rather that the yeoman was beginning, about the year B.C. 160, to find that his farm no longer paid, and was eager to get rid of it. He sold it to the capitalist at a ruinous sacrifice, since he was simply anxious to move on at any price. If the buyer threw several farms together, and worked them by cheap slaves in a ruthless way, he might make a profit for a time. Slave-labour on the Roman system had just one advantage—that the slave was the only unit in the population; he had no wife or children to keep, and every pair of hands represented only one mouth. Moreover, he had no standard of comfort whatever; he had to live as his master chose, herded together in dungeon-dormitories, half clothed and half starved, and sold, or left to die, the moment that he showed signs of wear and tear. The dispossessed yeoman had, at any rate, lived on a higher scale than this; he had wife and family to keep, and, however frugal his fare and garb, they were at least better than those of the slave. The farm, if bought at a sufficiently low figure, might be able to pay the capitalist long after it had ceased to pay the freeholder.

But it was only exceptionally that the new acquirers of the yeomen's homesteads tried to keep the land under tillage. It was much more common to throw many small holdings into a vast ranche or sheep-farm, worked by a few slave-herdsmen. Cattle and sheep, kept on a large scale, could pay, long after corn had become a hopeless failure. For while the Roman market was flooded with foreign wheat, there was no such competition in the matter of live stock. Ancient merchant ships were not large, swift, or commodious enough for the transport of beasts on an extensive scale. Hence the Italian cattle-breeder need not fear provincial or foreign competition in the local market. Beef and mutton, hides and wool, might still be grown at a profit, long after barley and wheat had been given up. Hence came the rise of the great ranches of Southern Italy which figure in so many descriptions.

That Italian agriculture was flagging in the middle years of the second century, even in quarters where the capitalist did not intervene, is quite clear. Cato in his younger days had practised farming for profit; in his old age he had to confess that it had become more interesting than lucrative; he kept up his farms by way of amusement, but put his spare capital into the purchase of house property, factories, woods, and baths. When Rome had once become acknowledged as the capital of the Mediterranean world, merchandise of all kinds had begun to

come to her market on a scale that had been unknown in
the third century. And of the imports that were poured
in from abroad, corn was one of the most prominent. The
city was only a few miles from the sea, and nothing
was simpler than to deliver this easily-packed commodity
at Ostia, or even to send it up the Tiber to the very doors
of the urban granaries. There were many countries
where wheat could be grown at a far cheaper rate than
in Central Italy. But it was not merely with the
speculative importer from Spain, Africa, or Egypt, that
the farmers of the Latin and Etruscan Campagna had now
to compete. Simple free trade was not their only bane.
They had also to face the state as a rival seller; the
tithe-corn of Sicily from the *civitates decumanae*, who paid
their tribute in kind instead of in money, was annually
shot upon the Roman market, and the state had to get
rid of it at what price it could. Experience shows that a
Government which sells always receives less than the ruling
rate for the commodity of which it is trying to get rid.
The Sicilian corn was purchased by the rich grain dealers
of Rome at a quotation which enabled them to put it upon
the market at an absurdly low figure. The Senate and
the urban populace did not care; there was a vague
notion abroad that if the corn did go cheap, it was Roman
citizens who bought it, and Roman citizens ought to get
as much as possible of the profits of Empire out of the
"*praedia populi Romani.*" Indeed, the city mob were
already clamouring for distributions of corn when any
excuse, adequate or inadequate, could be found.

It is scarcely necessary to point out the effect on
the agricultural classes of Central Italy of the appearance
of such huge masses of cheap corn in the great central
market of the capital. Mere foreign competitions would
have been very bad for them, but the interference of the
state as a seller made things hopeless. It is true that the

Roman farmer grew corn for his own consumption no less than for the purpose of selling it in the local market. This fact tended to make the working of the economic crisis slower. But the permanent fall in prices descended like a deadly blight on all the regions which had been wont to supply the city. It is necessary to remember, however, that it was not all Italy which was affected. The economic crisis mainly touched those regions which in older days had been the home-farm of the Roman people—the Latin and South-Etruscan lands. But it was felt also in Apulia and Lucania, where the majority of the soil was in Roman hands, owing to the confiscations that had followed the Hannibalic War. And Northern Etruria seems also to have suffered; it was a district which even in early days had been in the hands of great landholders who worked their farms with serfs, and now the serfs were being replaced by foreign slaves.

On the other hand, we must bear in mind that there were many parts of Italy where the agricultural depression does not seem to have been so much felt. Forty years later the Social War reveals to us the existence of a numerous free agricultural population all over the mountain-regions of the Apennines—Samnium, Picenum, the Marsian territory, and the rest. The Po valley in the north, too, was so fertile that it could compete in its own markets with any foreign seller. This region seems to have remained in a satisfactory economic condition long after depopulation began farther south. Roughly speaking, we may say that the economic crisis affected the land immediately round Rome, and certain other regions which were mainly in Roman hands. The Italian allies as yet suffered comparatively little; if they were sufficiently remote from the suzerain city, in a region of mountains and bad roads, they suffered not at all: for the fatal foreign corn could not creep among them on mule-back over the passes, so as to compete with the local produce. In many states the old economic conditions of the third century continued to prevail even down to the Social War. Rome's policy unconsciously helped them to survive; she jealously kept the Italians isolated, and excluded them from the profits of the Empire, with the result that they remained torpid but well preserved in their remote valleys.

Under the stress of the competition of cheap foreign corn, the rural population of the regions round Rome had to displace itself, much in the same way as the rural population of nineteenth-century England. Nowadays such folks take refuge in emigration to America or Australia, or still more frequently drift citywards and are absorbed into the industrial classes. These ways of escape were not so obvious to the Roman of the second century. The idea that the citizen might permanently remove himself from Italy, and settle down on better soil in Spain or Africa—the America and Australia of the ancient world—had not yet become familiar. It seemed abnormal and unpatriotic to a race who still cherished the notion formulated in the statement *omnis peregrinatio sordida est et inhonesta*. Unlike the Greek, the Roman was not content to go abroad for ever; the first great transmarine colony (as we shall see) perished of sheer superstition, and traditionary dislike for a settlement outside the sacred soil of the Peninsula.

Nor could the industrial remedy be fully utilised, owing to the inveterate prejudice against citizens taking to handicrafts—the special portion of the slave and freedman according to Roman ideas. The ruined farmers drifted to Rome, to live on the cheap corn, the doles of patrons, the frequent largesses of the state, and the distributions of candidates for magistracies. These migrants by themselves would have been enough to form the basis for a dangerous mob, but in Rome they mingled with and were demoralised by a far worse element, the great mass of manumitted slaves. The freedmen of the city were precisely the least promising section of the governing people. The slaves who made themselves acceptable to their masters, and won their freedom, were the clever subtle Greeks and Syrians who had served in the households of the nobility, not the barbarian field-hands, whom their owners never saw or regarded. There was a serious danger that Rome might become a Levantine city some day, though she was still far from the generation when men could truly say that "*in Tiberim defluxit Orontes.*"

For agricultural depression, such as there existed in Italy when Tiberius Gracchus first took to politics, there is only one certain remedy. If the citizens will neither emigrate nor turn themselves from agriculture to handicrafts, and if it is absolutely necessary that the farming class should be kept up, there must be Protection. The foreign corn must at all costs be kept out, so that the yeoman may make a margin of profit, and stay by his land. Here lay the one chance for preserving the old balance of classes in the Roman state. But unfortunately for those who had the interests of the farmer at heart, the constitution of Rome rested on a public assembly of citizens massed in the Campus Martius. On any ordinary day of meeting the assembly was entirely composed of the urban populace; it would require some very great matter to induce the farmers of the Campagna to trudge in many miles in order to exercise the franchise. The more distant voters in remoter corners of Italy were practically out of touch with politics altogether Accordingly, the statesman who wished to carry his law before the Comitia had normally to face only the *plebs urbana*. On rare occasions the outvoters might alter the composition of the assembly, but the everyday audience of the orator would consist only of the citizens who dwelt on the spot. How was it possible to propose Protection to such a body? They had come to Rome precisely in order to enjoy the cheap loaf, and they were already clamouring to have it larger and yet cheaper. They would have laughed to scorn any proposal to impose a heavy tax on their corn for the benefit of the rural voters. High patriotic appeals would have had little effect on them. Already, thirty years back, the elder Cato, declaiming in vain against a proposal for an unnecessary distribution of corn, had exclaimed in his wrath, "Citizens, I perceive that it is a difficult task to argue with the belly, because it has no ears." The city mob would never vote for the dear loaf.

The hopeless side of the agrarian problem, then, in ancient Rome, was that all legislation to support the farming class must be useless without Protection, and Protection could not be got. We do not hear even of an attempt to bring it into the sphere of practical politics.

Tiberius Gracchus was a perfectly honest and genuine enthusiast, who believed that he had a mission—the rehabilitation of Italian agriculture—and that he was quite competent to carry it out. It might be that his mission would lead him into trouble, and he was prepared to face the fact. He had had enough schooling in political philosophy from his numerous Greek friends to have freed his mind from the traditionary Roman horror of violent constitutional change. No doubt all the tags of Aristotle's school on χρεῶν ἀποκοπή and γῆς ἀναδασμός were familiar to him. It may not be out of place to remember that his tutor, Blossius, ultimately died an anarchist, fighting at the head of a band of revolted slaves. Yet, in spite of his studies in comparative politics and Greek philosophy Tiberius, by a strange contradiction, remained so much a

Roman legalist, that he held that what had once been made lawful must be morally justifiable, and that if the Comitia passed a law there could be no appeal to equity or common-sense against it.

Tiberius saw Italian agriculture languishing, the countryside occupied more and more every year by the huge estates of the capitalists, while in the city was accumulating the idle, half-starved mass of paupers who had once been Roman freeholders. His problem was, how to get the people back to the land. The end was laudable, the means which he adopted were astounding.

All over Italy there were large tracts of territory which were legally and theoretically the property of the state. Ever since the Republic became a conquering power, it had been wont to confiscate part of the soil of vanquished enemies. Sometimes this land was divided up into small farms for Roman citizens who engaged to settle thereon, sometimes a colony was planted on it, sometimes it was sold. But very often the state did not cede it in full property to any new owner, but simply proclaimed that any citizen who chose might "squat" upon it as a tenant at will, on condition of paying a rent. If it was arable, he was supposed to give the state a tithe; if it was open pasture, he was to pay a small capitation fee (*scriptura*) for every head of cattle turned out upon it. There existed a nominal check upon the accumulation of too much of this public land in the hands of single individuals, for the old Licinian laws had provided that no one should hold more than 500 jugera of tillage, or turn out more than 100 oxen or 500 sheep upon the pasture. But by the second century this ancient regulation was deliberately ignored; indeed, it had not been well observed even at the time of its enactment, and of late was only occasionally raked up by legalists like Cato the elder.

In the fourth century, and even in the third, the

tendency of the Roman state had been to divide up the larger part of conquered land *viritim*, or to put colonies upon it. But from B.C. 250 onwards the amount of new soil placed at the disposal of the Republic had been so enormous that it was not possible to find settlers ready to occupy it. A larger and larger proportion after each conquest had to be thrown open to the licensed squatter. This was more especially the case with the vast tracts that were confiscated in Southern Italy from the states that adhered too long to Hannibal. These had been the last of the distributions. Since B.C. 210 they had ceased; no new Italian land being available. Once and again there had been some talk of the inconvenience caused by the want of fresh soil, and the celebrated Laelius had thought for a moment of proposing a resumption by the state of part of the broad acres of the squatters. But he dropped the project after discovering its practical difficulties, and gained thereby his nickname of *Sapiens*.

The simple idea of Tiberius Gracchus was that the state should resume possession of all this land held by tenants at will—*possessores* was their legal name, and *possessio* their tenure—and distribute it up among the lately dispossessed farmers who were sitting idle in the streets of Rome. He announced that, as a matter of grace, and not of right, he should propose that the present occupiers might be allowed the terms granted by the Licinian Rogations. Each, that is, should be allowed to select and retain 500 jugera out of the land that he was holding; he might also (this was a new provision) set aside 250 acres more for each of two sons. The small estate thus created should be granted to the old occupier as private property, but the rest must at once be surrendered to the state. In the first draft of the law which Tiberius drew up, there would seem also to have been a clause providing for some compensation for unexhausted improvements on the surrendered land, such, we may suppose, as houses or farm buildings erected by the outgoing tenant. It was practically certain that the Senate would refuse its sanction to any such bill, but for that hindrance the reformer cared nought. He intended to carry it through the Comitia in spite of the Fathers.

With this, apparently, as his sole programme, he stood for the tribunate in B.C. 134, was easily elected, and entered into office in the succeeding year. The first announcement of his intention roused an opposition that he cannot but have foreseen, though he displayed considerable indignation at it. The eviction of all the *possessores* from the public land was not such a simple matter as it looked. When an estate has been occupied by the same family for many generations, without any reminder on the part of the landlord that they may one morning be requested to depart, ties both practical and sentimental grow up between the tenant and the soil, which it is idle for the lawyer to disregard. Of the public land held by *possessio*, some had been granted out as far back as the Samnite and Pyrrhic wars, and none had been distributed at a later date than Hannibal's expulsion from Italy. It had been held, therefore, by the tenants for terms ranging from seventy to two hundred years, without any interference on the part of the state. They had naturally expected that the system would endure, and had behaved as if they had a perpetual lease instead of a precarious license to squat.

The moment, therefore, that the bill was brought forward, Tiberius found that he had roused a hornets' nest about his ears. There was probably hardly a senator or a knight in Rome who did not hold some of his land by the mere tenure of *possessio*, and the fact that the tenure was precarious had (through the state's own fault) been completely forgotten. It was not merely the financial loss that angered the squatters, but the sentimental grievance. On the lands from which they were to be evicted lay, as they complained, their old family villas and the tombs of their ancestors. They did not want compensation for disturbance; nothing could make up to them for the loss of such things. Moreover, the legal difficulties that would be raised were unending; some had borrowed money on the security of such lands—were the creditors to lose the sum advanced? Others had charged upon them the dowries of their wives, or the portions of their daughters. Many had bought soil held by *possessio* at its full market value, under the impression—confirmed by the practice of two hundred years—that it was to all intents and purposes held under a perpetual lease. Some, occupying estates of this kind alongside of others held in full freehold, had pulled down the boundaries between them, and inextricably confused the holdings.

In short, the proposal of Tiberius to leave the *possessores* some remnant of their old acres, and to grant them a certain compensation for unexhausted improvements, failed (as was natural) to content them. How could it, when they were to be evicted from the main part of their land entirely in opposition to their own desire? Very reasonably, from their own point of view, they resolved to fight till the last gasp, and to fight in the old constitutional Roman fashion, by finding one of the tribunes who sympathised with them, and inducing him to put his veto on his colleague's proposed Agrarian-Law.

Now the tribunicial veto had by this epoch of the Republic's history grown to be a mere nuisance and an anachronism; yet it was so much tied up in men's memories with the ancient constitutional triumphs of the early centuries, that it was regarded much as the modern Englishman regards Trial by Jury or *Habeas Corpus*. To touch it seemed profane. Yet its employment had grown

THE AGRARIAN LAW OF GRACCHUS

casual and spasmodic. It was no longer used (as had been originally intended) for the protection of the plebeian from the patrician. Indeed patrician and plebeian were now inextricably confused in blood, and most of the staunchest oligarchs and reactionaries of the last century before Christ were of plebeian name and race. Of late the tribunate and the veto had been utilised in the most irregular and haphazard way, quite as often by the Senate against the Democrats as by the Democrats against the Senate. Sometimes it was used for purely personal ends by any vain, or eccentric, or ambitious person who had succeeded in obtaining the office. The quaintest tales may be collected, by those curious in the subject, concerning the use of the veto in these latter days. But on the whole the constitution had been saved, by a rough system of give and take, from the ever possible deadlock which the veto might bring about. The powers of the office had never been pressed to their logical extreme, though it was always possible that an obstinate man might bring matters to a crisis. At this particular moment, in B.C. 133, Rome was blessed not with one, but with two obstinate tribunes who held diametrically opposite views.

At the earliest opportunity, therefore, after his election to office, Tiberius brought forward his bill. Its most important clauses we have already noticed; but we must add that the confiscated land was to be cut up into farms of thirty jugera each, inalienable by the allottees, and charged with a small rent payable to the state. The former provision was intended to prevent applications by speculators, who might intend not to farm, but to sell at a profit; the latter was to keep before the eyes of the new settlers the fact that they were not freeholders, but tenants of the state. A permanent court of three commissioners "*Triumviri agris dandis assignandis,*" was to be created, not only to distribute land, but to sit as judges in all cases where there was a dispute as to what was and what was not state domain, or as to the fraction which the old tenant desired to retain, or as to any other point arising out of the law.

Both Plutarch and Appian have preserved scraps of the great speech with which Gracchus introduced his bill. They enable us to gauge perfectly the honest but emotional and high-strung temperament of the orator. "The wild beasts of Italy," he cried, "have their holes and dens to retire to, but the brave men who spill their blood in her cause have nothing left, when they come back from the wars, but light and air. Without hearth or home, they wander like beggars from place to place with their wives and children. A Roman general does but mock his army when he exhorts his soldiers to fight for their ancestral sepulchres and their domestic gods. For in these days how many are there of the rank and file who possess an altar that their forefathers reared, or a sepulchre in which their ashes rest? They fight and die merely to increase the wealth and luxury of the rich; they are called the masters of the world while none of them has a foot of ground of his own." Having thus painted the miseries of the present state of things, he began to explain his remedy for them. It was absolutely necessary that Rome should keep up the class from which her legions were drawn: land must be found for these landless men, and land was available. "Was it not most just to distribute the public property among the public? Had the slaves who now tilled the estate of the *possessores* more claims to consideration than citizens? Was not a soldier more valuable to the state than a man who could not fight, a Roman than a barbarian? Accordingly it was his duty to call upon the rich men who now held the public land to take into consideration the dangerous state into which the Republic was drifting, and to yield up their holdings of their own accord, as a free gift, if need be, to men who could rear children for the future benefit of Rome. They must be patriotic enough to subordinate their own profit to the good of the state. Surely it would be sufficient compensation that each of them was guaranteed the perpetual possession without payment of 500 jugera for himself and half as much for each of his sons."

The speech, as all our authorities agree, was moving and eloquent enough. It roused to enthusiasm the needy crowd of dispossessed farmers, who had never before heard their own case put so strongly. They fully believed that their ruin had come not from economic causes, but from the greed of the rich; they thought that, if started again with the state's aid and protection, they might yet live off the land. The purely urban multitude was moved with the emotional fervour of the harangue, and had no objection to confiscatory measures directed against its old enemies, the governing classes. Clearly Tiberius would not lack supporters, and the angry capitalists soon saw that they would have to fight to the death, if they wished to retain the broad lands which they had so long regarded as their own. Accordingly they had got their instrument ready. A tribune was at hand, prepared to veto the law. He was named M. Octavius: all agree that he was a perfectly honest and upright man. He had been a personal friend of Gracchus, but was a thorough conservative, and (what no doubt did much to settle his politics) a considerable holder of land in *possessio*. When, by the order of Tiberius, the clerk began to recite the preamble of the Agrarian Law, Octavius rose and bade him desist. Tiberius from the first showed signs of temper; he turned on his colleague, we are told, and used harsh and insulting words to him. Then he postponed the introduction of the bill to the next legal day of meeting, begging his friends to see that they came down in full force to the adjourned debate.

A vast crowd appeared on the appointed day, enough, as the reformer hoped, to overawe his recalcitrant colleague. But when the clerk again began to recite the preamble, Octavius again interposed his veto; then followed a violent scene, while the tribunes exchanged hard words and the mob raged and shouted. A most unhappy inspiration then came upon the reformer. Honestly unable to understand that his colleague could have any but selfish reasons for his obstinacy, he suddenly made a most offensive proposal to him. "You are," he said, "a considerable holder of public land. I will pay you the full value of it out of my own pocket if you will withdraw your veto." Naturally Octavius was deeply hurt, and put aside at once the insulting offer. His colleague had taken the very course which made it a point of honour for him to persist in opposition to the very last.

Again there was a deadlock. The condition of affairs raised wild anger in the breast of Tiberius. He was still convinced that only bad motives could lead men to oppose a law in which, as he considered, lay the sole hope of salvation for the Roman state. Accordingly he resolved that these enemies of the people should be chastised. He redrafted his bill, striking out the compensation clauses, and simply evicting the *possessores* as a punishment for their opposition. Moreover he resolved to show that if his adversaries could use the powers of the tribune, so could he. He determined to make all state business impossible, till his bill should have had a hearing. Using an undoubted constitutional right, but one which no man but a doctrinaire in a passion would have employed at such an early stage of the proceedings, he forbade all other magistrates to exercise their functions till the

THE WRATH OF GRACCHUS

Agrarian Law should have been discussed. He sealed up the state treasury in the temple of Saturn, to prevent any payments being made from it. He gave notice to the praetors that they must close the law-courts, and that if they allowed a case to be tried they should be punished by a heavy fine. In a short time every department of government was in confusion: public servants could not draw their pay; contractors could not continue their works; every litigant found his lawsuit hung up. The confusion and anarchy caused was out of all proportion to the gravity of the provocation which Tiberius had received. The main result of it was to estrange from the reformer's cause the greater part of his more moderate partisans. There were men who had thought that the law was desirable, if the *possessores* could be paid off and induced to depart without too much friction. But it was obviously iniquitous to abolish the compensation clauses merely because opposition had been offered. And to put a stop to all public business was mischievous and wrong-headed in the extreme. Tiberius, however, was wrought up to such a pitch of exasperation, that he utterly refused to press his scheme in a slower and less desperate fashion. He brought forward the new and harsher form of the bill, and laid it before the Comitia at the first opportunity.

Again Octavius interposed his veto. Rioting followed, and it is said that a gang of the clients and hangers-on of the *possessores* made a dash for the balloting urns, and tried to break up the Comitia in order to prevent the reformer from proceeding. They were routed, however, and the meeting continued. Two friends of Gracchus, a Manlius and a Fulvius, both consulars, are then said to have suggested to him that, before going further, he might ask the Senate to plead with his colleague to allow the bill a fair hearing. The proposal, if made in good faith, was not a very wise one, considering that most senators were holders, on a greater or lesser scale, of public land. Possibly, as Mommsen suggests, the more moderate men wished at all costs to give Gracchus time to get cool, and to allow him a chance of discussing his bill in a less electric atmosphere than that of the Comitia. It argues an honest simplicity on the part of the reformer that he accepted the suggestion, and hurried off to the Senate-house. Clearly he thought that his proposals must seem so reasonable to every good citizen, that the Senate would take sides in his favour, even against the private interest of the majority of its members. He was soon undeceived; there was much debate, but nothing was done. When he broached his request, he was met with insulting replies from prominent squatters, and finally the Senate refused to interfere with a tribune who was only exercising his undoubted constitutional privilege.

Convinced now that he would get nothing by quiet means, and that all the upper classes were leagued against him, Tiberius rushed into mere violence and illegality. At the next meeting of the Comitia he made one more appeal to Octavius, taking him by the hand, and imploring him not to stand between the people and their will. When the expected negative was given to his impassioned appeal, Tiberius suddenly produced a new and startling proposal. "Two colleagues of equal power," he said, "when they differ on a capital point, cannot work together. They must always be engaged in hostilities, and the public weal must suffer. It would be better that one should be removed." Accordingly he invited Octavius to take the sense of the meeting on their differences, with the understanding that the tribune found to be in a minority should abdicate from his office and withdraw. The notion was unprecedented and unconstitutional. Indeed, looking over the assembly, all clamorous for the Agrarian Law and new farms, Octavius must have

considered it a mockery as well as a solecism. Of course
he refused to have anything to do with such a scheme.
Tiberius told him to look out for the worst, and dismissed
the Comitia for that day.

On the following morning he put before the tribes
a very simple issue—Could the magistrate who opposed
the will of the people be the people's true representative?
If he was setting himself up in opposition to them, ought
he not to be removed? Of course the argument was
as illogical as it was unconstitutional, for "the will of
the people" in the mouth of Gracchus meant merely the
snap-vote of some particular assembly, of the 20,000 or
30,000 citizens who chanced to be in the Campus Martius
that day. There is an end to all government, if magistrates can be made and unmade at the whim of any
mob that gets together on a day of excitement. According to the Roman constitution, the idea of deposing a
tribune was unthinkable; once elected, he represented the
majesty of the people, and could not be touched; to harm
him was sacrilege. Voluntary resignation or death
were the only ways in which his place could become
vacant. To remove him by a vote of the tribes, before
his time was out, was as impossible as (let us say) it
would be for a mass-meeting of the electors of West-
minster to declare their member of Parliament deposed,
and then to fill up his place.

Nevertheless, when the adjourned assembly met,
Tiberius put before them the motion that Octavius
should be deposed from office. His colleague simply
observed that the whole proceeding was impossible and
illegal. But the voice of the multitude was with the
reformer. Seventeen tribes, one after another, gave
their votes for the proposal; before the eighteenth had
come up, and an actual majority had been registered (the
number of tribes was thirty-five at this period), Tiberius

gave Octavius a last chance, telling him that if his veto
were withdrawn the vote should proceed no further.
But the Optimate was neither to be intimidated nor to
be coaxed; he maintained his obdurate attitude until the
voting was over. Then, when told to depart, because he
had been deposed and was no longer a tribune, he clung
to the rostra, vociferating that the whole proceedings
were null and void—a statement which was undoubtedly
true, if there remained any force in the Roman constitution. Completely losing control of his temper, Tiberius
had him dragged off the platform and thrust away. The
mob below got him down, and nearly pulled him to pieces.
He barely escaped with his life, and a faithful retainer
who tried to protect him had his eyes torn out.

After this scandalous scene, in which he had narrowly
escaped the guilt of causing his colleague's death, Tiberius
proceeded to hold an illegal election meeting, and filled
up the place of Octavius in the tribunicial college with
an obscure client of his own, one Q. Mummius. There was
now nothing to prevent the passing of the Agrarian Law,
which was produced for the third time, and carried in its
revised form, with the compensation clauses left out. We
have already given its details. It only remains to add that
when the three commissioners, *agris dandis assignandis*, had
to be appointed, Tiberius showed a great want of political
wisdom. He named himself, his younger brother, Caius
—a youth of twenty—and his father-in-law, Appius
Claudius. He aimed merely at securing stringent efficiency in action, and did not see how invidious it was
to assign the grave and unpleasant work of confiscation
to a mere family party.

There would have been a serious financial difficulty in
starting the commission on its work, if it had not been
for an unforeseen chance. Even if the domain lands were
successfully torn from the *possessores*, and handed over to

THE PERGAMENE TREASURE 37

the would-be colonists, how were the latter to be fitted out for their experiment? Thousands of cottages must be built for them, tens of thousands of yokes of oxen purchased, hundreds of thousands of agricultural implements procured. How Tiberius had originally proposed to find the very large sums of money necessary for this purpose we are not told. The raising of the funds would certainly have involved him in a bitter conflict with the Senate, who always made finance their special province. But fortune intervened. Just at this moment there died Attalus III., the last king of Pergamus. He was an eccentric and tyrannical prince, who divided his time between the study of the fine arts and the extermination of his relatives. When he died suddenly of sunstroke, it was found that he had left his whole kingdom as a legacy to the Roman Republic. Those who knew him averred that he had often pondered over the most effective way of making his subjects unhappy, and had concluded that he could devise no better manner of doing so than this. There was an enormous accumulation of ready money in the coffers of Attalus. Tiberius resolved to seize upon it for his own purposes. Accordingly he brought forward a bill by which the Pergamene treasures were voted away to purchase ploughs and oxen, and to build barns and cottages for the new settlers. It mattered little that many districts of Asia broke out into rebellion rather than accept the Roman domination. The inland was up in arms under a certain Aristonicus (the son, it was said, of the daughter of an itinerant harper), who claimed to be a natural son of the father of Attalus III. But the capital, the coast cities, and, most important of all, the treasure, were safely made over to the Senate and People.

It was this ample stock which made it possible for Tiberius to set the Land Commission seriously to work. It is clear that before the end of his year of office a vast amount of land had been seized and distributed. But for one most important thing Tiberius made no provision. Evidently he had no conception of the need of it:—this was to secure that when the land was distributed, and stocked, and furnished with its barns and cottages, it should prove a paying concern. Yet one would have thought that even a rash experimenter might have reflected that if the older race of farmers, with all the accumulated experience of ages spent on the same soil, could not make both ends meet, it was decidedly unlikely that their successors—city-bred men, or at least men who had taken refuge in the city and lived there for some time estranged from rural pursuits—would be able to accomplish the feat. But it is clear that the fact that agricultural depression had its roots not in "the wickedness of the rich," but in obscure economic changes, had never entered the reformer's head. Of the friction that must have accompanied the confiscations our authorities tell us little. We only know that there were an immense number of complicated lawsuits, and that the bitterness of feeling among the expropriated *possessores* grew more bitter as the year rolled on. If they had raged at the threat of eviction, it was but natural that they should grow absolutely desperate as, man after man, they were actually expelled from their holdings. There is no reason to doubt the truth of the statement that plots were made to assassinate Tiberius. He himself certainly believed it; and when one of his friends died of an obscure distemper,[1] he accused his enemies of having poisoned him, and made

---

[1] The man died with symptoms which his friends could not understand, and spots broke out on his body. This in Roman folk-lore was supposed to betoken poison, but to us it has the opposite meaning, and would tend to show that he died of some sort of eruptive fever. Poisons do not (in spite of ancient tradition) manifest themselves by eruptions.

an inflammatory harangue at his funeral, in which he declared that he was obliged to place his life under the protection of the people.

Such a guarantee was not of much effective use, and Tiberius went about with the uncomfortable persuasion that he was a marked man. Bitter hatred followed him wherever he appeared. He had ruined too many prominent men to be able ever again to live in quiet. Angry senators insulted him in the streets, and asked him inconvenient constitutional questions on public occasions. No story was too silly or malignant to be told against him. One ridiculous Optimate solemnly declared that he had got from Pergamus, among the royal treasures, a crown and a purple robe, which he intended to use when he should proclaim himself king of Rome! The most threatening symptom, however, for Tiberius was that several resolute enemies announced that they intended to impeach him for *majestas*,—for unconstitutional conduct amounting to high treason,—the day that his office came to an end, because he had "diminished the majesty of the Roman people" by deposing a sacrosanct tribune from office. Tiberius, knowing that he was technically guilty, had no wish to face such a trial. He made an elaborate *apologia* for all that he had done in a speech which shows strong traces of his studies in the field of Greek political philosophy. "The person of a tribune," he said, "is no doubt sacred and inviolable, because he is the representative of the sovereign people. But if he manifestly opposes their interests and tyrannises over them, by refusing to allow them the liberty to vote on any project which they have at heart, he surely deprives himself by his own act of his sacrosanct character. If we were to find a tribune trying to pull down the temple on the Capitol, or to set fire to the arsenal, we should lay restraining hands on him in spite of his inviolability.

And in a similar fashion, he who is doing his best to diminish the majesty of the Roman people must be stripped of the power to do so. Is it not shocking to think that the people should not have the right of deposing one who is using his privileges against those who gave them to him? The kings of old held the most awful of magistracies, yet Tarquin was expelled. Can anything be more holy and venerable than the Vestal Virgins who keep the perpetual fire; yet if one of them breaks her vows she is buried alive. So, too, a tribune who injures the sovereign people can no longer be sacred and inviolable because of the investiture which the people gave him. He has destroyed the power in which alone his strength lay."

All this, and much more to the same effect, was eloquent and persuasive enough, but clearly it was not law, nor was it even common-sense. The whole argument rests on the assumption that a minority has no right to resist by the constitutional means which are at its disposal. It assumes that the verdict of the Comitia on some chance day of meeting is the same thing as "the will of the Roman people." It also presupposes that what the people desires is necessarily for its own best interests. From such views any amount of intolerant trampling on minorities might be logically justified. If anything more is needed to make the reformer's position absurd, it is that the body which he idealised into "the Roman people" was really the shifting urban multitude which his adversaries called "the mob"—*misera et sordida plebecula*, to use the words of a later politician.

The time for the election of the tribunes for B.C. 132 was now drawing near, and it was suggested to Gracchus that if he wished to preserve himself from prosecution for high treason, and if he desired to be sure that his Land Commission should go on with its work, the best thing that he could do would be to stand again for the tribunate, and to retain both his sacrosanct position and his power of dealing as a magistrate with the public assembly. By resolving to offer himself as a candidate for a second term of office Tiberius changed his whole political position. He had started as an enthusiast who had one single measure at heart, and merely desired to carry it through: the settlement of the Agrarian Question had seemed to him to be the one really pressing need of the Roman state. When his great bill had passed, he might logically have sung his *nunc dimittis* and retired into private life, to live down the hatred of the governing classes by proving that at least he had been wholly disinterested in all his actions.

But by asking for a second term of office Tiberius made himself into a permanent party leader. He saw this himself, and justified his position by putting forth a regular political programme. In the reforms which he announced that he intended to carry out in B.C. 132 we see foreshadowed the whole " Democratic platform " of the next fifty years. The planks of it included (1) the relaxation of the terms of military service; (2) the granting of a right of appeal from all law-courts to the sovereign people assembled in the Comitia; (3) the abolition of the monopoly, which the senators had hitherto enjoyed, of supplying all the jurors in the courts; (4) (if Velleius is to be trusted) the introduction of a bill for extending the franchise to Latin and Italian allies. How far this last proposal was to go is unfortunately unknown; indeed, we have only a very meagre outline of the whole set of schemes.

It would probably be doing Tiberius an injustice to suspect that the whole of this programme was drawn up in order to provide him with an excuse for asking for a renewal of his tribunate. He considered that his opponents had behaved so badly, that he was in duty bound to continue the campaign against them that had commenced with the Agrarian Law. He had gathered round himself a knot of partisans who looked upon him as their responsible leader, and would highly resent his retirement from public life. We may suspect also that the discovery of his own power to sway the multitude by his fervid eloquence had somewhat intoxicated him, and that he was not unwilling to accept the post of "friend of the people." To accuse him of mere ambition and love of authority would be unfair. Though he was busily engaged in breaking up the old constitution of Rome, he does not seem to have been aware of the fact. By legislating on such important matters as the Agrarian Law and the appropriation of the Pergamene treasures by mere "plebiscites," without the approval and consent of the Senate, he had practically ended the time-honoured compromise under which Roman politics had been conducted for the last two hundred years. If the state machine could be worked by an irresponsible tribune dealing directly with the sovereign people, the Senate became a useless wheel in the engine. But it seems probable that all these facts passed completely over the reformer's head; he was under the impression that he was no revolutionary, but merely a good citizen carrying out his obvious duty.

The news that Tiberius was canvassing for a second tenure of office brought the more or less suppressed wrath of his enemies to boiling-point. They had supposed that they would be rid of him as legislator at the end of the year, and they had hoped to do their best to get him tried for *majestas* when he was once more a private citizen. The prospect of a second year of democratic agitation appalled them. Accordingly they bent all their efforts to the end of frustrating his election. Owing to the season of the year, it was certain that very few rural voters would be present; they would not leave the vintage even to support their best friend. The matter would lie, as usual, in the hands of the urban populace, and the enemies of Gracchus were not without hopes that a combination of influence, intimidation, and bribery might secure them a majority in that very unsatisfactory body of voters. But when the reformer devoted himself for many days to a desperate personal canvass, it soon became evident that his popularity was too great, and that his triumph was more than probable. As a last resort his foes resolved to raise a constitutional question on a disputed point of election law.

When, among immense excitement, the poll began, the first two tribes gave their suffrages for Gracchus. It was so customary for the remaining tribes to follow the lead of those who had the " prerogative " of the first vote, that the return of the reformer seemed secure. But then the objection was made that it was not legal for the same person to hold the tribunate for two years in succession. This was a doubtful point of constitutional law; so much so, that a few years later the Democratic party took the trouble to pass a bill formally affirming its legality. But in B.C. 133 the question could still be debated. There were many precedents for a re-election; the case of Licinius, the author of the old Agrarian Law of B.C. 367, was especially apposite, as the people had returned him for ten successive years before he finally got his scheme carried out. On the other hand, there was an old law, dating from the generation after Licinius (B.C. 342), which discouraged re-election. It had not been invariably observed, but it was still on the Statute Book. Moreover, there was a constitutional theory that the practice was to be deprecated, because it prevented a magistrate from being made responsible for the acts of his year of office. A person who was perpetually re-elected could never be called to account. This theory was still worth defending if the Optimates wished for a fight.

When the point was brought up, the partisans of Tiberius raised loud cries of dissent, and such a tumult arose that the presiding tribune, one Rubrius, grew scared and refused to proceed. Then Mummius, the successor of the deposed Octavius, tried to take over the charge of the meeting, declaring that he saw no difficulty, and was prepared to go on with the election. But other tribunes intervened, declaring that either Rubrius must carry out his day's work, or else there must be a fresh casting of lots for the selection of a fresh president. While the magistrates wrangled, the people grew more and more turbulent, and when the meeting had degenerated into a riot it had finally to be adjourned.

This unexpected hitch in the proceedings struck dismay into the heart of Tiberius. He thought that he was lost if he should fail to secure his re-election, considering the fierce spirit which his enemies were displaying. Clothing himself in black, and leading his little son by the hand, he went round the Forum appealing to the multitude to save their friend from imminent peril of death. His indignant partisans closed around him, vowing that he should be preserved at all costs, and for the next few days he went about with a sort of bodyguard armed with staves and bearing torches after nightfall. This mob was a splendid mark for the satire and invective of the Optimates. Had there ever been before, they asked, a citizen of Rome who could not stir without a huge gang of bravos at his heels? What could such assemblies mean? If Greek precedents went for anything, the "friend of the people," who declared his life in danger and went about with an organised band of satellites behind him, would some day blossom out into a tyrant, seize the Capitol, and massacre the Senate.

TIBERIUS PREPARES TO FIGHT

We may be perfectly certain that Tiberius had no thought of emulating Cypselus or Peisistratus, but it must be confessed that his actions bore a most singular resemblance to theirs. Even those who sympathised with his ends were scared at his reckless proceedings, for in this last crisis of his life he showed a complete lack of coolness and self-restraint. On the night before the adjourned election meeting he collected a great crowd of his adherents, many of whom encamped before his house and slept in the street. He harangued them, told them that violence would probably be used against them, and added that in that case they must meet force by force. He arranged that his partisans should mass themselves in the front of the place of assembly before the Capitol, and keep off their opponents by their serried ranks. Appian adds that he agreed to give them a signal, if he considered himself in danger, by raising his hand to his head, as a token that his life was at stake. If they saw the sign, they must prepare to fight. All this was a deliberate provocation of civil war: to endeavour to pack a meeting and to come down prepared for violence means rioting and not politics. It was quite enough to give an excuse to men much less angry and unscrupulous than the opponents of Gracchus.

On the eventful day the tribune set out, accompanied by a mass of his supporters. We are told that all the omens were very dismal that morning; the sacred chickens had refused to eat; Tiberius stumbled on his own doorstep and cut his foot; crows scuffling on the roof dislodged a tile which fell almost on his head. His satellites muttered that ill-luck was in the air; but his old tutor, the philosopher Blossius, cried out "that the son of Gracchus and the grandson of Scipio, the protector of the people of Rome, would never be held back by any omen from going forth to help that people in the day of their need," and the *cortége* forced its way through the crowded streets toward the Capitol.

At first it seemed as if the reformer were about to carry all before him. His faithful tool Mummius had obtained the presidency for the day, and began to call over the roll of the tribes. There was a solid mass of democrats at the front, who received Gracchus with the loudest acclamations, and formed round him in a sort of battle array when he took his place with his colleagues. But presently it was seen that there was also a hostile element present; the *possessores* had sent down their clients and retainers, and scuffling and quarrelling began at half-a-dozen points, till all was clamour and disorder, and the voices of the tribunes could not be any longer heard. At this moment Tiberius descried a friend of his own, a senator named Fulvius Flaccus, making frantic signs and beckonings to him, over the head of the crowd, from a point of vantage on to which he had climbed. Flaccus, one of the few really warm partisans of reform in the Senate, had news for his leader. When he had been with difficulty thrust to the front, he gasped that danger was imminent, for the *possessores* were trying to induce the Senate to declare Tiberius a public enemy, and since they could not move the consul to action, were threatening to arm their friends and servants and to sally out into the streets to murder him. Without waiting to see whether or no the report was exaggerated or the enemy really at hand, Tiberius gave the signal for hostilities by making the preconcerted sign of raising his hand to his head. In an instant all was in confusion; his friends girt up their gowns, broke up the fasces of the lictors, and any other woodwork they could find, to make bludgeons, gathered in a compact mass and drove the partisans of the *possessores* out of the field with bruises and broken heads. The other tribunes fled, the priests hastened to shut up the temples, and all

THE RIOTERS AND THE SENATE 47

peaceable citizens ran home to get out of the trouble, spreading various absurd rumours as they fled.

While all this was in progress, the Senate had been sitting in the temple of Fides, receiving from time to time more or less accurate accounts of what was going on before the Capitol. The news that Flaccus had carried to the assembly seems to have been somewhat highly coloured, for though the *possessores* had been denouncing Tiberius in the bitterest terms, they had not succeeded in moving the consul Scævola to take any action against him, nor had the Senate shown any willingness to pass a decree of outlawry. There were still many moderate men in it, who shrank from the responsibility of commencing civil strife. The debate in the Senate was only brought to a head when the clamour of the multitude who were fleeing from the scene of riot was heard. Inquiries made of the fugitives elicited the wildest statements; some said that Gracchus was deposing all the other tribunes from office (as he had once deposed Octavius); others cried that he was appointing himself without election tribune for the ensuing year. The most absurd version was that, when he had been seen raising his hand to his head, he was asking for the kingly crown.

The opponents of Gracchus were already wrought up to such a pitch of wrath by the financial ruin that he had brought upon them, that they readily believed—or professed to believe—even the wildest of these rumours. Their spokesman, L. Cornelius Scipio Nasica, a consular who had been a great holder of domain land, leapt to his feet and once more adjured Scævola to take up arms against the "tyrant." But the imperturbable magistrate merely announced that if Gracchus was persuading or forcing the people into irregular courses, he should take care to annul his proceedings, but that he would not be the first to have recourse to violence, nor would he ever put any citizen to death without a trial. Then Nasica cried aloud that since the consul refused to defend his country, he adjured all who wished to save Rome and her laws to follow him to the Capitol. So saying he girt up his toga, and cast the purple border of it over his head, that all might see his rank. He rushed into the street followed by many scores of the younger senators, who were joined outside by a crowd of their clients and attendants. They soon made their way to the Capitol, where they found Gracchus haranguing his partisans; the multitude was thinning out after the election proceedings had come to an end, and it is said that the reformer had now no more than 3000 or 4000 men around him.

Without any attempt at parley, Nasica charged at the Democrats, with his followers streaming in a wedge behind him, the senators at their head. Neither side was armed, save with staves and broken chairs and benches. Quite contrary to what might have been expected, the Optimates cleft through the mob of Gracchus's partisans without much difficulty. It is said that many instinctively gave way before the rush of furious senators, out of inbred reverence for the purple stripe. This much is certain, that, belabouring their opponents with their improvised weapons, Nasica and his followers cleared the Capitol, driving the Democrats before them and casting some over the cliffs of the ascent. The fray was very bloody, for the assailants knocked on the head every man that fell; nearly 300 persons were killed; not one, it is recorded, by an edged weapon, but all by sticks and stones. Among the victims was Gracchus himself, who had been thrown down near the door of the Capitoline temple, in front of the statues of the ancient Roman kings. He had stumbled over a corpse, and as he strove to rise, a senator named Publius Satureius beat out his brains with a footstool.

Thus miserably perished a young man of excellent intentions and perfect honesty, who thought himself destined to be the regenerator of Rome, and merely succeeded in launching the state upon a hundred years of bitter civil strife. No man is fit for a party leader who combines an emotional temperament, an impatience of opposition, and a complete inability to look at contested questions from his opponent's point of view as well as his own. It is probable that Tiberius was attempting an impossible task: without the introduction of Protection agriculture was doomed in Central Italy, and Protection could not be got, because it was against the interests of the urban multitude. But the agrarian question had to be fought out, and the contest, if waged with the usual gravity and self-restraint of ancient Roman politics, need not have ended in confiscation without compensation on the one side, or riot and massacre on the other. For the course that events took Gracchus himself must bear the responsibility: his enemies were greedy and narrow-minded, but he himself was harsh, reckless, and provocative beyond measure. When, in a moment of pique, he struck out the compensation clauses from his bill, he challenged the *possessores* to a fight to the death. Morally speaking there can be no doubt that they were entitled to some sort of amends for being evicted, without warning, from estates which they and their fathers had occupied for several generations. Having ruined many men of mark and impoverished many more, Tiberius had secured for himself an enmity that was bound to end either in his death or exile, or in his being compelled to seize autocratic power. His means were even worse than his ends: no statesman has a right to pull down the constitution about the ears of the people, the moment that he finds himself checked in his designs. However bad a constitution may be, the man who upsets it, before he has arranged for anything to put in its place, is a criminal and an anarchist, if he knows what he is doing, a mischievous madman if he does not. It would seem from the general bent of the reformer's character that it is to the latter class that he must be consigned. He had many private virtues,—but so had Robespierre: a man may be eloquent, incorruptible, and thoroughly convinced of his own good intentions, but if he is sufficiently reckless, vain, and autolatrous, he may blossom out into the worst sort of tyrant—the philosophic doctrinaire. Looking at the emotional and impatient character of Tiberius, it is quite possible to conceive that, if that scuffle on the Capitol had had another result, he might ultimately have become that which his enemies declared that he wished to be—the tyrant of Rome.

CHAPTER III

CAIUS GRACCHUS

IN studying the career of Tiberius Gracchus we were investigating a very simple phenomenon. The great tribune was aiming at nothing more than the redress of social and economic evils, and had no thought of reconstructing the Roman constitution. When the provisions of that constitution stood in his way, he recklessly overrode them; but when they chanced to suit his purpose, he utilised their most tiresome and absurd formalities to the utmost limit. It was characteristic of the short-sighted Tiberius to press the tribunicial authority to its most exaggerated extension one month, by shutting up the law courts and the treasury, while in the next he struck at the very roots of that authority, and taught men to despise it, by illegally deposing a tribune by the vote of the Comitia. Whether such conduct was likely to strengthen the position of future tribunes, he does not seem for one moment to have reflected. But as a substitute for the old constitution, which he was so ruthlessly breaking up, Tiberius had nothing to put forward. When we examine his programme—the list of reforms that he intended to bring forward in his second tribunate—we find that it does not include any scheme for rearranging the machinery of the state, but only certain proposals to change points of detail, such as the composition of juries, the conditions of military service, and (perhaps) the limits of the franchise. There was no attempt to settle the great problems of sovereignty and imperial administration, which were the really pressing questions of the day. Apparently he was prepared to entrust the unwieldy Public Assembly with the details of the governance of the empire, for which it was even more unfitted than was the oligarchic Senate.

But, in spite of Tiberius's short-sightedness, the after-effects of his career were such as to make constitutional changes likely, and even necessary. He had broken up for ever the tacit agreement between Senate and People, by which alone the clumsy machinery of the Roman administration could be kept working. He had shown that the Comitia, if galvanised into activity by a reckless and restless tribune, was capable of reasserting its old theoretical powers, and of passing laws in defiance of the Senate, and in opposition to the Senate's dearest interests. No state can contain two sovereigns, and it had now to be settled which was really supreme at Rome—the Senate, according to the practice of the last two centuries, or the People, as theory required. It was only necessary that a capable leader should again come forward to put himself at the head of the Democratic party, and then the struggle for sovereignty must force itself to the front as the main problem of the day.

Leaders of a sort were not long wanting, but at first they were mere noisy agitators, who only stirred the surface of things. C. Papirius Carbo and M. Fulvius Flaccus, the immediate successors of the elder Gracchus, were not men of mark or ability. Their doings had little practical importance. Carbo tried to pass a declaratory law, to the effect that tribunes might legally be re-elected year after year [B.C. 131]. He failed, fell away from his Democratic beliefs, and relapsed, for reasons obscure but probably discreditable, into the ranks of the Optimates. A few years later, however, the bill was passed by other hands. Flaccus, who was a genuine enthusiast, but fickle of purpose and lacking in perseverance, began to meddle with another and a much more important question—the enfranchisement of the Italian allies. He brought in a bill for this very just and wise purpose, saw it blocked by the tribunicial veto, and then, instead of persevering with it, suddenly left Rome, and plunged into a series of campaigns in Southern Gaul [B.C. 125]. The Senate deliberately threw the chance of military glory in his way by assigning him the Gallic province; he could not resist the opportunity, and disappeared from home politics for two years. The only practical result of his agitation was the rebellion of one isolated Italian city, Fregellae, which was crushed with ease by the praetor Opimius [B.C. 125-4].

Ten years passed away from the death of Tiberius, and then there arose a man who knew his own mind, who accurately gauged the problems of the time, and saw that not only the social and economic difficulties of Rome, but also the question of sovereignty must be faced, if the Democratic party was to triumph.

Caius Gracchus was nine years younger than his brother Tiberius, and had been too young to aid him in his schemes, though not too young to be appointed one of the famous triumvirs of the Land Commission—that family party which had given so much offence to the Optimates. When the powers of the Commission were gradually whittled away, and its judicial duties assigned to the consuls (who simply refused to discharge them), Caius sank for a moment into obscurity. But it was not for long; like every other young Roman of good family and active spirit, he put himself in the regular political career, and sued for the quaestorship, as the first step in the *cursus honorum*. Once started he was bound to go far.

Caius was not a mere enthusiast and humanitarian like his brother: he was a clever, many-sided, wary man, who saw all the dangers of the task he was going to take in hand, and faced them, under the stimulus of ambition and revenge, rather than from benevolence and patriotism. We shall see that all his career was coloured by these motives, a fact which accounts for the many deliberately immoral measures that are to be found in his legislation.

For some years after his brother's death he took no very prominent part in public affairs; yet he did not keep himself so secluded and obscure as Plutarch makes out. We know, for example, that he made an oration in favour of Carbo's bill concerning re-election to the tribunate, and that he spoke against the detestable law of Junius Pennus [B.C. 126], which expelled Italian residents from Rome.

Caius took the quaestorship in the year of the law of Pennus, and was sent to serve in Sardinia under the proconsul Aurelius Orestes. He was kept in that unhealthy and uninteresting island for two years, as his office was prolonged for a second term, owing to the jealousy of the Senate, who were glad to keep away from the capital one who bore the dreaded name of Gracchus. Thus, as it chanced, Caius was absent from Italy during the franchise agitation of Fulvius Flaccus and the revolt of Fregellae. This fact did not prevent the Optimates from accusing him of having had a guilty knowledge of the intentions of the rebel city. He won golden opinions for his efficient financial administration in Sardinia, as well as for his personal integrity; he was the only quaestor—as he himself said—who went out with a full purse and came back with an empty one.

After returning from Sardinia in B.C. 124, Caius stood for the tribunate for the ensuing year, and obtained the office without much trouble, so popular was his name among the multitude. The only effect of a bitter opposition to him, started by the Optimates, was that he was returned fourth on the list, instead of at the head of the poll.

THE CHARACTER OF CAIUS

When once launched on the sea of domestic politics, Cáius atoned by his unceasing activity for the long delay that he had made before plunging into the troubled waters. He was the most restless and eager of men: beside him, we are told, his brother Tiberius had always appeared mild, moderate, and conciliatory! These are hardly the epithets that we should apply to the author of the confiscation of the domain-land and the deposer of Octavius, but the comparison enables us to understand the terrible vehemence of his younger brother. Caius had no moments of rest or quiet after he had once put himself forward as the friend of the people. His activity was militant and aggressive, his eloquence bitter and vituperative. He was always working himself up into the fine fury that ends in hysterics. We are told that he was aware of the fact, and that when he came down to the Comitia to speak, he stationed a discreet retainer with a pitch-pipe behind him, whose duty was to give a warning note whenever the oration was tending to become a screech. Unfortunately—like the Archbishop of Granada in Lesage's story—he did not invariably accept the criticism of his underling. He was always on the edge of over-emphasis. First of all Romans, as we read, he strode from one end of the rostra to another while speaking, and cast his toga from off his shoulders by the vehemence of his action. His enemies compared him to Cleon, the blustering demagogue of ancient Athens.

It is strange that a man of such a high-strung nature should have kept back from politics so long. His own explanation of the abstention was that he felt that he was well-nigh the last of his race: save himself and his young son, the male line of the Gracchi had died out, though his father, the consul, had left behind him no less than twelve children. Cicero used to tell a story that Caius had sworn after his brother's disastrous end to hold aloof from the political life, but that his resolution was broken down by a vision. He thought, as he slept, that Tiberius stood before him, and cried, "Why this long lingering, Caius? There is no alternative. The fates have decreed the same career for each of us—to spend our lives and meet our deaths in vindicating the rights of the Roman people." Dreams are often the reflection of the subjects on which the mind has been perpetually brooding in the waking hours, and the tale well expresses the blending of motives in the mind of Caius. He felt that it was his duty to avenge his brother, and he was deeply stirred by seeing the Democratic party mute and helpless, for lack of a leader and a programme, when he felt that he could so easily supply both these wants. Ambition and revenge were probably at the bottom of his resolve to a greater measure than he himself was aware.

Whatever was the spark that kindled this eager and susceptible temperament into a flame, there can be no doubt that, from the first moment of his election to the tribunate, Caius displayed the restless energy of a fanatic. He took in hand no less a scheme than the absorption into his own hands of the whole administration, foreign and domestic, of the Roman Empire. His plan was to overrule the Senate by the simple device of keeping perpetual possession of the tribunate, a thing which was now perfectly legal owing to the law which had been passed since his brother's death. As tribune he would bring in an unending series of laws and decrees dealing directly with all the departments of state, so that the Senate should have no right to meddle with anything. If the sovereign people claimed and used its power to settle every detail of the governance of the empire, there would be no room for senatorial interference. Mommsen has maintained that this scheme was a deliberate anticipation of the monarchy of

THE FIRST MEASURES OF CAIUS 57

the Cæsars, and that Caius, by proposing to hold perpetual office, as the sole guide and arbiter at whose fiat the assembly should pass laws, was practically intending to make himself tyrant of Rome. This, however, is unfair to Gracchus: it would be more true to say that he aimed at occupying at Rome somewhat the same position that Pericles had once held at Athens. The Athenian had been *Strategos* year after year, and had guided for half a lifetime the votes of the Ecclesia. Yet no one save comic poets called him a tyrant: he was προστάτης τοῦ δήμου, as the Greeks phrased it, but that is a very different thing from holding a tyranny. What Caius Gracchus craved was much the same position; but he had not the calm wisdom of Pericles, and a man of his vehement and reckless temper was certain ere long to fall out with his supporters and wreck his career.

We have said that there was a strong element of revenge among the motives which stirred up Gracchus to put himself at the head of the Democratic party. His two first laws display it very clearly. One of them was a declaratory bill, which re-enacted the old constitutional principle that any magistrate who in his year of office had put to death or banished Roman citizens without a trial should be called to account before the Comitia. This measure was aimed at the Consul Popilius, who, though he had not been concerned in the riot where Tiberius met his end, had subsequently seized and executed many of the reformer's partisans. The ex-magistrate recognised the intent of the law, and was perfectly conscious of the flagrant illegality of what he had done ten years before, and of the probability of his conviction for high treason. He fled out of Italy into exile, without waiting to be indicted. His fate was well deserved, for the conduct of his party had been abominable; after the death of Tiberius further executions had not been required; and if they had been, there was no excuse for not proceeding according to proper legal forms of trial.

But the second law of Caius was by no means so righteous. It was aimed at the perfectly respectable and blameless tribune Octavius, who had opposed Tiberius on the question of the Agrarian Law, and had been deposed by him in such an illegal fashion. The bill now brought forward was to the effect that any magistrate whom the Roman people had removed from office, for any cause, was to be for the future incapable of holding office again. This was mere persecution, for Octavius had done nothing more than exercise a right, which he undoubtedly possessed, in a conscientious if somewhat obstinate fashion. All our authorities agree that there was no ground for believing that he had been actuated by spite or corrupt motives. It would appear that Caius found that public opinion was not with him when he attacked Octavius, or that he grew ashamed on second thoughts of this vindictive measure. At any rate, he dropped the bill, announcing that he did so in deference to the wishes of his mother Cornelia, at which (as we are told) the people showed themselves perfectly satisfied.

The other legislative proposals of the first tribunate of Caius Gracchus are of very various kinds, covering all sorts of different spheres of imperial and domestic administration. They plainly show that the vehement young tribune thought nothing too small or too great to be dealt with by the assembly, under his own superintendence as prime minister of the people. It is unfortunate that the historians on whom we have to rely for information do not enable us to make out the exact sequence in which the various laws were passed. We have to deal with them in classes rather than in strict order of time.

In some ways the most important of all was a bill which (in spite of all that the advocates of Caius can allege)

THE CORN-DOLE INSTITUTED 59

appears to have been simply and solely intended to commend him to the populace, as the true friend who had once and for all filled their stomachs. He proposed a *lex frumentaria*, which provided that corn—the tithe-corn of the Sicilian cities stored in the granaries of the state—should be sold to any citizen who applied for it at $6\frac{1}{3}$ asses per *modius*. Each man was allowed to buy five *modii* a month. In order to prevent swindling and speculation, the buyer had to visit the granary himself and receive the corn in person. Thus the bill profited the urban mob alone, since they were the only citizens who lived near enough to the fount of supply to be able to turn it to account.

Now, $6\frac{1}{3}$ asses per modius was, as it would appear, a rate which represented about one-half the normal price of corn in the Roman market during an average year. The measure was equivalent, therefore, to the free gift of half his daily loaf to every urban voter. The proletariate thought the bill a most admirable one, and its author was hailed, wherever he appeared, as the true friend of the people. He had appealed to them in a manner which even the simplest could understand, and their gratitude reminds us of the famous cry of the Portuguese army when it saluted its commander with the shout, "Long live Marshal Beresford, who takes care of our bellies."

The voters of the Suburra were blameless. They knew no better, when they aided their leader to carry through this most unhappy bill. But Caius must bear a very heavy burden of reproach for this miserable bid for popularity. Not only had he devised the surest means of demoralising the urban multitude, but he also dealt the last death-blow to Italian agriculture. More than any other single man, he was responsible for the growth of that mass of paupers asking for nothing but *panem et circenses*, which in a few generations was to represent the sovereign people of Rome. When once the indigent multitude had begun to expect food from the state at an artificial price, it was not likely that they would stop clamouring till they got it for nothing. The demagogues who pandered to them by continually increasing the dole were the legitimate offspring of Caius Gracchus.

The case against him is made even worse by the fact that at the same moment when he began to distribute the tithe-corn at half-price, he also made a great parade of re-enacting his brother's Agrarian Law. He declared that the restoration of the old yeoman class was as dear to his heart as it had been to that of Tiberius. He restored the full powers of the Land Commission, for the distribution of what remained of the public domains, and commenced once more to plant out farmers on small allotments.

This was sheer economic lunacy, for how could farming pay in Central Italy, if the state entered the field as a competitor against the local agriculturist, and swamped the Roman market with corn sold at half-price? If Caius really supposed that it was any use to send forth new farmers, at the moment when he was underbidding them by the institution of the corn-dole, he must have been an idiot. If he set the Land Commission to work with a full knowledge that all its efforts must be futile, he must have been a deliberate impostor. Knowing the cleverness of the man, we are forced to conclude that the latter alternative is the nearer to the truth. He probably re-enacted his brother's law for purely political reasons, not because he thought that it would have any good effect, but because it looked well in the Democratic programme. His real scheme for relieving the economic pressure was of quite a different kind. He intended to despatch the ruined Italian farmers over-seas, to form new colonies in the provinces, where their efforts would not be sterilised by the unnatural condition of the local Roman market.

This was the true way of relieving the distress of the

yeoman class: they could not hold their own in Italy without Protection, which it was certain that Caius's friends in the urban multitude would never grant them. But on the fertile soil of Africa they might do well enough. Accordingly, Caius set his colleague, the tribune Rubrius, to introduce a bill for the founding of a colony on a very large scale—there were to be allotments for no less than 6000 citizens—on the deserted site of ancient Carthage. If the settlers failed to maintain themselves as agriculturists, they would have a good second chance of succeeding as traders, for it was inevitable that some great town must grow up again at a point of the Mediterranean so central and so well suited for maritime traffic. So far Caius was right: within two centuries the restored Carthage was to be one of the greatest cities of the empire, but it was not to call a Gracchus its founder.

Other colonies were to be planted in Italy itself: the places chosen were Tarentum and Capua. These new settlements can never have been intended to live on agriculture; they were clearly designed to become (what each of them had been in the past) great urban centres of trade. The old Capua and Tarentum had not died natural deaths. The one had come to a violent end because it had in the hour of danger deserted Rome during the Hannibalic War. The other, though not quite so harshly treated in a political sense, had been practically ruined by its protracted sieges and the forcible diversion of its commerce to the rival port of Brundisium. Now Capua was an open village without even a legal existence, and Tarentum a decayed fishing-haven. But Caius thought that there was an opening for a great market-town in the midst of the Campanian plain, and for a flourishing port on the Ionian Sea. If strengthened by a draft of Roman citizens, the cities might rise again, if only from the mere convenience of their sites.

For the colonial schemes of Caius, both in Italy and in Africa, we have nothing but praise. He had hit upon the true method of relieving the misery of the proletariate, and if he had been enabled to carry out his designs, there would have been an opening provided for every citizen who was willing to work, and disliked the miserable life of the dole-fed pauper. There are other laws to be placed to his credit which show that when his mind was not warped by revenge or ambition he was a true statesman of the first rank. One was destined to complete the road system of Italy, which had grown up very much at haphazard, and still left many regions practically isolated from the main arteries of communication. Admiring biographers describe to us the excellence of his roads, "drawn in a straight line throughout the country, wonderfully built, with a bed of binding gravel below and a paved *chaussée* above. When a ravine was met, it was filled up with rubble ; when a watercourse, it was spanned by a bridge. Levelled and brought to a perfect parallel, the highroad presented a regular and even elegant prospect for mile after mile. There were pillars of stone to mark the distances and directions, and horse-blocks at convenient spots to enable the traveller to mount with ease."

Another law that was obviously beneficial, and had been long called for, was one for relieving the rank and file of the army from the burden of providing themselves with clothing. In the old days, when the citizen-soldier spent a few months in the field, at no great distance from his home, and was disbanded at the coming of winter, the custom had been natural and reasonable. But to expect a conscript sent for six years to Spain to keep himself clothed from his modest pay was absurd. Not only was this boon secured to the soldiery, but other laws of Gracchus mitigated the severity of the conscription, securing that no man should be forced to serve before he had attained the legal age, and reducing the number of years for which he could be kept on continuous service. Less happily inspired was another bill, which seems to have given the soldiers at the wars the right to appeal against any sentence of death passed by their general. Such a provision would certainly prove detrimental to discipline. There are occasions when it is absolutely necessary that the commander should be able to punish mutiny or cowardice on the spot by the extreme penalty, and to allow an appeal against him is preposterous.[1] As a matter of fact, the law was not always observed. There are cases known, long after this time, in which military executions took place on the largest scale. Crassus, in the Servile War, once decimated a whole cohort for gross cowardice in the field.

But the most important of all the legislative enactments of Caius Gracchus were those by which he set to work to modify the constitution, by cutting down the powers of the Senate. His chief device for this purpose was to raise up a new corporation in the state, with interests which should be so different from those of the Senate that it might be trusted to act as a check on that body. It was in the Equestrian Order that he found the materials for this counterpoise.

In early days the Equites were simply the cavalry of the Roman army; every man with the "equestrian census," had to serve as a horse-soldier, whether he were senator, landholder, or capitalist. But by B.C. 123 the Equites had become a very anomalous body. They had practically ceased to have a military organisation; the last occasion on which we hear of them taking the field as a separate corps was at the siege of Numantia. The Roman burgess-cavalry had been entirely superseded by squad-

[1] I am following Mommsen in ascribing the grant of appeal from the imperator's sentence to a Gracchan law *De Provocatione.*

rons raised from among the allies. Nor did the Equites any longer number senators in their ranks; since B.C. 129 no senator could be a knight. The body now consisted of those men of wealth who had not been called up to sit in the senate. It was heterogeneous, containing two very different classes of members. The more reputable half of it comprised the larger landowners of non-senatorial rank throughout Roman Italy. The other half was composed of the great capitalists, merchants, and contractors of the city. The urban and the rural knights had few common privileges or functions. The only occasions when they had occasion to meet was when the censor called them up to his quinquennial review, or when the "equestrian centuries" had to give their vote in the Comitia Centuriata. They had very little cohesion or *esprit de corps.*

Caius resolved to make this wealthy but ill-compacted class into a corporation with common honorary rights and practical advantages. The part of it with which he had mainly to deal was the capitalist class in the city, for just as the urban proletariate, being always on the spot, came to style itself the Roman people, so the speculators and contractors of the capital came to speak of themselves as if they were the whole equestrian body.

The most important of the laws by which Gracchus designed to sow discord between the Senate and the Equites was that by which the control of the law courts was transferred from the one to the other body. Hitherto senators alone were placed upon the *album judicum,* and allowed to serve as jurymen. The results had been discreditable of late years, and in particular the provincials complained that a senatorial jury would never convict a defaulting governor for embezzlement and oppression. There had been a particularly bad case of the sort just before Caius received the tribunate. M'Aquilius, governor of Asia, had been acquitted, in spite of the fact that the provincials proved against him a number of scandalous acts of misgovernment. His acquittal had been secured by wholesale bribery, and the decision had been so iniquitous that the reputation of senatorial juries had sunk to a very low ebb. It was easy, therefore, to attack them on high moral grounds, and Caius's talent for vituperative eloquence had free scope. His line of argument may be guessed from a fragment of one of his speeches against the Senate which has survived:—" No senator troubles himself about public affairs for nothing," he observed, "and in the case before us (an arbitration concerning territories in Asia Minor) the honourable gentlemen may be divided into three classes. Those who voted *aye* have been bribed by one claimant, those who voted *no* by the other, and those who did not vote at all by both; and these last are the most cunning of all, for they have persuaded each party that they abstained in his interest, saying that if they had voted at all, they must have done so for the other side."

The senatorial juries had undoubtedly been most unsatisfactory. But the equestrian juries which Caius substituted for them were even worse: there is no reason to believe that the tribune was unaware of this fact, for in reference to this law he is recorded to have remarked that "he had cast daggers into the Forum with which the two orders should lacerate each other." Clearly his purpose was to brew mischief for the benefit of the Senate, rather than to secure any advantage for the citizens or the provincials. To put the control of the law courts into the hands of the urban knights (for the rural knights did not count) had the worst possible effect. The typical *eques* was a good deal more of a money-lender, speculator, and financial agent than of a mere merchant. His interests were as much opposed to those of the provincials as they were to those of the Senate. His main wish was to exploit the empire for the benefit of his own class. It

is difficult to construct any parallel from modern times
which can bring home to the reader the exact meaning
of the surrender of justice into the hands of the Equites.
Some faint adumbration of the results may be realised
by imagining what might happen in England if all juries
had to be chosen exclusively from members of the Stock
Exchange. Whenever any financial question might be in
dispute, there would be a tendency, even in honest men,
to decide in favour of their own class interests. The
Roman *publicanus* was little influenced either by delicacy
or by regard for public opinion. The result of giving
him judicial omnipotence was merely that he abused it
for his own interest rather more than his senatorial predecessors had done. "The Equites," says Appian, "soon
adopted the senators' system of bribery, and no sooner
had they experienced the pleasures of unlimited gains,
than they proceeded to strive after them far more shamelessly than had ever been done before. They used to
set up suborned accusers against the senators; they not
merely tyrannised over them in the law courts, but
openly insulted them." The old grievance had been that
bad provincial governors escaped punishment for their
misdeeds, owing to the misplaced tenderness of their
friends on the jury. The new grievance was that any
one who did not play into the hands of the Equites,
and grant them whatever they asked, was prosecuted and
condemned, however blameless his conduct might have
been. It took some years for the system of blackmailing
to reach its perfection, but what it grew to may be
judged from the case of Rutilius Rufus. This virtuous
administrator had set himself to protect the provincials
of Asia from the extortions of the *publicani*. He came
home bringing with him the blessings of the whole land;
but on his return the financiers had him accused (of all
things in the world) of embezzlement and extortion. He

THE ASIATIC TITHES 67

was promptly condemned, though he brought representatives of every class of the provincials to bear witness that he was the best friend they had ever known: and retired to live in honoured exile among the very people whom he was supposed to have oppressed.

Doubtless Caius did not foresee the full harvest of scandals which was destined to spring up from his treatment of the law courts. But he must have known that he was putting power into the hands of a class that could not be trusted. For the results, therefore, he must take the responsibility. Meanwhile he obtained the immediate profit that he had desired: "the Equites supported the tribune when votes were required, and received from him in return whatever they wished."

How harmful to the state were these "things which they wished" may be seen from the case of the Asiatic taxes. Since their annexation in B.C. 133, or rather since their rescue from the hands of the rebel Aristonicus in B.C. 129, the cities of Asia had been paying to Rome a fixed tribute of moderate amount. But the knights loved the system of tax-farming, and suggested to Caius that it might be introduced into this wealthiest of all the provinces. He consented, and by his law *de Provincia Asia censoribus locanda* instituted a most detestable form of it. Not only was the tithe system imposed on Asia, and the administration of it farmed out, but it was ordained that the bidding for the tithes should take place before the censors at Rome—not at Pergamus or Ephesus—and that the whole revenue of the province should be contracted for *en bloc*. The object of this strange arrangement was that provincial competition for the contracts might be excluded, firstly, by the fact that the auction was held in Italy, and, secondly, by the enormous capital required. For only a syndicate of Roman millionaires could afford to contemplate the tremendous sums that had to be dealt with, when the land revenues of the whole of the two hundred cities of Asia were handled in a single contract.

By means of Caius's law the old kingdom of Pergamus, the last region of the Hellenic East which had preserved its prosperity, was reduced in a single generation to a deplorable state of misery. The best commentary on the new system of government is that when, in the year B.C. 88, a foreign enemy entered Asia, the whole country-side rose like one man in his favour, and massacred in a single day the 80,000 Roman traders, officials, and tax-collectors who dwelt among them.

The great tribune was re-elected for a second term of office without any difficulty, and his work in B.C. 122 was a continuation of that of the previous twelve months. Several of the laws of which we have already spoken only came to full fruition in the latter year. Caius was now thoroughly well established in power as the people's prime minister: he was commencing to add a whole bundle of standing offices to his main title of tribune, being triumvir on the agrarian board, chief commissioner of roads, and official superintendent of the new colonies that were to be founded. Plutarch, speaking in a somewhat exaggerated strain, asserts that he was occupying a quasi-royal position, that he had $\mu o\nu\alpha\rho\chi\iota\kappa\eta$ $\tau\iota\varsigma$ $\iota\sigma\chi\upsilon\varsigma$. But he forgets to point out that he was destitute of one most important element of power—he had no regular armed force at his back, only the fickle bands of the urban multitude. The Roman constitution, as time was to show, could only be overthrown by an *imperator* with legions at his heels: the orator, who had but his ready tongue and his chance mob of partisans, was really unequal to the task of upsetting the old *régime*. But meanwhile his power and activity were very terrifying to the Senate. "Those who most feared the man were struck with his amazing

THE COLONY OF JUNONIA

industry, and the facility with which he despatched the most diverse kinds of business." He lived in the centre of a sort of court, frequented equally by foreign ambassadors, architects, engineers, military men, and philosophers. He had business with all these classes, received them all with urbanity, and surprised them all by his interest in and mastery of their various provinces of knowledge. It was easy for his enemies to say that there was a royal court already established in Rome, with nothing wanting save the diadem.

During his second tribunate Caius was engaged both in completing his legislation in behalf of the Equites and in developing his great colonial schemes, especially that for the establishing of the new city that was to be called Junonia, on the site of Carthage. But he was also launching out on to the development of another item of the Democratic programme: he wished to carry out that liberal extension of the citizenship to the Italian allies which had been growing more and more of a necessity during the last fifty years. Tiberius Gracchus, if we may trust Velleius, had broached the idea in B.C. 133: Fulvius Flaccus had certainly brought it to the front in B.C. 125, with no result save the unfortunate revolt of Fregellæ. But Caius had much more favourable opportunities than either his brother or Flaccus, for he had secured a much more complete hold over the Comitia than either of them had ever possessed.

The project was one which was eminently deserving of support. In former days the Roman people had been fairly generous with the franchise; not only had all the Latin and Etruscan districts around the city been granted the full citizenship one after another, but there were ways provided in which individual members of allied states further afield might become incorporated in the body of Roman burgesses. But this wise liberality had gradually

CAIUS GRACCHUS

gone out of fashion. Just as Roman citizenship grew more and more valuable, owing to the ever-increasing profits of empire, it became more and more difficult to obtain. No new territory in Latium or Etruria had been taken into the state boundary since B.C. 188, and it was growing much harder for the individual citizen of an allied community to slip into the burgess body. The fact was that the Romans in ancient days, when fighting for existence, had been eager to strengthen themselves by multiplying their numbers: now that they had acquired an empire, they were less eager to share their advantages with others. The knowledge that discontent at their niggardliness was ever growing more lively among the Italian states, had not yet begun to alarm the ordinary Roman, whether Optimate or Democrat. The city rabble were just as unconcerned about it as the most purblind reactionary in the Senate.

Caius Gracchus, therefore, had to convert his own party to the policy of liberal treatment for the allies. It was true that his brother may have advocated their cause, and that others among the leaders of the party, notably the energetic but unstable Fulvius Flaccus, were convinced of its righteousness. But the weapon with which Caius had to win his victories was the urban multitude, the one constant element in the composition of the Comitia. He thought that he could carry it with him, even when he was advocating measures which were not directly and obviously profitable to itself. Indeed, he imagined that he had bought it for ever, belly and soul, by the gift of the corn-dole. He was so far right that a great portion of the populace was ready to stick to him through thick and thin, and to vote for whatever bill he might chose to bring forward. Unfortunately for himself and for Rome, he was to discover that the whole body was not so loyal, and that men who could be bribed once to vote for the

PROPOSAL TO ENFRANCHISE THE ALLIES

Democratic side, might be influenced on another occasion by equally corrupt inducements held out by the enemy. Caius was always styling the urban multitude "the people." He was destined to find that it might be truer to call it "the rabble."

The very moderate and statesmanlike form in which Caius proposed to deal with the franchise question was to bestow the full citizenship on the Latins, and the rights hitherto held by the Latins on the remainder of the Italian allies. The "Latins" now represented not the old thirty cities of the Latin League, which had long been taken into the Roman state, but the numerous colonies with "Latin rights," *i.e.* the *jus connubii* and *jus commercii*, which were scattered all over Italy. They only wanted the power to vote in the Comitia to make them full citizens; the practical as opposed to the political advantages of the status were already in their possession. On the other hand, the main body of the Italian allies were to receive the commercial and civil privileges hitherto confined to the Latins, but were not to be introduced into the tribes, or permitted to swamp the public assembly by their enormous numbers. No doubt Caius contemplated the arrival of the day when they too might become Romans. But he had no wish to hurry matters, and intended to bring about the complete Romanisation of Italy by gradual emancipation; only after a longer or shorter training as Latins would the multitudes of Central and Southern Italy be permitted to obtain the full franchise.

All this was prudent, moderate, and far-sighted; but unfortunately there was little in the scheme to rouse enthusiasm among the more sordid members of the Democratic party—the mass of demoralised urban voters who formed the habitual majority in ordinary meetings of the Comitia. In their ignorant selfishness, they looked upon the matter from a very narrow point of view. The individual Roman citizen, they thought, would suffer if the number of his equals were increased. There would be more hands among which the bribes of the would-be consul and praetor, and the public distribution of money and food made by the state, would have to be divided. The Consul Fannius, though he had been elected by the assistance of Gracchus himself, led the opposition. He put the question in a nutshell when he asked the multitude whether they had reflected that by passing such a bill they would soon have the Latins elbowing them out of their places in the Comitia, crowding them out of the circus and theatre, and eating up their corn. This sordid and cynical appeal went to the heart of the plebeians, and the majority of them soon showed that they were ready to refuse support in this matter to the leader who vainly believed that he had purchased their perpetual allegiance.

While the franchise question was still in an early stage, a new figure appeared upon the scene, to the great perplexity of Gracchus. This was a certain Marcus Livius Drusus, a tribune of whom little had hitherto been known. He did not attempt to resist Caius by the method of mere stolid opposition, which Octavius had used ten years before against the reformer's elder brother. His plan was one which had often been tried in Greek politics. The counter-demagogue had been a well-known figure at Athens, though he was as yet unfamiliar at Rome. Drusus professed to be even more devoted to the people than his colleague, and to be ready to go yet farther in the paths of innovation. Only on two questions—that of the founding of colonies beyond the sea, and that of granting the franchise to the Italians—did he profess to differ from him. Of both these measures he disapproved, but he had his own substitutes ready, both for propitiating the allies and for providing land for the would-be colonists.

DRUSUS OUTBIDS GRACCHUS

With the object, then, of showing that he was a truer and more liberal friend of the people than Caius himself, Livius Drusus announced his intention of bringing forward a whole series of popular measures. Perhaps the most prominent of these was a huge scheme for colonisation inside Italy. Instead of choosing only two places with particularly favourable sites, as Gracchus had done, he announced that he would establish no less than twelve colonies in the peninsula, each of them to hold no less than three thousand citizens. The scheme was wholly impracticable, for these were to be agricultural and not trading centres, and agriculture, as we have already seen, was ruined beyond redemption. But the populace had not yet grasped the fact, and the plan seemed to them far more attractive than anything that Caius had proposed. Equally popular and equally futile was another bill, which was to turn all the farms which had already been distributed by the Land Commission into the private property of their occupiers. Tiberius Gracchus had made a great point of imposing a rent upon them, in order to remind the farmers that they were the tenants of the state and not full freeholders. He had also prohibited them from selling their land, for he had feared that they would be prone to dispose of their holdings at the first bad season, if they were given the chance, so that the *latifundia* would in a short time be reconstituted. It is probable that ten years of unprofitable farming had already disgusted great numbers of the settlers of B.C. 133-132, and that they were now wishing to throw up the holdings for which they had once clamoured so loudly. At any rate, there is no doubt that Drusus's proposal to make the land alienable, and to abolish the modest rent imposed by Tiberius, acquired a certain cheap popularity. There were other bills brought forward at the same time of which we have no accurate details·

one was intended to propitiate the allies for being refused the franchise; it provided that Latin soldiers should no longer be liable to the punishment of scourging by Roman officers—and probably their status in other ways was to be brought nearer to that of their comrades who possessed the full citizenship.

In proposing each of his laws, Drusus took great care to point out to the people that he was acting with the full consent and approbation of the Senate. He wished to produce the impression that popular legislation could be procured from other sources than the Democratic party, and succeeded in his aim. The majority of the urban multitude were too stupid to see that when the competition was ended by the removal or death of Gracchus, their noble friends would relapse into their former state of apathy as to the needs of the people. It has been suggested by some historians that Drusus was not a deliberate charlatan playing a part, but a real, though misguided, enthusiast, who was unconsciously made the tool of the Senate. It has been pointed out that several of the laws which he proposed in B.C. 122 were reintroduced a generation later by his son, who was a genuine Democrat of the most enthusiastic sort; and it is suggested that the elder Drusus believed in his own panacea, and passed it on as a sacred secret to his son and heir. But on the whole it is safer to believe the Roman historians when they tell us that the colleague of Gracchus was well aware of what he was doing, and had no more worthy aim than to undermine his rival's position by out-bidding him in the market of popular favour.

The waning power of Caius over the multitude was shown most clearly by the fate of his bill for the enfranchisement of the Latins. When it was brought forward, Drusus announced that he should veto it. There was no explosion of popular wrath, for the fact was that the majority of the multitude was apathetic on the point, or even held that the good things of empire had better be distributed among a few than among many Roman citizens. Caius saw no opportunity of assailing his colleague; he made no attempt to demolish him, as his brother of old had demolished Octavius; public feeling would have been against him if he had tried. Instead of starting a furious agitation on behalf of the Italians, as his friend and colleague Fulvius Flaccus proposed, he went off to Africa to superintend the foundation of his new colony of Junonia. Thus the Democratic party in the city was left in the temporary charge of Flaccus; this was unfortunate, for the ex-consul was a man equally devoid of tact and of prudence, and prone to plunge into profitless violence when freed from the restraints imposed by his more statesman-like friend.

Caius probably supposed that nothing would commend him more surely to the people than the sight of the new Carthaginian colony inaugurated with all possible pomp and splendour, and flourishing from the first, as it was bound to do, if only it obtained a fair start. He marked out the site on an even larger scale than the Rubrian law had named, and made a great parade of assembling colonists from all over Italy, apparently permitting Latins as well as Romans to send in their names. All the proper ceremonies were carried out: the flag was planted, the furrow driven round an enormous space of ground, and the boundary stones set up.

When, however, Gracchus returned from Africa to Rome, he found that his demonstration had completely missed fire. The most absurd rumours had been put about by his opponents: a legend had cropped up that Scipio had solemnly cursed the site of Carthage when he captured it in B.C. 146, and that nothing could prosper on such unlucky ground. It was said that a gale had torn down the standard which Gracchus had erected—a fact quite possible in itself, but rendered less likely by the additional garnishment of the story, which said that the boundary stones of the new colony had been dug up at night by wolves. If wolves there were, they must clearly have been two-legged Roman wolves of the Optimate breed. Nevertheless these silly tales seem to have had their effect, and to have loosened the hold of Caius on the Comitia. When the tribunicial elections came on, and he stood for the third time, he failed to be chosen. It is said that he had really a majority of votes, but that Drusus or some other tribune who presided at the poll made a fraudulent and unjust return. That such a thing should have been possible shows that at least the suffrages of the people must have been much divided, for if Caius had possessed his former ascendency, no one would have dared to juggle with the votes.

Gracchus was appalled with this misadventure. "He bore the disappointment with great impatience, and when he saw his adversaries laughing, told them with an air of insolence that they should soon be laughing on the wrong side of their mouths." Meanwhile he had only a short time left in which the invaluable tribunicial position was still his own: on the 10th of December B.C. 122, he would become a private person again, and would not only lose his power of legislation, but become liable to prosecution for any illegal acts which his enemies might choose to allege against him. The last months of his office seem to have been spent in a bitter personal struggle with Drusus. Each produced strings of popular laws to tempt the appetite of the people, and Caius had the disappointment of seeing himself outbid by a rival whose main advantage was that he was prepared to bring forward projects, possible or impossible, with no thought of the consequences

As a good Greek scholar, Gracchus must have recognised that he had fallen into the unenviable position of Cleon in the *Knights* of Aristophanes. His stewardship was about to be taken from him, and he would soon be obliged to give an account of all his doings.

At last the fatal day came round, and Caius ceased to be the sacrosanct representative of the Roman people, and became once more a private citizen. It is probable that, even if he had kept quiet, his adversaries would now have found some excuse for falling upon him: like his brother Tiberius twelve years before, he had made too many enemies. But he did not give them the opportunity of leaving him alone; within a few days of the coming of the new year, B.C. 121, he was engaged in bitter civil strife with them. For he had still plenty of partisans at his back: the better men of the Democratic party still believed in him, and among the multitude there were many whose profound hatred for the Senate and all its works had led them to distrust the gifts of Drusus. Most important of all, there was a lively agitation outside Rome: the Latins were bitterly vexed that the citizenship, which had been dangled before them for the second time, had now been again withdrawn from their reach. Their old friend, Fulvius Flaccus, got into communication with them, and assured them that he had not forgotten them, and still hoped to defend their cause. But organisation was needed to bring their forces to bear, and of organising power there seems to have been little or none on the Democratic side.

The moment that the new magistrates of B.C. 121 were installed in office, an effort was made by the Optimates to rescind as much as they dared of the Gracchan legislation. The Equites were too strong to be lightly meddled with, and the laws passed in their favour were left alone. It was still necessary to keep the urban multitude divided, so no attempt was made to touch the corn-dole. Any hint of such a design would have thrown the whole mass back into the arms of Gracchus. It was accordingly against the colonial scheme that the Optimates opened their batteries. Formal representations were made to the augurs that the omens at the foundation of Junonia had been unfavourable, and all the stories about the gale, the broken flag-staff, and the uprooted boundary stones, were brought forward. The augurs made the reply that was required: "The auspices of Junonia had been most unfavourable, and clearly showed the anger of the gods at the unhallowed attempt to build upon the cursed soil." Accordingly the Consul Opimius, who assumed the lead in all the proceedings against Gracchus, took the opinion of the Senate on the question whether it would not be right to annul the Rubrian law and disestablish the new colony. The Fathers fell in with his design, and granted him an *auctoritas* for the introduction of an act of repeal. It was accordingly brought before the people by the tribune, M. Minucius.

This brought Caius to the front. The scheme for transmarine colonisation was very dear to him. In it, as he believed, lay the true remedy for the economic distress of the Roman people. "When Gracchus and Fulvius Flaccus," says Appian, "discerned that their great project was to be thwarted, they became like madmen, and ran about declaring that all the stories about the evil omens were lies invented by the Senate." They announced their intention of opposing the Act of Repeal by every means in their power, and began, when it was too late, to organise their partisans for the fray. This was precisely what their enemies had hoped. If they could be goaded into any act of violence, they could be accused of treason, and doomed to suffer the same lot that had fallen on Tiberius Gracchus and his followers twelve years before. Neither party made any attempt to disguise their intention of using force if it should become necessary. The Optimates secretly armed their clients and slaves. On the other hand, Flaccus sent the word round rural Italy that strong arms were needed at Rome. It is said that hundreds of his partisans, disguised as labourers, came up to the city on the day when the Bill was to be brought forward, and that there were more allies than citizens among these able-bodied visitors. Caius appears to have disliked this open appeal to violence. He felt that the Democrats would be putting themselves in the wrong if they began the fray, and seems to have discouraged his followers by his fervid appeals to them not to take the offensive. But the die was cast. The more enthusiastic Democrats were determined to fight, and came down to the assembly armed with daggers and staves as if a conflict was absolutely certain. They were so far right, and their leader so far wrong, that in the present strained situation of affairs there was no hope of a peaceful issue.

On the day of voting the Optimates and the Democrats faced each other more like two armies than two orderly political factions. On each side the lethal weapons were barely disguised beneath the broad folds of the togas. The only doubt was whether the enemies or the partisans of Gracchus would strike the first blow. As a matter of fact, the Democrats put themselves in the wrong by opening the battle by a wanton murder.

The Consul Opimius had opened the proceedings by the usual sacrifice in the porch of the Capitoline temple. When he had done, one of his servants—a certain Q. Antullius—who was carrying away the entrails of the victim, rudely pushed through the front rank of the Democrats, crying, "Stand off, ye bad citizens, and make way for honest men." It is said that he emphasised his insulting words by making a gesture of contempt in the very face of Gracchus. At this Caius gave him a fierce look, whereupon an over-zealous follower stepped forward and stabbed the man through and through with a dagger. Antullius fell dead between the two parties, with the sacred entrails still in his hand.

Prepared for strife as all those present had been, they were yet shocked by this sacrilegious murder. No mêlée followed, but the enemies stood gazing upon each other, and no one dared to strike a second blow. At this moment a sudden thunderstorm burst over the Capitol, and, awed by the manifest wrath of Jupiter, the whole armed multitude melted homeward in the drenching rain.

The day ended without the expected battle, but blood had been shed, and the Optimates were able to cast the responsibility for the commencement of civil strife upon their adversaries. It is certain that if Antullius had been left alone, the contest would merely have broken out a few minutes later, for both crowds were bent on mischief, and the most trivial incident would have sufficed to set them by the ears. Morally speaking, the guilt may be equally divided between them, for each had come down prepared to fight, and if the Democrats had not struck the first blow, the Optimates would have done so a little later. Both the Consul Opimius and the headstrong Fulvius Flaccus had deliberately got ready for battle, and whatever may have been the private feelings of Caius, it is certain that he came down armed to support his friends. His admirers have alleged that he was precipitated into civil war against his will; his detractors have quite as much to say for their view when they assert that he lost his opportunity for carrying out a *coup d'état* because a reckless fool struck too soon, and placed his whole party at a moral disadvantage.

There can be no doubt that the dagger-thrust dealt by

this over-zealous Democrat ruined his party. It was to little purpose that Caius went down to the Forum that same afternoon, and tried to explain away what had happened as a deplorable accident, for which he was not responsible. Many who might otherwise have supported him had been profoundly shocked, and it is impossible for the man who has placed himself at the head of an armed mob to disavow any connection with its atrocities. Just as Robert Emmett was responsible for the murder of Lord Kilwarden, though he may not himself have thrust a pike into the old judge, so was Caius Gracchus responsible for the murder of Antullius. It is useless in such cases to plead blameless character and patriotic intentions. Moreover, the friends of Caius did not even take the trouble to excuse themselves. Fulvius Flaccus, when the assembly had broken up, called together a mob of his supporters, harangued them, and armed them with a store of weapons which lay in his house, for he possessed a complete arsenal of Gallic broadswords and lances, the trophies of his successful campaign of B.C. 125. He and his reckless satellites passed the night in noise, riot, and carousing; the ex-consul himself, it is said, was the first man drunk, and in his cups uttered many *obiter dicta* most unbecoming in one who was about to plunge the city into war next morning. The behaviour of Caius was very different; he burst into tears on leaving the Forum and shut himself up in his room, gloomily pondering over the end to which two years of civic power had brought him. But though he did not commit himself to any overt course of action, a great mob of his partisans gathered round his house, and encamped about it all night. Another mass collected in the Capitol before dawn, to occupy the points of vantage for the struggle which was expected to break out in the morning.

Meanwhile Opimius and the other foes of the Democratic party had been making much more practical preparations. The consul had ordered every senator and every knight of the Optimate party to provide two fully armed men; he had taken command of a body of Cretan mercenaries who chanced to be passing through the city, and had ordered a general muster of the clients and retainers of his friends. They were a formidable band, and, with the magistrates at their head, they had the inestimable advantage of appearing to represent law and order.

Protected by this mass of special constables the Senate met next morning. The consul began to lay before them the desperate state of affairs, and the necessity for outlawing the Democratic leaders. At this moment, by a preconcerted arrangement, the bier of Antullius, followed by his mourning friends, was borne past the doors of the Senate-house. The Fathers rushed out and burst forth into exaggerated demonstrations of horror and sympathy. Then flocking back to their seats they passed the *senatus consultum ultimum*, which empowered the consuls, in the usual terms, "to take care that the republic might receive no harm." Rome was thus put under martial law, and as a last formality messengers were sent to Gracchus and to Fulvius Flaccus, bidding them repair in person to the Curia in order to give an account of their doings.

Frightened at the great armed force around the Senate-house, the Democrats had begun to concentrate on the Aventine. They were almost destitute of guidance, for Caius was sunk in a melancholy apathy, and Flaccus was barely recovered from the effects of last night's debauch; it was with difficulty that he could be roused at all that morning. The only intention displayed was to stand at bay on the old plebeian stronghold; no offensive action seems even to have been contemplated. But the temple

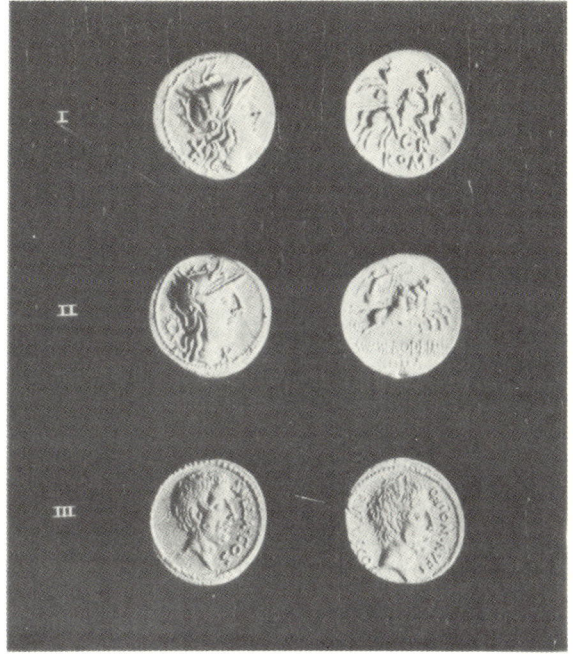

Roman Coins from the British Museum. (Plate I.)

I. Denarius of Ti. Gracchus the Elder, father of the two Gracchi.
II. Denarius of L. Opimius, the slayer of Caius Gracchus.
III. Denarius with Portraits of Sulla and of Pompeius Rufus, his colleague as consul in B.C. 88.

THE FIGHT ON THE AVENTINE

of Diana and the neighbouring streets were barricaded, and emissaries ran round the city calling the multitude to arms, and even promising freedom to any slaves who should join them. This last anarchic proposal must have disposed of any chance that Caius might gain support among his old allies of the equestrian order. The very name of a slave-rising was enough to make an Optimate of every man of independent means.

It was probably the perception of the fact that the number of their partisans on the Aventine was much smaller than they had expected, which led the Democratic leaders to negotiate before opening hostilities. When they received the message from the Senate, which bade them come down and justify their actions, Caius, it is said, seriously proposed to take his life in his hands and obey the summons. But Flaccus objected to put himself in the power of the enemy. He would only consent to send his son Quintus with a reply, in which the garrison of the Aventine offered to lay down its arms and disperse, if a complete amnesty was offered to every citizen, small or great. It is said that many of the senators were not indisposed to accept these terms: except to fanatics, anything is better than civil war. But Opimius carried a majority with him when he declared that traitors could not send ambassadors, but should come in person to surrender themselves to justice before they sued for mercy. The young Flaccus was sent back to his father, and told not to come again, unless he brought with him an offer of unconditional surrender.

After some futile debating between the leaders of the Democrats, the proposal to capitulate without terms was negatived, and the son of Flaccus was once more despatched to the Senate with a second set of offers. Opimius told him that he had been warned not to return, and that he had forfeited any claims to be considered an ambassador. He cast the young man into prison, and ordered his armed bands to converge upon the Aventine. Then he published a notice that any one who laid down his arms before fighting began should be granted an amnesty, but that Gracchus and Fulvius were public enemies, and that whoever brought their heads to the consuls should be paid for them their actual weight in gold.

The rumour of this proclamation, and the sight of the Optimate bands working upwards among the streets that lead to the summit of the Aventine, was too much for the resolution of most of the Democrats. A great many slunk off to their houses while yet it was time. But enough remained to defend the barricades, and for some little space there was sharp fighting between the two parties. But the Cretan archers so galled the Democrats that ere long they gave back from their position, and the assailants stormed the hill-top and burst in among them. Then followed a massacre; no less than three thousand persons are said to have been slain, and their bodies cast into the Tiber. Fulvius Flaccus and his elder son Marcus hid themselves in the house of a client, but when their pursuers threatened to burn down the whole street unless they were given up, an informer was promptly forthcoming. They were beheaded on the spot without form of trial. Caius Gracchus was not found upon the Aventine. No one had seen him during the fighting: he had shut himself up in the temple of Diana, and proposed to commit suicide when the barricades were forced. But two of his friends, the knights Pomponius and Laetorius, took his dagger from him, and persuaded him to fly before it was yet too late there was still a way of escape by the Porta Trigemina and the Sublician bridge. Before leaving the temple, Caius is said to have fallen upon his knees, and with upraised hands to have prayed to the

THE DEATH OF CAIUS

goddess "that the people of Rome, for their ingratitude and base desertion of their friend, might be slaves for ever." If the story is true, it well explains the mood of sullen despair which had lain heavy on his soul for the last twenty-four hours. He had pushed things to extremity, and then his party had melted away from him. All his plans, as he now saw, had been futile from the first, because he had mistaken the urban rabble of to-day for the ancient citizens of Rome.

Caius and his two friends were sighted by some of the victorious Optimates as they fled down towards the Tiber. They made what speed they could, but the reformer presently stumbled and fell, spraining his ankle, so that he could no longer move with ease. By the river gate the pursuers were nearing them; thereupon Pomponius bravely turned to bay, and held them back for a moment at the cost of his life. Laetorius did as much on the Sublician bridge, and by their sacrifice Caius, now accompanied only by a single slave,[1] reached the suburb under the Janiculum beyond the water. As he hobbled on, supported by his retainer, the streets were full of idle spectators, who shouted to him to run his best, as if he were a competitor in the circus. But no one gave him the least assistance, though he kept calling for a horse as he went. Before the Optimates came up, he had got beyond the last houses, and reached the Grove of Furina, just outside the city. He was seen to enter it, but when the pursuers burst in after him, they found both him and his companion lying dead. At his master's orders the slave had stabbed him to the heart, and had then turned his weapon against himself. The head of the reformer was cut off and carried to the Consul: his body was cast into the Tiber Opimius carried out his promise, and gave the bearer of

---

[1] Some call him Philocrates, others Euporus.

the head its weight in gold—seventeen pounds eight ounces, as tradition recorded.[1]

Thus miserably ended the career of the younger Gracchus, a man who, both as a politician and as an individual, was strangely compacted of strength and weakness. Clearly he was no single-minded enthusiast like his brother. He had studied statecraft, and had learnt not to be over-scrupulous in his methods. If, indeed, he was set on regenerating the people of Rome, he chose the strangest allies and employed the most doubtful means. He must have been perfectly well aware of what he was doing, when he purchased the support of the urban rabble by the gift of the corn-dole, and that of the greedy Equites by surrendering to them the unhappy province of Asia. When the means are so obviously immoral, one is driven into doubting the purity of the end which they are intended to subserve. Was Gracchus really set on saving Rome from the economic and constitutional perils which were sapping her strength? Or was he rather an ambitious politician yearning for power at all costs, and eager to revenge on the Senate his brother's death? It is easy to read his career in either light, yet each reading must be full of contradictions. If we hold, with Mommsen, that Caius was deliberately trying to make himself tyrant of Rome, we can easily understand all the less worthy episodes of his career. The man with such an idea in his head would not have shrunk from using unworthy tools or practising any sort of political charlatanry. To purchase the aid of the rabble or the knights by bribes, to flatter the hopes of

[1] A well-known story relates that the recipient of this sum, one L. Septimuleius, had taken out the brains and filled the cavity with lead, in order to defraud the consul. But how could the man have gone through this elaborate and disgusting operation in the crowded street, encompassed by the other pursuers who had been "in at the death?"

the Italians who desired the franchise, would be appropriate moves for one who aimed at repeating the career of Cypselus or Peisistratus. But this theory leaves unexplained the reluctance which Caius manifested at the end to engage in actual civil war, the want of energy which he displayed in organising his party for the final conflict, and the melancholy apathy which he showed during the last twenty-four hours of his life. If he had really aimed at supreme power, such conduct could be explained by physical cowardice alone, and of that not even his enemies dared to accuse him. A would-be tyrant would have armed and organised bravos, have attacked the Senate instead of assuming the defensive, and have thrown himself into the battle with frantic energy. All the doings of Caius, on the other hand, are those of a man forced into violence against his will, and obviously doubting whether death was not preferable to the guilt of stirring up civil war. They are not the acts of one who wishes to grasp at supreme power and cares not how it is attained.

On the other hand, as we have already seen, it is still more impossible to explain his career by representing him as a single-hearted friend of the people, who thought nothing of himself, and only aimed at regenerating the Roman state. Ambition, revenge, the reckless use of unworthy methods, are too easily discernible in many of his actions.

Probably the true way of reconciling the contradictions of the life of Caius is to realise that though he possessed many of the instincts of the tyrant and the demagogue, there was also latent in him much of the ancient Roman civic virtue. He loved to rule, he was unscrupulous in his methods, he hated fiercely the Optimates and all their works; but at the same time he had a genuine wish to serve the state; he showed it by persisting in his schemes for transmarine colonisation and the enfranchisement of the Italians long after they had become unpopular. A mere self-seeker would have dropped them the moment that he was certain that they failed to please the rabble of the Comitia. When at last he found himself borne on irresistibly toward civil war, Caius was deeply grieved. He faced it with reluctance, and finally had it thrust upon him, against his will, by the reckless folly of his subordinates. The responsibility, no doubt, must ultimately rest upon his shoulders: he might have retired to bide his time instead of fighting. But to do so was almost impossible: he was surrounded by excited partisans whom he could not control, and if he had gone back, he would have seemed to be betraying them to his and their enemies. The outburst of actual war and the reformer's dreadful end were melancholy but inevitable.

CHAPTER IV

FROM THE GRACCHI TO SULLA

B.C. 121-88.

CAIUS GRACCHUS was a striking example of the truth of the melancholy adage that

> "The evil that men do lives after them,
> The good is oft interred with their bones."

For among all the many measures that he brought before the Roman people, precisely those which were evil in their tendencies survived him, while those wherein lay the seeds of good were thrust aside and ignored for another generation. The corn-dole which he had invented proved so popular that the victorious Optimates dared not meddle with it. It remained as a permanent curse, pauperising and demoralising the city multitude, and ruining what was left of Italian agriculture. The new equestrian jury-courts sold justice so shamelessly, for the next thirty years, that men began at last to talk of the period when the senators had been judges as the good old times. The Asiatic tithe-farming went on, and gradually ruined that fine province, besides provoking therein such a virulent hatred of Rome, that (as we have already pointed out) when the Asiatics got their first chance of revolt, in the days of King Mithradates, they rose like one man and massacred 80,000 Roman citizens in a single day.

But the two really valuable remedies for the ills of the state which Gracchus had advocated were thrust aside, if not forgotten. Transmarine colonisation was stopped, and the new settlement at Carthage was destroyed. The Italians were commanded to give up all idea of obtaining the franchise; indeed, special care was taken to close the various avenues by which individuals had hitherto found it possible to slip into the citizen body.

As to the Agrarian Law, which Tiberius had framed and Caius had re-enacted, the Senate did not formally repeal it, nor did they give back the confiscated land to the *possessores*. They simply removed, one by one, the Gracchan checks on the economic tendency of the times, and allowed the new farmers to die out by slow extinction. Livius Drusus, it will be remembered, had made the Gracchan allotments alienable, and abolished the ground-rent due from them, even before Caius fell. In B.C. 119 a law was passed which dissolved the Land Commission, so that no further distribution could be made; it also provided that such domain land as still remained in the hands of the original *possessores* should be secured to them on condition of their paying a small rent, which was to be employed in subsidising the ever-growing needs of the corn-dole. Lastly, in B.C. 111, a third law was passed, which removed this rent and made the land into the freehold private property of the occupiers.[1] The moment that they got the opportunity of alienating their farms, under the law of Drusus, the Gracchan holders began to dispose of them. Agriculture did not, and could not, pay; political economy exerted its iron law, and the allotments were sold, for what they would fetch, to the nearest capitalist. The *latifundia* once more commenced to grow up, and the decrease in the number of small landowners is marked from B.C. 118 onward by the regular shrinkage of the census-returns. By the end of the century it is probable that the whole effect of the Gracchan

[1] The territory of ancient Capua, the Ager Campanus, was now the only important tract of public property remaining.

redistribution of land had passed away. Only a few years later it was said, doubtless with gross exaggeration, that the larger part of the land of Roman Italy was in the hands of no more than 2000 proprietors.

Meanwhile it must be remembered that the Senate never thoroughly recovered that undisputed control of all the machinery of the state which it had possessed in the old days before the appearance of the Gracchi. It never dared to strike at the Equestrian Order, which remained as a permanent check on its omnipotence. Even when the abuse of the law-courts by the knights had grown into a perfect scandal, the Senate refused to commit itself to an attack upon such a powerful body of enemies. Apparently the leading Optimates lived in a state of constant apprehension that a new Gracchus might at any moment arise to dispute their authority, and wished to do no more than to avoid friction and hang on to the emoluments of power. They managed, by a policy of short-sighted opportunism, to maintain their ascendency from year to year, till at last, after a considerable interval, the Democratic party again found leaders and a programme, and civic strife recommenced.

From the death of Caius Gracchus in B.C. 121, down to the appearance of Marius on the political stage in B.C. 106, the Democratic programme lay dormant. The history of the time turns mainly on questions of foreign policy, and it was by their incompetent management of those questions that the Optimates finally gave their adversaries a chance of raising their heads. It was not an age of peace: all through these years the people were muttering and murmuring; occasionally there were riots, or an unpopular magistrate was impeached, or a law backed by the Senate was rejected in the Comitia. But there was no continuous agitation for any definite political end, nor did any leader succeed in rallying the Democratic faction for a new attack on the Senate. As the constitution then stood, a single omnipotent leader, provided with the tribunate or some other important magistracy, was needed to galvanise the sovereign people into activity. It could only put forth its strength if guided by an autocratic chief, using the "one-man power" which a democracy really loves. And the chief was long in coming.

Meanwhile the main thread of the annals of Rome consists of the history of two long foreign wars, both grossly mismanaged by the Senate at home and by the incapable oligarchs who were sent out to bear rule in the provinces. These were the lingering Jugurthine troubles [B.C. 117–105] and the dangerous Cimbrian war [B.C. 113–101]. It is unfortunate that while we possess an elaborate (if not altogether trustworthy) narrative of the African affair in Sallust's *Jugurtha*, the story of the far more important Cimbrian campaigns has to be gathered from imperfect notes in Plutarch, Appian, and the Epitome of Livy.

It was in consequence of the Jugurthine war that the Democrats first began to raise their heads again. The facts of the Senate's maladministration were sufficiently disgraceful. The king of a not very powerful subject state had broken all his treaties, slain off the cousins whom the Senate had made his colleagues, and done whatever he pleased in Africa, without paying the least attention to the commands of the suzerain power. When embassies of remonstrance were sent him, he had merely quieted the envoys by judicious bribes combined with lavish promises of submission. He carried on this shameless policy for five years (B.C. 117–112), and might have persisted even longer in it, if he had not let the savage break out in him at an inauspicious moment. When he crushed his last surviving cousin by the capture

THE JUGURTHINE WAR 93

of Cirta in B.C. 112, he massacred not only the Numidian garrison, but a great number of Roman and Italian residents in the place. This atrocity so much aroused the anger of the Roman people that the Senate was forced to declare war on Jugurtha. It was abominably mismanaged; of the two imbecile generals to whom the subjection of Numidia was first entrusted, one granted the king terms of peace which the indignant people refused to ratify. The second so misconducted himself that his army was scattered, beaten, and sent under the yoke.

These disasters roused a tempest of wrath at Rome; public opinion was so strongly excited that under a temporary leader—one Mamilius Limetanus—the people created a Court of High Commission, which raged against the prominent members of the Optimate ring, sent into exile the two incapable generals Bestia and Albinus, and revenged an old grudge by packing off after them Opimius, the consul who in B.C. 121 had put down Gracchus and his friends with such cruel zeal. But in spite of this outburst the Senate was not yet deprived of the control of foreign affairs, and was allowed to send forth against Jugurtha its best fighting man, Q. Caecilius Metellus [B.C. 109].

The new general was fairly successful, but he did not work quickly enough to please the angry critics of the forum. He took most of Jugurtha's fortresses, but the king fled into the Atlas and the Sahara, and maintained a desperate guerilla warfare which seemed likely to linger on for ever. The people were, perhaps unjustly, dissatisfied; they did not understand (as we understand only too well in this year of grace 1902) the difficulties of hunting down elusive bands of marauding light horse.

It was at this moment that there at last appeared a serious candidate for the headship of the Democratic party. Caius Marius was a man of a very different type from his predecessors in that post; he was a rude soldier who had risen from the ranks by his hard head and undaunted courage. He had none of the literary polish, the philosophic training, or the lofty eloquence of the two Gracchi. As a politician he can only be described as a blatant demagogue; he had not the brains or the imagination to sketch out a political programme. He was no more than a discontented and ambitious veteran, with a personal grievance. His simple method of achieving notoriety was to declaim to the multitude concerning the very real abuses of the senatorial government, and to promise to set all to rights if he were made consul. He most unjustly blamed Metellus for the protraction of the war, and promised to end everything in a year if only he were placed in office. He had been provoked by the aristocratic hauteur and quiet insolence of the proconsul, and was thinking quite as much of revenging personal slights to himself as of giving the Democratic party an opportunity of seizing the reins of power.

The vulgar self-assertion and coarse invective of Marius did not disgust the multitude; he was duly elected, and straightway went over to Africa to supersede Metellus. The province was not assigned to him by the Senate. In spite of their opposition he had a bill passed in the Assembly, which gave him charge of the Numidian war. But though he took large reinforcements with him, legions raised on a new system, by volunteers from the lower orders of the city, he was not at first much more successful than his predecessor. He scoured the whole country-side with movable columns, but he could not catch the evasive Jugurtha. His reputation might have been wrecked if chance had not come in to his aid. His quaestor, L. Cornelius Sulla, at last succeeded in capturing the Numidian king, not by force of arms, but by treachery. He bribed Jugurtha's Moorish allies to seize and surrender their guest; the king was kidnapped and made over to Marius, and then the war came suddenly to an end [B.C. 105].

Marius had redeemed his promise to put an end to the Numidian struggle, though the method in which it closed was neither glorious nor dignified. But he had saved his reputation, and was able to celebrate a triumph, and to pose before his supporters as a successful general. At the moment of his return he had the state at his mercy, for the Senate was cowed, and the people would have been ready to grant him anything he asked. Moreover, he had legions at his back; the democracy for the first time was armed with sword and shield, and did not depend on the stones and staves of riotous mobs.

If external troubles had not intervened there must have been a political explosion of some sort in B.C. 105–104; it might very possibly have ended in the installation of Marius as temporary ruler of Rome. But neither he nor the Senate had the leisure to turn their attention to domestic politics. For the first time since the fall of Hannibal a serious danger from without was impending over Italy. The year B.C. 105 witnessed the most dreadful disaster to the Roman arms, with the possible exception of Cannæ, that ever occurred in the days of the Republic. For the last eight years there had been unrest along the northern frontier of the empire, both in the Balkan Peninsula and in the Alpine lands. All the unknown barbarism of Central Europe was on the move; tribe was thrusting against tribe, and the outer waves of the seething whirlpool of nations were washing against the borders of the provinces of Macedonia and Narbonese Gaul. At first the troubles were not serious; the attention of Rome was distracted to the Jugurthine war, and little attention was paid to the raids of the Celts or Germans. But things gradually grew worse: several small Roman armies were cut to pieces: there were mishaps of some importance in 113, 109, and 107. At last the situation grew so threatening that the Senate despatched two large armies—a dozen legions of raw recruits — to defend the frontiers of Gaul. For the originators of all the stress and turmoil, the great mass of migratory bands whom we vaguely know under the name of the Cimbri and Teutons, had thrust aside the lesser tribes and were marching against Italy itself.

An awful disaster ensued: the two incapable and quarrelsome generals, Mallius and Caepio, found the invaders on the Lower Rhone, and attacked them with foolhardy confidence. They did not even combine their forces, though their camps were less than a day's march apart. Caepio, in disobedience to the orders of his superior, attacked the enemy's camp in the morning: he was defeated and his legions annihilated. In the afternoon the Germans threw themselves upon Mallius, slew him, and cut to pieces the whole of the second Roman army. Eighty thousand men fell in the two battles of Arausio [Oct. 6, 105]: not a cohort remained to guard the passes of the Alps: the only hope of Rome was in the army which Marius was bringing home from Africa. If the barbarians had marched at once for Turin or Genoa, it is hard to say what they might not have accomplished. But they lingered long in the valley of the Rhone, and then, to the surprise of all men, drifted away towards the Pyrenees instead of crossing the Alps.

Thus Rome was given the chance of re-organising the defence of her frontiers, and Marius, instead of practising demagogy in the Forum, hurried northward with his troops, to interpose between the barbarians and the gates of Italy. The Cimbrian war, contrary to all expectation, was protracted for five summers (B.C. 105–101), and Marius, re-elected year after year to the consulship, was kept perpetually in the field, watching for the moment when the enemy should at last make up their minds to deliver their great stroke. It was not till they had wandered far and wide in Spain and Gaul, spreading devastation around them, that the barbarians turned back at last to the true objective, and marched in two vast columns against Italy, the Teutons by the nearer route through Provence, the Cimbri by the longer sweep that leads through Southern Germany, by the Brenner Pass and the line of the Adige, down to Verona.

Marius now showed that at least his reputation as a soldier had not been exaggerated. We must not linger over the details of his two great victories. In 102 he warred down the Teutons in a long running fight among the hills of Provence, which ended with their complete destruction at the battle of Aquae Sextiae. In the following spring he crossed the Alps into Italy to meet the Cimbri, who had at last completed their long circular march, and had descended into the plains of the Po. At Vercellae he annihilated them, with a slaughter as great as that of his Teutonic victory in the preceding year. The disaster of Mallius and Caepio was revenged, and Rome was safe from the Northern invader for another five hundred years.

The man who had put an end to the long nightmare of fear which had hung over the city from the day of Arausio to that of Vercellae, might have asked and obtained from the people any reward that he might choose. They offered libations to him, as if he were a god, and hailed him as "the third founder of Rome:" he might have been her eighth king had he known the right way in which to sue for the sceptre and the diadem. But the great general was the most bungling and incompetent of politicians. His naïve vanity and clumsy ostentation made him ere long ridiculous—a grave fault in a pretender to supreme power. The Optimates sneered at his solecisms in grammar and in dress: these might have been imperceptible to the multitude, but even they were forced to laugh at a consul who was always trying to make great political harangues and breaking down hopelessly in the middle. "The firmness which he displayed in battle did not accompany him into the assembly, and the least interruption or distraction disconcerted him, so that he promptly became incoherent." Moreover, even the rabble would have preferred a leader who did not mix vulgar familiarity and vainglorious ostentation in such a curious measure, and who could have concealed more successfully his growing addiction to the wine-cup.

But, in spite of all his obvious defects, Marius was firmly convinced that he was to be not only the preserver of Rome from the barbarians, but also the destined "saviour of society," who was to take up the task of the Gracchi and to tear the administration of the empire from the incapable hands of the Senate. A little experience convinced him that he was not really suited for the work of a mob orator, nor for the drawing up of an elaborate political programme of reforms. But the only result of this discovery was to make him resolve to take into his pay useful persons capable of writing his speeches and drafting his bills for him. He must find tools and mouthpieces who would act as his agents in the work of revolution.

Unskilful in every political action, Marius enlisted as his managing partners two able and reckless scoundrels, whose disreputability was to be the ruin both of himself and of the Democratic cause. These two choice spirits, L. Appuleius Saturninus and C. Servilius Glaucia, were the Roman counterparts of the Cleophons and Hyperboli of Athens. The former was a contentious, obstinate man,

SATURNINUS AND HIS LAWS

who (as quaestor in 104) had a quarrel with the Senate, in which he considered that he was ill-treated. Since then he had devoted himself to the career of malcontent and exposer of abuses. In B.C. 103 he had obtained the tribunate, and had used its powers by bringing perpetual charges of bribery or misconduct against unpopular Optimates, by raising mobs, and by sweeping the streets whenever the spirit seized him. He was now anxious to take another turn of tribunicial power. His colleague, Glaucia, seems to have been a shade less violent, but even more insolent and disreputable. His special talent lay in the direction of vulgar and indecent stump oratory, with which he could always keep the multitude on the roar.

Having enlisted the support of this precious pair, Marius started on his career as a Democratic reformer. He allowed Saturninus to draw up the programme for him; he for his part was to support it with the majesty of his military reputation, and, if necessary, by calling in the aid of his disbanded veterans, who were loafing about the city by thousands, living on the great donatives which they had received at the end of the Cimbric war. The "platform" of the revived Democratic party consisted of a reproduction, with some slight variations, of the schemes of Caius Gracchus. The permanent support of the urban mob was to be bought by a grotesque exaggeration of that statesman's detestable corn-law. The dole had been issued to the citizens since B.C. 122 at the rate of $6\frac{1}{2}$ asses per modius. Saturninus proposed to sell the corn for the ridiculous price of five-sixths of an as; he might as well have given it away for nothing. Less objectionable by far was the revival of Gracchus's great scheme for transmarine colonisation. Saturninus had already[1] proposed to revive the Gracchan scheme of colonising Africa, for the benefit

[1] As early as B.C. 103, it would appear.

of the veterans of the Jugurthine war. Now he produced a grandiose plan for transmarine colonisation on the largest scale. It included a law for the planting of colonies in Achaia, Macedonia, and Sicily, and another for the distribution of great regions both in Gaul and in Africa among the victorious soldiery of the Cimbric war. Marius was to be entrusted with the execution of the whole vast scheme. The Italians were also to be pacified by this measure, for they were to be included in the Gallic distribution, and each settler was to receive full burgess rights. Saturninus had grasped the fact that the city rabble, on whose votes he had to subsist, objected to the enfranchised Italians at home, who might cram the Forum and scramble for doles, but had no objection to the enfranchised Italian who had been packed off to Africa or Central Gaul. Out of sight would be out of mind. His colonisation scheme, therefore, was contrived to play a double part, in satisfying the veterans and in pacifying the allies. In strict accordance with Gracchan precedents, bills were added to strengthen the already over-great power of the Equites in the law-courts. But there was a most original novelty included in the Appuleian Law: the reckless tribune subjoined to it a clause compelling every senator to swear obedience to the whole code within five days of its passing the Comitia, on pain of losing his seat. For intolerant suppression of adverse opinion no more stringent device had ever been invented. The Senate as a power in the state would have been annihilated, if it had been forced to submit to such ordinances.

But it was not so much the contents of the Appuleian Laws which proved fatal to their framer and his patron, as the way in which the laws were carried. Saturninus's whole career was a carnival of violence and outrage. He habitually went about attended by turbulent mobs, who

OUTRAGES COMMITTED BY SATURNINUS

beat or slew any one who dared to differ from their idol. His followers were capable of anything: in the tribunicial elections for B.C. 100 it seemed probable that he would fail to be chosen. Thereupon a band of his satellites fell upon and stoned to death Q. Nonius, one of the successful candidates. Saturninus was elected to fill the vacant place. It was just possible to look upon this sinister coincidence as the work of chance; but no one could mistake its meaning when precisely the same thing happened at the consular elections for the succeeding year. Glaucia was a candidate under the protection of Saturninus and Marius. It seemed likely that he might be beaten by Caius Memmius, a man who, though now a moderate member of the Optimate party, had been a very popular Tribune of the Plebs eleven years before, and had headed the agitation against the mismanagement of the Jugurthine war. The moment that his candidature was seen to be dangerous, Memmius was set upon by a gang of ruffians and beaten to death.

These were perhaps the most shocking of the deeds of Marius's enterprising lieutenant, but his general behaviour was quite in keeping with them. When the law dealing with the corn-dole and the Gallic colonies was before the Comitia, some Optimate tribunes tried to interpose their veto. Saturninus did not take the trouble to deal with them as Tiberius Gracchus had dealt with Octavius; he simply had them thrown off the rostra and went on with the proceedings. The evicted magistrates, though much knocked about, struggled to the front and began crying that "they heard thunder on the left," which should have brought the meeting to an end. But Saturninus, pointing with a menacing gesture to the stones which his followers were gathering up, told them that they had better beware, or it would not only rain but hail. The tribunes discreetly fled; but a hot-headed young Optimate, the quaestor Q. Caepio, collected a band of his clients and supporters, girt up his toga and stormed the rostra, upsetting Saturninus and those about him. The assailants were but a handful, and the demagogue, rallying his forces and putting Marian veterans in his front rank, charged back, drove off Caepio and his gang, and completed the formalities of passing the bill among desperate noise, confusion, and tumult.

It was farcical to call such a mere riot a legal meeting of the Comitia, or to hold that bills which had been vetoed by half-a-dozen tribunes had any binding force. But it was for refusing to swear obedience to them that Quintus Metellus, the haughty but honest and capable predecessor of Marius in Numidia, was driven into exile.

There seemed to be no length to which Saturninus and Glaucia would not go. But their triumphant violence defeated their own ends: Marius was prepared to wink at a good deal of ruffianism on the part of his supporters, but he drew the line at the systematic murder of respectable opponents, and would have preferred to see the opposite party in the assembly overawed by threats rather than driven out with sticks and stones. Clearly he began to fear his own lieutenants, and to doubt whether they might not turn against him instead of merely carrying out his plans. He suddenly dropped his support of them, secretly informed the Optimates that he would not be responsible for their acts, and passed the word round among his veterans that they were to remain neutral.

Exasperated at being disavowed by their employer, Saturninus and Glaucia tried to continue their wild career on their own behalf, and in December B.C. 100 brought matters to a head by seizing the Capitol with the object of carrying through a regular *coup d'état*. What exactly they intended to accomplish we cannot guess; certainly it can hardly have been (as their enemies asserted) to proclaim

Saturninus king, or even dictator. But deprived of the aid of the veterans of Marius, they proved no more able to defend themselves than Caius Gracchus and Fulvius had been in B.C. 121. The Optimates easily shut them in and held them beleaguered, while the Senate proclaimed martial law. Marius, much against his will, was forced to lend his sanction as consul to their proceedings. When the besiegers had succeeded in cutting off the supply of water from the Capitol, Saturninus and his crew were forced to surrender. They were placed under a guard in the Senate-house by the orders of Marius; but the Optimate mob tore off the roof, and pelted the prisoners to death with tiles before the consul could interfere.

Thus ended the third attempt of the Democratic party to seize the conduct of affairs, and to make an end of the Senate as a governing body. It failed mainly from the incapacity of Marius either to conduct a political campaign himself, or to select agents who would be competent to do so in his behalf. If he had known how to secure men of tact and discretion instead of reckless incendiaries, he might have done what he pleased: for the strength of his reputation would have carried everything before it in B.C. 101, and the arms of his veterans were at his disposal. But Saturninus, in spite of a certain ability and energy, was frankly impossible either as leader or lieutenant. He would have wrecked any cause by his insolence and recklessness.

Marius, much disappointed by the failure of his schemes, and more or less conscious of the ridiculous figure which he had cut, retired from Rome when his consulship was over, and went for a long tour in Asia, under the pretext of fulfilling a vow which he had made during the Cimbrian war to the gods of the East. When he returned, he found that he had been half-forgotten, and that the Senate was more powerful than it had been at any time since the fall of the Gracchi. There was a gap of more than eight years before any serious political strife again arose at Rome; but the unsatisfactory economic and constitutional position of the Republic once more produced its inevitable result, and a new reformer arose.

Marcus Livius Drusus differed from his predecessors in that he was in no sense a legitimate descendant of the Gracchi. He was what in modern phraseology we should call a "Tory-Democrat." He believed that the Senate was far more fitted than the assembly to administer the empire. He had taken part against Saturninus in B.C. 100, and his views, as to what were the main dangers of the state and how these dangers should be met, differed from those which were held by the Democratic party. In personal character he was as unlike Saturninus and Glaucia as can well be imagined, being a man of very staid and even haughty carriage, extremely strict in his morals, and self-conscious beyond the limit of priggishness.[1] He was so well aware of his own virtues that his dying words are recorded to have been that "he wondered how many years would elapse before the state would get another citizen as good as himself."

After having studied for several years the unsatisfactory condition of the Republic, Drusus had come to the conclusion that its main dangers were the ever-growing power and insolence of the Equestrian Order, the corpora-

[1] That Drusus was a well-developed specimen of the prig is indubitably shown by the delightful story concerning his interview with the architect. Part of the tribune's house was much overlooked by his neighbour's windows. The architect who was rebuilding it came to him with a plan showing how, by judicious alterations, he could prevent his domestic doings from being witnessed. Drusus rejected the idea with scorn, saying "Nay, use your skill to build so that all that I do may be visible to all my neighbours!" If they would study his acts they would see exactly how the life of a Roman citizen ought to be managed.

M. DRUSUS AND HIS SCHEMES

tion of financiers to whom Caius Gracchus had sacrificed the state, and the discontent of the Italian allies. He also thought that something might still be done to re-establish the yeoman class by providing new colonies at Capua (an old idea of C. Gracchus) and in Sicily. There was nothing in these views which might not be held by a sincere Optimate, and Drusus found that he might look for support from all the more enlightened members of the Senate. For the first time a reformer was backed by a large proportion of the most important men in the state. The better sort of senators had long been chafing at the corruption of the equestrian law-courts, and of late the condemnation of the virtuous Rutilius Rufus for his blameless government in Asia had provoked them beyond endurance. As to the question of giving the franchise to the allies, any sensible Optimate could see that the existing constituency in the Comitia was as bad from his point of view as any other body that could be created. It could do no harm if the urban multitude were diluted, or even swamped, by the sturdy farmers of those parts of Central Italy to which agricultural depression had not yet penetrated. The Agrarian Law, too, which Drusus proposed had not the confiscatory character of that of Tiberius Gracchus. The Campanian state-domains and the other small remnants of public land in Italy were being held on lease; they had not practically passed into private possession, as had the estates which had been resumed by the Gracchan law of B.C. 133; and to colonies in Sicily no one could have any rational objection. The fertile island had been so wasted by the slave war of B.C. 104-101 that it could afford to take in a very large body of new settlers.

It is impossible to deny that the reforms of Drusus were less objectionable, and had a more respectable and influential set of supporters, than any other of the programmes which were laid before the Roman people during the last century of the Republic. Unfortunately their author did not introduce them in the best or wisest fashion. The bills had to pass the Comitia, and that corrupt constituency had to be conciliated. Thinking that the Agrarian Law would not suffice to buy it over Drusus linked to his other proposals one of a most openly immoral sort. He offered to increase the pernicious corn-dole, by adding to the amount of state grain which each citizen was allowed to purchase every month. It was represented to him that the treasury could not stand the expense, wherefore he enacted that the coinage should be debased in order to find the extra money. Of every eight denarii issued by the mint, one was to be of copper plated with silver, and to refuse the base coin was to be a high offence. Evidently Drusus was no economist; but even though the ancient world had not discovered "Gresham's Law," that the bad money drives out the good, he must have known that his bill would cause grave financial troubles. It was clearly a case of doing evil that good might come.

Drusus found himself at the head of a very heterogeneous body of partisans. His proposals had caused a cleavage in both of the old factions. He was backed by the better half of the Senate, by the Italians, and at first by that blind and greedy majority in the assembly which would vote anything that was sweetened by a corn-dole. Against him were the Equites and that section of the Senate which was simply reactionary, and opposed to all manner of change merely because it was change. He had also to reckon with that part of the urban multitude which regarded the extension of the franchise to the Italians with such distaste that they feared and shunned any one who might propose it.

Quite conscious of the existence of this latter body,

Drusus (with more wiliness than honesty) brought forward together his laws for depriving the Equites of the control of the courts, for planting the colonies in Italy and Sicily, and for increasing the corn-dole. To do so directly contravened the *Lex Caecilia Didia* passed in B.C. 98, which forbade the introduction of clauses dealing with several distinct subjects under a single preamble. Nevertheless the proposals were carried, in face of a bitter opposition, headed by the consul Marcius Philippus. The meeting at which they passed was much disturbed, and the adversaries were so vehement that at last Drusus had Philippus dragged off the rostrum by his apparitors, an outburst of temper which unhappily recalled the doings of Saturninus. His bill passed, but its legality was very doubtful in face of his opponent's contention that subjects so different could not legally be linked together in one enactment [B.C. 91].

Victorious thus far, Drusus then began an agitation to prepare the people for the second part of his programme, the great law which was, in his idea, to regenerate the Roman people, by introducing into the citizen-body the great mass of Italian allies. Aware of the difficulties of the task, he got into communication with the chief men in each state throughout the peninsula. They visited his house, and formed an association for the purpose of pushing their claims. It is said that in every country town there was a branch started, whose members swore to live and die with Drusus, to spend life and fortune in behalf of him and of all other brethren who had taken the oath, and to enlist in the bond every possible helper. To institute such a society was to go perilously near the edge of conspiracy and high treason, and its framer can hardly have supposed that he had made the oath harmless and constitutional by adding a clause in which the members bound themselves, "when they had received the franchise, to regard Rome as their fatherland and Drusus as their patron." The association was soon well rooted in every corner of the land, and provided the Italians with the bond of organisation and the common executive whose want had hitherto been their weakness.

Drusus had not been wrong in thinking that the proposal to enfranchise the allies would shake the allegiance of many of his followers, and gain him bitter enemies. Both in the Senate and in the urban multitude there were many who began to fall away from him when he insisted on the necessity of this great measure. After a time he lost the control of the Senate, and a majority in it voted that his first set of laws had been invalid, owing to the informal way in which they had been passed *en bloc* under a single preamble.

But the resolution of the haughty tribune was not in the least shaken. He announced his intention of persisting with his schemes in spite of all opposition: he made no attempt to dispute the legality of the Senate's decision as to his laws, but determined to bring forward the question of the Italians. How far he would have carried the matter we cannot tell, for one evening as he was returning to his own house, after making a harangue in the Forum, he was murdered. A multitude was pressing around him, when he was seen to stumble and fall: he had been stabbed in the groin with a cobbler's knife, which was found sticking in the wound. Within a few hours he was dead, and all his plans perished with him. His enemies of the Equestrian Order succeeded in getting a bill passed by the Comitia to the effect that the association which he had formed had been treasonable, and that both his friends in the Senate and his chief agents among the allies should be prosecuted for conspiracy.

The news that Drusus had been murdered, and that a Special Commission had been appointed to try his

GENERAL REVOLT OF THE ITALIANS 109

supporters, was the signal for the outbreak of rebellion all over Italy. The chief men of all the allied cities had learnt to know each other in the reformer's house, and had ascertained that they all had the same grievances and the same desires. The desperate meaning to the Italians of the present crisis was that they had now ascertained that neither party in the Roman state would ever help them. They had long supposed that they might count on the aid of the Democrats, for both the Gracchi and Saturninus had promised them relief. The Optimates, as they had supposed, were their enemies: but now the best of the Optimates had taken up their cause: Drusus had been supported by men such as Crassus the orator, Aurelius Cotta, and the aged M. Aemilius Scaurus, the *princeps senatus*. It was the main body of the Democratic party, and its allies, the Equites, who had foiled the plans of Drusus. The urban multitude in its narrow jealousy had deserted him, lest it might lose some portion of its shows and its corn-doles. The tribune Varius, who had proposed the bill against the friends of Drusus, was a well-known Democrat, and his chief supporters were Equites.

Realising that the Democracy was really as hostile to them as the most bigoted conservative in the Optimate party, the Italians saw that they could only hope to gain their rights by unsheathing the sword. Within three months of the death of Drusus, the whole peninsula from Picenum southward was in arms: few states save the Latin colonies continued faithful to the Roman cause.

With the details of the fierce but confused campaign which raged all over Italy during the years B.C. 90–89 it is not necessary to deal. The odds were against Rome: the sturdy yeomen of the Apennine valleys were individually better men than the town-bred legions whom the consuls, Lucius Cæsar and Rutilius Lupus, led against them. It must be confessed, however, that the Romans fought far better than might have been expected: even the urban multitude displayed a savage determination worthy of their ancestors, and offered to give up even their cherished corn-dole in the day of necessity. But the citizens were opposed by superior numbers; their officers were for the most part incapable; the campaign presented a thousand difficulties because of the necessity of endeavouring to relieve the many outlying garrisons—Latin colonies for the most part—in remote corners of Italy.

If Rome was not crushed in the first year of the war, it was because she still retained many advantages. She had the undisputed command of the sea, and by means of it could send succours round the peninsula, even when the central lines of communication were held by the enemy. The provinces, fortunately for her, did not choose this moment to revolt; from them she drew not only numerous auxiliary troops, but also the ample supply of money and food by which alone the war could be maintained: the revolted Italians were terribly handicapped by their poverty. Rome had also a considerable number of officers—headed by Marius himself—who were accustomed to commanding and moving large bodies of men: none of the Italian generals had ever headed any force larger than a cohort, and they had to learn the art of handling armies numbered by tens of thousands without any previous experience. But the most important factor of all in the struggle was that Rome represented unity of action and organisation, as opposed to a heterogeneous mass of tribes of very different races, divided by local interests and old grudges. The Italians did not succeed in setting up a vigorous federal government: the constitution which they devised for themselves was a slavish and stupid imitation of that of Rome, which failed to give

THE ITALIANS OBTAIN THE FRANCHISE

them either a vigorous executive or a capable administrative council.

Yet, in spite of all these advantages, the experiences of the first year of war so tried the strength of Rome and broke down her haughty spirit, that she practically consented to grant the allies the franchise which they had demanded. The *Lex Julia*, passed in the winter of B.C. 90, gave the citizenship to all the Italian communities who had remained faithful, including the whole of the populous Latin colonies. Having once surrendered the principle for which they had entered on the war, the Romans did not hesitate to go farther. Only two or three months after the *Lex Julia* had been enacted, there followed the still more important *Lex Plautia Papiria*, which granted the franchise to every individual Italian who should lay down his arms and appear before a magistrate to crave enrolment as a Roman citizen. This law saved the existence of Rome, at the sacrifice of her old claim to dominate Italy as a mistress. The rebels flocked in by tens of thousands to give in their names and to take up the long-coveted status of citizen. The power of the insurrection was so much thinned that the second campaign of the war, that of B.C. 89, went almost entirely in favour of the Romans. District after district was subdued, and at the end of the year only the obstinate Samnites and the less important tribes of Lucania remained in arms. It was clear that the fate of the war had been decided, and that the crushing of the last desperate rebels could only be a matter of time. The Romans once more breathed freely, and, contented to have saved the existence of the city and the empire, contemplated with comparative equanimity the crowd of new citizens with whom for the future they had to share the dominion of the world.

At this moment, the most inappropriate one that could

have been chosen—for Samnium had still to be subdued, and a great foreign war with King Mithradates was just breaking out—civil strife recommenced at Rome. The conduct of the two parties was absolutely insane: there is no parallel for it in history save one: the state of France in 1793-94, when foreign invasion, domestic insurrection, and bloody proscriptions in the capital were all in progress at once, bears much similarity to the state of Italy in B.C. 88-87.

That civil war should arise, when every man and every sesterce was still wanted to preserve the state from dangerous external troubles, is all the more astonishing because in B.C. 88 both the Optimate and the Democratic parties were in a deep state of discredit. No one could say that the rule of the Senate during the last thirty years had been anything but feeble and incompetent. On the other hand, all the main items of the Democratic programme had been tried and found wanting. The agrarian and colonial schemes of the Gracchi had failed to regenerate the state—farming was as unprofitable as ever. The corn-dole of Caius Gracchus had been in working order for a whole generation, and had been carried to its logical extreme by Saturninus and Drusus; yet the urban population was as miserable and as discontented as ever. The franchise had now been granted to the Italians, who had obtained possession of every personal immunity and political privilege that they could wish—save indeed that they had been enrolled in eight tribes only, so that their voting power in the Comitia was not fully equivalent to their numbers. But it had always been the practical advantages of citizenship rather than the right to register their suffrages that they had desired.

But a party does not necessarily cease to exist because its programme is played out, more especially a party of criticism and discontent, such as that of the Roman *populares.* They were, if anything, more violent than they had ever been before, though all the constructive items in their political creed had been tried and had proved futile, so that nothing really remained of it save the single destructive cry of "Down with the Senate." But if no longer a party with measures, they were now a party with men. The great civil war that was approaching was to show that the personal ambitions of a Marius, a Sulpicius, or a Cinna supplied enough of a war-cry to unite the turbulent elements in Rome, and that the *populares* could continue to exist even without a popular programme.

Hitherto all the really important constitutional and economic quarrels between Optimates and Democrats had been fought out by mere rioting and chance medley; but now a fierce and prolonged civil war, which was to put scores of legions in the field, was to follow on a mere personal rivalry for a military command. A tribune named Sulpicius Rufus, to whom the mantle of Saturninus had descended, was busy in formulating some new reforms of second-rate importance. The most prominent of them was a bill for distributing the freedmen (who had hitherto been confined to the four city tribes) and the new Italian citizens (who had in a similar way been told off to eight tribes only) among the whole of the old constituencies. There was no great point in the bill so far as the Italians were concerned, for they would rarely if ever come up to vote, on account of the mere difficulties of distance. As to the freedmen, they were the worst element in the state, and to propose to give them more power in the Comitia than they already enjoyed was the act of the most unscrupulous demagogy.

Sulpicius, as it would seem, was a man from whom such legislation might be expected.[1] We have no unbiassed account of his character and his plans, but the records

[1] Cicero alone speaks well of him in the *De Oratore.*

which his enemies have left behind paint him in the most
lurid colours. "He was inferior to none in desperate
attempts," writes Plutarch, inspired by some Optimate
authority. "He was a compound of cruelty, insolence,
and avarice, and could commit the most infamous crimes
in cold blood. He openly sold the citizenship of Rome
to persons who had been slaves, and received their money
told out on a table in the Forum. He always went about
with a band of 300 armed satellites, and had a council of
young Equites whom he called his anti-senate. Though
he got a law passed that every man who owed more than
2000 denarii should be expelled from the Senate, he had
debts himself to the amount of three millions." There
seems no doubt that he could vie in ruffianly violence
with Saturninus and Glaucia. Several times he cleared
his adversaries out of the Comitia with staves and daggers.
On one occasion, it is said, he tried to murder the consuls
Pompeius and Sulla during the actual session of the
assembly. The son of the former was killed in this
desperate riot.

However exaggerated may be the language of Plutarch,
it is at least clear that Sulpicius was a man of violent and
unscrupulous character: but for the moment he had
control of the streets and the assembly, and it was to him
that those who had something to gain addressed themselves. Accordingly it does not surprise us to find him
adding to the many laws which he passed one intended
for the private and personal benefit of one of his friends.
It was a decree appointing Caius Marius to the command
of the army which was to be sent to the East to repel
King Mithradates. The old general had recovered from
the shock of his political humiliation in B.C. 99. He had
been entrusted with a considerable body of legions during
the Italian war, and had fought with success against
the rebels, though he had not gained any very striking

victories. He felt that he was only half rehabilitated in the eyes of his fellow-citizens, and was anxious to close his career with a series of brilliant campaigns which should cause them to forget the names of Saturninus and Glaucia. The King of Pontus was, he thought, the kind of enemy who would provide a Roman general with the opportunity for winning a sensational triumph, annexing whole provinces, and accumulating untold stores of plunder and trophies. If he returned to Rome laden with the spoils of the East, he would once more occupy the commanding position in the state which he had enjoyed at the end of the Cimbric war.

The army which was destined for the Asiatic campaign was at present lying under the walls of Nola, the last fortress in the lowlands which was still in the hands of the rebellious Samnites. But it was believed that the place would soon fall, and then the six legions which formed the besieging force would be disposable for service over-seas. They were at present under the command of the consul L. Cornelius Sulla, to whom the charge of the Mithradatic war had been duly assigned by the Senate. He was a prominent member of the Optimate party and an old enemy of Marius. In displacing him, the aged general would not merely secure the command of the best Roman army then existing, but would also disappoint and humiliate a personal foe.

Accordingly Marius allied himself to Sulpicius Rufus and paid his enormous debts, while in return the tribune passed the decree which deprived Sulla of his army. They little knew the manner of man they were provoking. Their bill was to cost one of them his life, and to cause the other to be hunted out of Italy and driven into a miserable exile. They had stirred up into action the most capable and the most relentless enemy that the Democracy was ever to know.

CHAPTER V

SULLA

LUCIUS CORNELIUS SULLA, the man whom Sulpicius and Marius had so recklessly challenged to mortal combat, is one of the most striking figures in Roman history. For mere psychological interest, there is no one who can be compared with him save Cæsar alone. He combined in the most extraordinary degree the old Roman political virtues with the personal vices that the new Rome had borrowed from the Hellenised East.

To his credit it must be granted that, throughout his career, he displayed the main qualities which had distinguished those generations of men who had built up the Roman domination in Italy during the fourth and third centuries before Christ. He had an enormous sense of the dignity and importance of the Roman name: the welfare of the state, as he conceived it, stood before any private or party interest. He was entirely lacking in personal as opposed to national ambition: the crown and the purple robe had no attraction for him; in this respect he must be reckoned superior even to Cæsar, who was not insensible to such things. Nor was he affected by the more insidious craving for power; he was one of those rare spirits who, after they have achieved the highest things, and risen to practical sovereignty in the state, are content to step down from the throne and to retire into private life. Moreover, he had the solid military ability, the steadfast level-headed perseverance, the freedom from vain theory, which had distinguished the best men of the elder days of the Republic.

Mixed with these old Roman characteristics were all the vices of the decadent half-Hellenised generation into which he had been born. Sulla had learnt to be regardless of human life, not merely of the lives of aliens or barbarians (most Romans were that), but of the lives of citizens also. If a man, great or small, stood in way of his schemes or his reforms, he doomed that man to perish with entire nonchalance. He had the most profound belief in the all-importance of the Roman state, but the sacrosanctity of the individual citizen seemed to him a farce. The old shibboleth, *civis Romanus sum*, had no protective power against his ruthless hand. Another modern trait in his character, which could only have come from the habitual study of destructive and doubting Greek philosophy, was a frank disregard for the law of the constitution—a thing for which the old Roman had as slavish a reverence as had his contemporary the Pharisee for the letter of the law of Moses. While other men still wrangled over forms and ceremonies, vetoes and auspices, Sulla quietly marched an army against Rome, and showed that neither religious sanctions nor tribunicial mandates had any power to stop a commander with loyal troops at his back. Sulla had a supreme contempt for forms that had grown meaningless, though the majority of the men of his generation were still in bondage to them.

Very un-Roman, again, was another of Sulla's characteristics—a smooth, plausible, utterly hollow urbanity, the deceptive courtesy of the diplomat. The Roman of the elder republic had been brutally straightforward: his notion of diplomacy was summed up in the two handfuls of "peace" and "war" which Fabius offered to the Carthaginian senate, or in the line which Popilius Laenas drew around the astonished Antiochus Epiphanes. Sulla, on the other hand, took an artistic pleasure in circumventing and cajoling those with whom he had to deal. To out-manœuvre Jugurtha at Bocchus's court, to talk round the Parthian ambassador (whom his master afterwards executed for being so outwitted), were great delights to him. To outdo the wily barbarian in his own field of lies had an intrinsic pleasure in the execution.

Another and most unamiable side of Sulla's disposition may be summed up in saying that he was an epicurean both in the best and the worst sense of the word. He had a keen enjoyment of artistic and intellectual pleasures: he loved beautiful things for their own sake, was an enlightened student of literature, and appreciated and collected Hellenic works of art. He liked to converse with philosophers and authors, with actors and artists, and willingly sharpened his brains and increased his knowledge of every side of life by mixing with all sorts and conditions of men.

But at the same time he had the bad side of the artistic temperament. He was frankly vicious in his private life, as evil a liver as any Greek tyrant of old. He was perfectly destitute of any sense of chastity or shame, and, moreover, habitually indulged to excess in the banquet and the wine-cup. This it was that ruined his splendid constitution, and turned his handsome face into the "mulberry spotted with meal," to which it was compared in his middle age.

To complete this strange and repulsive character we must add a curious strain of wild superstition. Of the simple and stolid religiosity of the old Roman there was no trace in him: but, like Napoleon, he believed in his star. Though, as far as deeds went, he was a scoffer, yet he professed a belief that he was the chosen tool of the gods. Venus, he said, was his special patroness, and gave him good fortune; he sometimes called himself in grati-

THE YOUTH OF SULLA

tude "Epaphroditus." He claimed to have dreams, omens, and premonitions. He took as surnames the adjectives Felix and Faustus, "the lucky." His most hazardous steps were made, as he said, under direct inspiration from above. He wrote in his autobiography that his resolutions taken on the spur of the moment, and his enterprises begun without any proper preparation, always succeeded far better than those on which he had bestowed the most time and forethought. We might perhaps have imagined that he assumed this rôle of the favourite of fortune merely to encourage his followers, had it not been that he carried it into private life, when no end was to be gained by proceeding with the farce. There seems to have been a genuine fantastic vein of superstition in this otherwise practical and cynical mind. We know, for example, that on battle-days he wore under his corslet a small golden image of Apollo which he had got at Delphi. But the strangest development of his beliefs has yet to be told. On his death-bed, when one would have expected that his mind should have been filled with the memory of all the horrors that he had committed, he was visited with comforting visions. He told his friends that he faced the other world with equanimity, for his dead wife and son had appeared to him and had bidden him hasten to join them in a life of perfect rest and happiness beyond the grave. Truly this was a strange ending for the blood-stained author of the proscriptions of B.C. 81!

Sulla had spent his youth in dire poverty. His family was ancient but impoverished: no man of this branch of the Cornelii had held curule office for six generations. He had not even a paternal mansion or a hearth of his own, but lived, as we learn from Plutarch, in a set of lodgings one storey removed from the garret, and hired at the meagre rent of 3000 sesterces (about £26) per annum. He was a man who yearned after all the comforts and elegancies of life, who loved good dinners, good wine, and other less reputable luxuries, and who in his youth could not get them. It is this poverty of his early years that accounts for his insatiable addiction to pleasure in middle age, when most men have lost their taste for frivolity. He was making up for the enjoyments of which he had been defrauded in his young days.

Men of the type of Sulla, able, impecunious, and destitute of any family influence, were generally the stuff from which demagogues were made. There are a dozen instances in Roman history of young and penniless aristocrats who started on the career of mob leader and champion of the rabble. It was the easiest trade on which to embark if one loved notoriety, had no scruples, and lacked wealthy relatives to push one forward. But Sulla was above all things an aristocrat: he loathed the urban multitude and all its works, and when he put himself forward as a candidate for the quaestorship in B.C. 107, it was as a strict Optimate. How such a poor and unknown young man ever succeeded in obtaining a magistracy we do not know. That he was able and eloquent is clear enough, but a full purse, or a programme of confiscation and corn-doles, was a much better commendation to the electors than mere ability. How one who was an Optimate, and yet had not the money to buy his way to power, got his foot on the first rung of the ladder that led to the consulship, it is hard to conceive. But the feat was accomplished: Sulla became quaestor, and served under Marius in Numidia during the last year of the Jugurthine war [106-105].

It was here that he won his first distinction, and earned the undying enmity of his superior in command. While the struggle with the evasive Numidian seemed likely to drag on for ever, Sulla suddenly brought it to an end by his clever and unscrupulous diplomacy. By a combination of bribes and cajolery, he induced Bocchus the Moor, Jugurtha's chief ally, to kidnap his guest and relative, and to hand him over in chains to the Romans. The war came to an end, and Marius took the credit to himself, but he was well aware that Sulla had really brought it to a finish. The quaestor made no attempt to disguise the fact; he took as the device of his signet-ring a picture of Jugurtha surrendered by Bocchus to himself, and he persuaded the Moor to dedicate on the Roman Capitol a group of statues reproducing the same composition. Marius was bitterly vexed; it was probably for this reason that Sulla took a particular pride in the statues; they were placed long after as the device on Cornelian coins. We may still see Sulla in his chair, the captive Numidian king in chains before him, and the Moor in front waving the olive branch with which he sued for peace with Rome.

Once launched on an official career, Sulla came steadily to the front; his only drawback was his want of funds. The first time that he stood for the praetorship he was rejected, because the people had expected from him, and had not received, a great show of African wild beasts. But finding money necessary, he finally succeeded in scraping it together, partly as spoils of war, partly in less obvious and reputable ways. His public services, however, were distinguished in the highest degree: nothing that he took in hand failed to come to a good end; already the "luck" on which he was so fond of insisting made itself felt. He won golden opinions in the Cimbric war while serving under the Consul Catulus. In B.C. 93 he at last obtained the praetorship, and in the following year held as propraetor the turbulent and newly formed province of Cilicia. He had been sent there without an army or a proper supply of money, yet he made his name feared all around. He frightened away Mithradates, who was trying to annex Cappadocia; he restored the rightful king of that country, and protected him against an Armenian invasion. First of all Romans he came in touch with the formidable Parthian power, which was just advancing to the line of the Upper Euphrates. He met the ambassador of King Arsaces IX., and not only cajoled him into a friendly agreement, but induced him to allow the Roman to have the place of honour over the Parthian name in their negotiations. The great king executed his envoy, when he returned, for permitting this humiliation of his majesty, but the peace between the two powers stood firm. In short, Sulla had pacified South-Eastern Asia Minor, and strengthened the boundaries of his province, with no other resources than his ready wit, his capacity for "bluffing" Orientals, and a handful of untrustworthy native auxiliaries. His self-confidence, never weak, is said to have been confirmed by the prophecies of Eastern wizards. The chief soothsayer of the Parthian ambassador was struck by his invariable good fortune, cast his horoscope, and told him "that he was destined to be the greatest of men, and that it was strange that he could endure to be anything less at the present moment."

When Sulla returned to Rome, it was natural that he should take a high place among the Optimate party: he was the only man among them who had built up a reputation for unvarying success. Hence he was naturally entrusted with high command in the Italian war. He fully justified his promotion, won battles over the Samnites and the Lucanians which far surpassed the successes of any other Roman general in these campaigns, Marius not excepted, and gained such a reputation that he was elected as consul for B.C. 88. It was natural that when the Italian war died down he should be chosen to march against Mithradates, for he was the only living general who knew the East, and had already made a name in that quarter of the world. Sulla was quite satisfied with the commission; he believed that he was competent to save Asia, and he had been deeply grieved by the humiliation which the Roman arms had been suffering in the Mithradatic war.

Hence it was that he was moved to ungovernable wrath when he was informed that Sulpicius had passed a law to remove him from command, and to make over his army to Marius. He had already been in violent collision with the demagogue, who—as it is said—had tried to get him assassinated in broad daylight during the meeting of the Comitia. But there is no reason to suppose that he would have interfered with the sword in domestic politics if he had not been deprived of his Eastern commission. He believed that the turning back of Mithradates was a far more important duty than the quelling of demagogues. Sulpicius had had many predecessors who had all come to a bad end: if sufficient rope was given to a turbulent tribune, he was certain to end by hanging himself. But it was a different matter when he intervened between Sulla and his cherished project of reconquering Asia and Greece from the Pontic king. When the news reached the consul he behaved in the most unexpected fashion. He began by drawing off the greater part of his army from the siege of Nola and bringing it up to Capua. There he harangued the soldiers, told them that he was the victim of the intrigues of bad citizens, and asked them whether they were prepared to follow him. The men were devoted to the general who had led them so well during the Italian war: they cared little for the difference between Optimate and Democrat, but they remembered that Sulla had always been the most indulgent and good-humoured of chiefs, that he had kept their stomachs full and their pockets well lined. They believed, like himself, in his luck, and they had been looking forward to easy victory and endless plunder in Asia. The legions shouted that they would follow him anywhere, even if he marched against Rome itself—which was precisely what he was intending to do. When the praetors Brutus and Servilius met him, forbidding him to advance further, the soldiers fell upon them, tore their robes, broke their fasces, and stoned them out of the camp, glad to escape with their lives. This violence frightened many of Sulla's chief officers, who slunk away from him lest they should find themselves involved in high treason. But the rank and file stuck firmly to him, and with 30,000 men at his back he began a rapid march on Rome. To those who were appalled at his project, he merely said that all the omens were favourable. The Asiatic Moon-Goddess, who had been so friendly to him in Cappadocia, had appeared to him in a dream, had promised him victory, placed a thunderbolt in his hand, and bade him use it to annihilate his enemies.

When this wholly unexpected news reached Rome, Marius and Sulpicius sent out several embassies one after another to endeavour to stop Sulla. But he deceived them by fair words, inviting them to induce the Senate and the Democratic leaders to meet him in a conference, while he continued to advance at full speed towards the city. As he was approaching it he was joined by his colleague, Pompeius Rufus, a very determined Optimate, whose presence was invaluable to him, for when the two consuls acted together it gave a false air of legality to their proceedings.

Marius and Sulpicius had barely time to barricade the streets and to arm their followers from the state arsenal, when the arrival of the Sullan army in the suburbs was reported. Without the least hesitation the legions crossed the sacred *Pomoerium* and pushed into the city. The Democrats, surprised as they were, made a desperate resistance; but though swords and pikes had been served

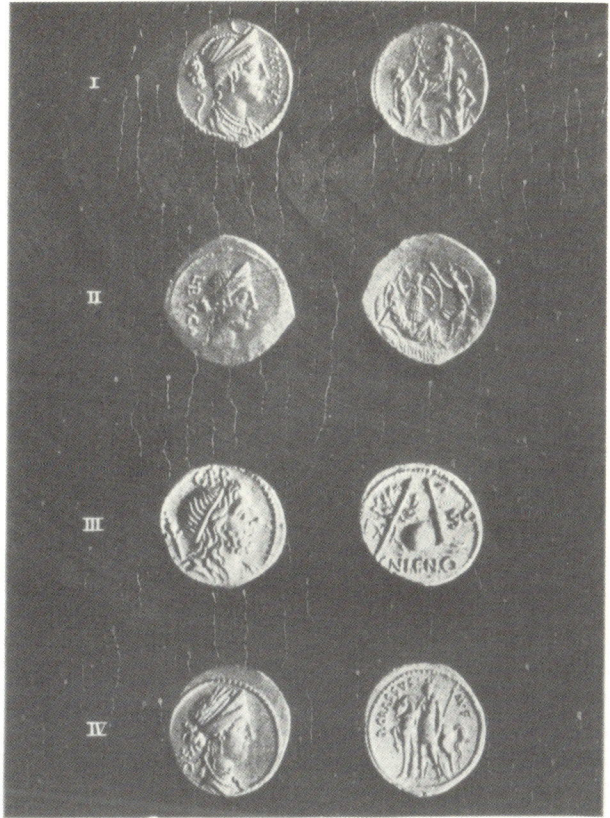

Roman Coins from the British Museum. (Plate 2.)

I. Denarius with representation of Jugurtha surrendered by Bocchus to Sulla.
II. Denarius with representation of Sulla's Vision in B.C. 88. Selene appears to him and presents to him Victory armed with thunderbolts.
III. Denarius struck by the restored Oligarchy in B.C. 80-70. Obv. Head of the Genius of the Roman People. Rev. Emblems of Empire by sea and land (globe, rudder, and caduccus).
IV. Denarius of Crassus. The rev. a knight leading his horse, commemorates his censorship.

SULLA STORMS ROME

out to them, they were but untrained rioters contending with disciplined soldiery. There was fierce fighting around the Esquiline market and the temple of Tellus, but it did not last for long. When Sulla brought forth torches, and told his men to burn out the enemy if they could not expel them in any other fashion, the Democrats gave way and fled.

The victors bivouacked that night in the squares and along the streets, ready to fight again next morning if necessary: but they soon discovered that the leaders of the enemy had left the city, and that the mob had dispersed. Sulla had broken up the dearest traditions of ancient Rome; he had brought armed legions into the Forum. To lovers of the constitution, whether Optimates or Democrats, it seemed that the abomination of desolation was in the Holy Place. But no thunderbolt descended from heaven to annihilate the impious consul. His luck was still with him, and he faced the situation, which would have appalled any one less cheerful and unscrupulous than himself, with perfect equanimity.

The Senate was assembled by the consuls, and informed that the "tyrants" had been expelled from the city. It voted that the Sulpician laws had been passed without the proper formalities and were null and void. It also passed a decree of outlawry, by which Sulpicius, Marius and his son, and ten other persons, were declared public enemies, and a price was set on their heads. The tribune was caught lurking in a villa at Laurentum. He was beheaded, and his head was set upon the rostra from which he had so often declaimed, a ghastly innovation in the etiquette of massacre which was to be regularly followed hereafter. But most of the other Democratic leaders escaped from Italy. Marius, after a long series of adventures, culminating in his celebrated mud-bath in the marshes of Minturnae, made his way to Africa, where he was ultimately joined by his son and several others of the outlaws.

It would now have been in Sulla's power to assume the permanent control of the state. He might have proclaimed himself dictator, or have renewed his consular authority, and have settled down to rule as an autocrat with the swords of his legions propping up his throne. But he had no personal ambition. He was a Roman and an Optimate, who desired the triumph of his country and his party, and was determined to do his best for both. But there was nothing of the tyrant in him: his present duty, as he supposed, was to restore his party to power at Rome, and then to sally forth to save the Eastern provinces from Mithradates. These two ends he proceeded to carry out, with no concern for his own private profit.

The executions, as he supposed, had crushed the Democrats. Marius he despised, and considered a negligible quantity; there was no other surviving chief of any note to resuscitate the vanquished faction, and the Senate ought to be able to take care of itself for the present. Accordingly he contented himself with making some comparatively unobtrusive changes in the constitution before his departure. The chief of these was a law providing that the approval of the Senate—*senatus auctoritas*—had for the future to be granted to any bill brought forward by tribunes, or other magistrates, before it could be laid before the assembly. Another law restored the old order of things in the Comitia Centuriata, where the wealthier classes were replaced in the preponderant position which they had enjoyed under the early Republic. But it was not really by these slight alterations of existing custom that he imagined that the Senate could defend itself. He left behind for their protection two armies under Optimates of assured fidelity and ability—his late colleague in the consulship, **Pompeius Rufus, and Q. Metellus Pius**,

SULLA SAILS FOR GREECE

the son of the conqueror of Numidia. For the Mithradatic war he withdrew from Italy only five of his own veteran legions, which had served with him throughout the campaigns of B.C. 90–88, and had won so many successes over the Samnites. With this force he thought that he could master all the Asiatic hordes of Mithradates; nor, as the event showed, was he wrong.

The moment, however, that he set out for the East all went wrong in Italy. He had, as it seemed, taken his good fortune away with him. The Senate proved far too weak to maintain the position to which he had restored it, and the Democratic faction found a new leader in the consul for B.C. 87, L. Cornelius Cinna, a vain heady man, who seems to have been carried away by a sudden lust for establishing a personal domination in the style of Caius Gracchus, rather than by any true zeal for the popular cause. As an Optimate, no statesman could hope to be more than a member of the governing ring; as a Democrat, it was possible to exercise a quasi-monarchical power; hence came the temptation to men of vulgar and unscrupulous ambition to enlist on the Democratic side.

Even before Sulla left Italy, his colleague, Pompeius Rufus, on whose ability to keep order he most relied, had been murdered in a military riot in Picenum. Gn. Octavius, who was consul for B.C. 87 along with Cinna, proved too weak for the task of controlling his exuberant partner, when the latter openly took arms on behalf of the Democrats. A sporadic civil war began to spread all over Italy, which became really formidable when Cinna made an alliance with the Samnites, and called back Marius and the rest of the exiles. The Optimates lost ground; at last Octavius and his army were actually besieged in Rome, and, weakened by desertion and famine, the Senate capitulated. Cinna and Marius entered Rome in triumph, and celebrated their victory by a wholesale

massacre, not a mere attack on a dozen leaders, such as
Sulla had carried out in B.C. 88. Marius went about
at the head of a band of slaves, slaying every man with
whom he had ever had a personal quarrel, whether he was
a prominent politician or not. Indeed, the old general
acted more like a lunatic afflicted with homicidal mania
than a responsible party leader. Every prominent man in
Rome who had not taken sides with the exiles was doomed
to death: not only was Octavius put to death, but a number of respectable ex-consuls were murdered, among them
Lucius Cæsar, who had enfranchised the Italians in B.C. 90;
Catulus, the colleague of Marius in his Cimbrian victory;
Antonius, the orator; and P. Crassus, the father of the
Triumvir. The Optimate wing of the Senate was almost
exterminated; none escaped save a handful of fugitives,
and the officers whom Sulla had taken with him to the
East. Marius caused the head of every senator who had
been slain to be hung up in the Forum, so that for many
weeks it resembled the precinct of the king of Dahomey
after the "Great Customs," rather than the meeting-place
of a civilised people. The atrocities only ceased when
Marius died, on January 13th, B.C. 86, just after he had
caused himself to be elected consul for the seventh time.
Cinna, glutted with blood, now turned from the work of
massacre to the more practical task of taking measures
for the suppression of Sulla, who had sailed for the
East in the previous year to take up the war against
Mithradates.

When Sulla had started from Brundisium for Greece in
the spring of B.C. 87, he had taken with him no more than
five of his own veteran legions—some 30,000 men at
most—and a moderate supply of money. He had supposed
that he might look for a regular supply of recruits and
subsidies from the Optimate government which he had
left behind him at Rome. He found the eastern pro-

vinces in a desperate condition; not only had the whole
of Asia been lost, but the Pontic armies had crossed into
Europe, and had overrun the greater part of Thrace and
Macedon. The fleet of Mithradates had subdued the
whole of the Cyclades, and had sacked the great central
emporium at Delos, where 20,000 Italians are said to
have been massacred. Athens had fallen into the hands
of the tyrant Aristion, a humble imitator and admirer
of the Pontic king. Nearly all the smaller states of
Greece had hastened to do homage to the invaders.
Sentius, the governor of Macedonia, and his legate,
Bruttius Sura, with a handful of Roman troops, were
holding out in Thessaly, but would certainly have been
overwhelmed had not Sulla come to their aid.

The great proconsul had marched south from Epirus
and recovered part of the western regions of Greece, as
far as Delphi and the borders of Bœotia, when he received the appalling tidings of the outbreak of the new
Democratic rising in Italy and of the treason of Cinna.
Many men would have turned back to crush the rebels at
home before grappling with the external enemies of the
state. But Sulla thought even more of the danger to the
Roman empire than of the danger of the Optimate party.
Instead of returning to Italy, he pressed with all vigour
the campaign against the generals of Mithradates. Without his help Octavius and the Senate were lost, and at mid-
winter in B.C. 87-86 he learnt that Rome was in the hands
of the Democrats, that his friends had been massacred,
and that he himself and his chief officers had been declared public enemies and outlawed. Decrees passed at
Rome to that effect did not much injure him, for his
army was thoroughly loyal, and not a man left him. But
the dreadful part of the situation was that he had for the
future to depend entirely on his own resources. He had
no money and no fleet, the bulk of Greece was in the

I

hands of the king's generals, and 100,000 Pontic troops occupied its chief fortresses.

But Sulla showed no sign of discouragement. He paid his legions by the desperate expedient of seizing the temple treasures of Delphi and Olympia. To raise a fleet he sent forth his legate, L. Lucullus, bidding him appeal to all the smaller powers of the East, who were frightened by the conquering career of Mithradates. But the Oriental states were cowed, and Lucullus at first met with many refusals; he could only procure a few galleys from the Rhodians and the Phœnicians, with which he could not make any head against the large Pontic fleet. The armies and supplies of Mithradates continued to pass and repass the Ægean without hindrance during the first two years of the war.

But on land, where Sulla was at work himself, things looked better. The generals of Mithradates were beaten at Mount Tilphossium in Bœotia and pressed back towards Athens. Then the greater part of the Greek states sent to ask for terms: they had not liked their experiences of the last year, while they were under the Pontic yoke. Sulla let them buy safety at a price: he wanted money above all other things, and consented to overlook their treason in consideration of huge fines. Having secured his rear, he proceeded to lay siege to the strongholds of the enemy, the city of Athens and its port the Piraeus. They were two fortresses, and no longer one, for the "Long Walls" which had connected them in the days of Pericles had disappeared, so that their defence was carried out on separate lines.

The first great episode, therefore, in Sulla's Greek campaign of B.C. 87–86 was the double leaguer of Athens and the Piraeus. He had with a very small army—for many of his troops were detached in the direction of Thessaly—to besiege superior numbers in two strong places, of which one was perpetually receiving succour from the sea. The Pontic garrison and the Athenians held out with great resolution, knowing the massacre that awaited them if they gave way. The walls were too strong for Roman siege-craft, and the city had to be starved out, while at the same time several attempts to relieve it both from the inland and from the side of Piraeus had to be beaten back. But Sulla never despaired, and after many months the garrison of Athens grew so weak from famine that they failed to guard the circuit of the walls with sufficient care. The Romans entered by escalade at a point near the Dipylon gate, and met with little resistance in the streets. Sulla allowed his men to plunder the place as a reward for their long endurance in the trenches, and to put to the sword many of the citizens. When at last he ordered the sack to cease, he observed that "he spared the living for the sake of the dead," *i.e.* the degenerate Athenians of his own day obtained mercy in memory of Pericles and Plato [March 1, B.C. 86].

Hardly was Athens won, when a great army of succour, over 100,000 strong, came down from Macedonia, driving before it the Roman corps which had been detached on the side of Thessaly. Sulla hastened up from Athens with reinforcements; whereupon Archelaus, the governor of Piraeus, came round by sea with his garrison and joined his colleague, Taxiles. The armies met at Chaeronea, one of the inevitable battle-spots of Greece, where an invader advancing from the north can be brought to action in the narrow space between Lake Copais and the Phocian foot-hills. Sulla had only 15,000 foot, and less than 2000 horse, but he never doubted for a moment of success. He had seen Asiatic armies before in their own land, and had the greatest contempt for them. But at first he had some difficulty in bringing over his own men to his opinion;

they feared the masses of cavalry and the many regiments of mercenaries equipped in the Macedonian fashion with the brazen shield and the long *sarissa*. To quiet their minds Sulla had to cover his flanks with entrenchments and stockades; but presently the men grew tired of the spade and asked to be allowed to fight. Sulla told them that they should have their will, "though it seemed that it was not so much courage as dislike for digging that made them so eager." The event showed that an Oriental army when manfully faced, even by very inferior numbers, would never stand firm before a resolute attack of European troops. There was much confused fighting, but the story of the battle reads like that of the early British victories in India. The odds seemed hopeless, but the balance of courage compensated for them. The scythe-chariots of the Asiatic turned out as great a fraud as they had been at Cunaxa or Arbela. The legionaries soon learnt their futility; "they clapped their hands and asked for more, as if they had been looking at the races in the circus." The unwieldy phalanxes of infantry got into disorder, and when the line of pikes was broken, fell an unresisting sacrifice to the Roman sword. Only the cavalry of Archelaus gave some trouble; it pierced the Roman line at one point and had to be driven off by hard fighting. But, seeing his infantry cut to pieces, the Pontic general rode off the field and escaped.

We can hardly believe Sulla's allegation that he slew 100,000 men in this battle, more especially when he couples it with the astounding statement that he himself lost but fourteen legionaries, of whom two were only "missing" and turned up next morning. Even Asiatic armies cannot be routed with such a light butcher's bill, and the wild lie must have been put about merely to cheer the spirits of the army, and inspire them with contempt for the miserable enemy [March B.C. 86].

FLACCUS AND SULLA

But just when the subjection of Greece seemed complete, a new danger fell upon Sulla. The Democrats at Rome had just landed an army in Epirus under the Consul Flaccus, in order to attack him in the rear. For Cinna and his friends had not the magnanimity of Sulla, and would not reserve their swords for the foreigner, or defer civil strife till the state was free from external enemies. Fortunately for the victor of Chaeronea, Flaccus proved a feeble foe, as was to be expected from a hero of the Forum,—one whose only achievement had been to pass a disgraceful law which allowed debtors to pay off their liabilities by tendering one-fourth of what they owed to their unfortunate creditors. The consul marched into Thessaly, spreading proclamations which invited the legionaries of Sulla to desert the standard of an outlaw and to join the legitimate representative of the Roman people. But when the two armies faced each other near Melitaea, Flaccus's raw levies showed no eagerness to fight; they began to pass over to Sulla, whose reputation as a general and notorious liberality impressed their minds The Optimate, on the other hand, could thoroughly rely on his men, though he had bought their loyalty by methods of very doubtful morality, not only by paying them well but by allowing them to live at free quarters, to pillage every place that offered resistance, and to maltreat the inhabitants to their heart's content. Flaccus found his own army much more likely to melt away than that of his rival, and hastily sheered off towards Macedonia, giving out that he would march against Mithradates instead of against the Optimates. This he actually did, to the great relief of Sulla, who not only was relieved of an enemy, but saw that enemy doing good work for him by making a diversion in Asia. For Flaccus crossed the Hellespont, and though he was soon after murdered in a mutiny, his successor, the demagogue Fimbria, continued his policy, left the Optimates alone, and began harrying Mysia and Bithynia.

But long ere Flaccus reached Asia, Sulla was compelled to fight one more great battle in Greece. While he had been marching into Thessaly to face the Democrats, Mithradates had sent reinforcements to join Archelaus, who after his defeat at Chaeronea had taken refuge at Chalcis in Euboea. To watch this new army Sulla had fallen back to Athens, where he spent the winter of B.C. 86–85, waiting for the enemy to make a move on to the mainland. For as long as the Pontic troops were protected by the channel of the Euripus they were unassailable. Sulla had no fleet to ferry him over the strait, and the sea belonged to his adversaries. The Pontic ships wandered far and wide, even as far west as Zacynthus, and there was no Roman squadron to keep them in check.

But in the spring of B.C. 85 Archelaus had been strengthened by new levies, till he had 80,000 men in hand. The king wished him to fight, and he had been sent a colleague named Dorylaus, who was eager to take the offensive. Accordingly the Pontic army crossed the straits into Boeotia, and gave Sulla the opportunity for which he had been longing. His second great battle was fought in the marshy plain near Orchomenus, only ten miles away from the spot where he had won his first victory in the preceding year. The decisive engagement was brought about by the Romans commencing to run lines across the plain, so as to hem in the enemy with their backs to the morasses of Lake Copais. As Sulla had expected, this manoeuvre compelled his adversaries to attack him. The Pontic cavalry came suddenly charging down on the half-completed entrenchments, and drove back for a moment the cohorts which were covering the work. Seeing them give way, Sulla sprang from his horse, seized a standard, and ran to the front. "If any one asks you where you deserted your general," he shouted to the recoiling battalions, "say that it was at Orchomenus." The taunt recalled them to their duty, the line was re-formed, the reinforcements brought up, and in the pitched battle which followed the whole Pontic army was hurled into the lake and annihilated. "Even two hundred years after that day," writes Plutarch, "bows, helms, broken mail, and swords are still continually discovered in the mud, where the fen was once choked with the bodies of the barbarians." The whole horde perished: only their general Archelaus escaped, as he had done in the previous year at Chaeronea.

Mithradates was now much cowed in spirit. All his chosen mercenaries had been destroyed, his foothold in Europe was lost, and he saw the war about to be transferred to Asia. For Lucullus had at last collected a fleet, which gave Sulla that power of crossing the Ægean which he had not hitherto possessed. Moreover, Fimbria was already across the Hellespont, and though his army was small and raw compared with that of Sulla, it was already giving the king much trouble. Accordingly he sent to ask for peace, offering to abandon all that he had conquered in Europe if he were allowed to retain the province of Asia. He promised in addition to lend the Optimates a fleet, a great sum of money, and an auxiliary army for use against the Democrats in Italy. But Sulla was far too good a Roman to allow the empire to be shorn of its wealthiest province, and scorned to march against Cinna at the head of a barbarian force. He rejected the terms proposed to him, and offered the king merely the restoration of the boundaries that had existed before the war. He might keep his ancestral kingdom, but he must evacuate Asia, surrender his fleet, and pay a heavy war indemnity.

The Pontic monarch at first thought that these terms were harder than his adversaries had any right to ask. He declared that he would continue the war rather than accept them. Sulla then began to make active preparations for crossing the Ægean : at the same moment a great number of the states of Ionia, Lydia, and Caria revolted against Mithradates, whose rule had been rapidly becoming unbearable, as his temper grew worse and his financial demands more pressing. Moreover, Fimbria's army had pushed south and occupied Pergamus, after defeating the king's son in a pitched battle.

With a sudden descent from swollen pride to abject servility, very characteristic of an Oriental prince in his day of trouble, Mithradates sent to tender acceptance of the original terms that had been offered him. He evacuated as much of the Asiatic province as was still in his hands, gave up seventy war-galleys, and paid a fine of 3000 talents. He had a formal conference with Sulla at Dardanus in the Troad, where he promised everything that was asked of him, and bore with humility the haughty and trenchant harangue of his conqueror, who told him that he was fortunate to escape so easily as he was now doing, after his unprovoked attack on Rome in the day of her necessity, and his wanton massacre of the Italian residents in Asia during the first year of the war.

The honour of the Roman name being now fully vindicated, and the boundaries of the empire restored, Sulla was at last able to turn against the Democrats. He had first to deal with Fimbria, whose army had pushed southward and was now lying at Thyatira, in Lydia; but when he drew near, the soldiers of his adversary refused to bear arms against the saviour and champion of the Roman cause in the East. Their general, seeing his men melting away from him, made an attempt to get Sulla murdered at a conference, and when this miserable plot failed, fell upon his own sword. The submission of Fimbria's legions was a godsend to the Optimates, for Sulla was able to leave them behind to garrison Asia, so that the whole of his own veterans could be utilised for the approaching invasion of Italy.

Having completely pacified the East, and carried out in its entirety the programme which he had set before himself when he left Rome in B.C. 87, Sulla now turned his face homeward. He was aware that he had no light task before him: his military chest was full, for he had levied an enormous fine of 20,000 talents on the Asiatic cities which had joined in the massacre of B.C. 88. But his army was very small: he had no more than his original five legions, kept up with difficulty to their full strength, for Roman recruits were hard to find in the East. Even counting a few mercenary troops which he had levied, he had no more than 30,000 men—about the same number with which Hannibal had invaded Italy a hundred and thirty-five years before. They seemed but a handful, when it was borne in mind that Cinna could dispose of the resources of the whole peninsula, not to speak of those of the provinces of Gaul, Spain, and Africa. But Sulla had three causes for confidence—his own generalship (or, as he preferred to call it, his luck), the absolute fidelity of his legions, and the knowledge that comparatively few of those who were to be opposed to him were particularly zealous to fight for the Democratic cause. In military efficiency each of his men was worth two or three of the raw recruits with whom they would have to deal; and what soldier was likely to desert the general who had been giving him of late no less than sixteen denarii a day, just thirty-two times the normal pay of the Roman legionary?

Sulla gave his enemies fair warning of his intentions. Before he set sail he sent a despatch to Rome, in which he laid before the Senate a detailed account of his four successful years of campaigning in Greece and Asia. He then announced that he was approaching to chastise those who had been guilty of the massacres of the winter of B.C. 87–86, not to harm the Roman people. He should not meddle with the rights of the newly enfranchised Italian citizens, nor should he do any wilful damage to Italy. He was the enemy, not of the many, but of the few, and only those who had blood on their hands need fear him.

Such a declaration was well suited to frighten the Democratic government at Rome, for Cinna and his friends knew that they were no longer popular with the country at large. Their three years of rule had been a disastrous failure; it started with a bloody massacre which alienated every citizen of moderate mind. Then, when constructive measures were necessary, the famous Democratic programme had ended in a fiasco. Cinna had no genius in him, and the code of laws which he produced turned out to be no more than a *rechauffée* of the out-of-date expedients of Sulpicius and the Gracchi, which had already been tried and found wanting. The one startling novelty had been the dishonest debt-law of Valerius Flaccus, which (as we have already mentioned) permitted those who owed money to demand a receipt in full from their creditors when they had paid one-fourth of what they had borrowed. It may be guessed what was the effect of this law on the money-lending Equites, who had hitherto been staunch supporters of the Democratic cause.

Cinna and his friends, in short, had staked their success on their power to satisfy all Italy, and to provide a purer and a more efficient government than that of the old senatorial oligarchy. In this they had notoriously failed. So far from being a return to the Golden Age, the three

CINNA ARMS AGAINST SULLA

years domination of the Democratic party had been a time of massacre, bankruptcy, and discontent. The chiefs of the dominant faction had proved windbags, and dishonest windbags too. Of all the men who emerged as leaders in these troublous years, none showed the least sign of genius save the praetor Q. Sertorius; the rest were noisy rather than energetic, and bloodthirsty rather than resolute. Indeed, the only men who fought with zeal against Sulla were those who had compromised themselves in the massacre, and knew that they were beyond the hope of pardon.

Sulla's great advantage, then, was that he and his followers meant business, while the majority of those arrayed against him were lukewarm. But still the odds seemed so desperate, in point of mere numbers, that it was thought that his little army would be overwhelmed. Cinna had 100,000 men enrolled in B.C. 84, and in the next year it is said that his successors hurried double that number into the field. But few were eager for the fray. It seemed that they were to be sacrificed to save the necks of their leaders, not to defend Italy, for Sulla kept asserting that he came as a friend to every one but the fanatics who had murdered his friends, razed his house to the ground, and declared him a public enemy. Noting the slackness of the people and the army, the majority in the Senate, who felt themselves less compromised than their leaders, voted that an embassy should be sent to Sulla, to see if he could not be reconciled and brought home without a war. But when, amid many protestations of his moderation and good intentions, the proconsul answered that he must bring his army at his back to give him security, and that the guilty must be punished, it was evident that there was no way of avoiding the struggle.

Cinna meanwhile had been seized with the idea that the

best way to keep Sulla out of Italy would be to attack him in Greece. He collected an army at Ancona, with the intention of crossing over into Epirus. The first cohorts sailed, but when the main body was ordered to embark in very stormy weather, the men mutinied. Cinna came hurrying down to appease them, but was received by a volley of stones and beaten to death. The control of his party fell into the hands of men even less capable than himself, the chief of whom were his colleague, the consul Papirius Carbo, Marius, the son of the great general, and L. Junius Brutus Damasippus. The Democratic party had no longer a single autocratic leader—Cinna's three consulships had been styled a *dominatio* and almost a tyranny—but was ruled by a council of war destitute of any commanding personality.

In the spring of B.C. 83 Sulla landed in safety at Brundisium, which opened its gates without opposition— an event of evil augury for the Democrats. It was his object to show from the first that he came as the friend of Italy, and the enemy only of those who had proscribed him. All through his first campaign he was fighting with his brains as much as with his sword, by proclamations no less than by battles. He began by granting the Brundisians immunity from all taxation as a reward for their surrender. As he marched through Apulia he kept his army in such order that neither man nor beast, cottage nor cornfield, was harmed: yet it must have been hard to hold in veterans accustomed to the plunder of the East. Wherever he came, he announced that there was full amnesty and pardon for every one who did not actually appear in arms against him. This conduct had the most marked effect on the hostile army: from the very first the Democratic legions showed great lukewarmness in the cause of their commanders. The two consuls for the new year, C. Norbanus and L. Cornelius

SULLA DEFEATS THE CONSULS

Scipio, were entrusted with the opening of the campaign against the invader. They were both very incompetent officers, and foolishly separated their armies by such a wide gap that Sulla was able to deal with them in detail. Norbanus was defeated near Canusium, in Apulia; he hastily fell back across the Apennines, but received a second beating at Mount Tifata, after which he shut himself up in Capua. His colleague Scipio marched to his aid, but his army was dispersed more by intrigue than by fighting. For Sulla proposed an armistice, and took advantage of it to tamper with the consul's men, who, when the resumption of hostilities was proclaimed, refused to fight. Part of them dispersed, part went over to Sulla, and Scipio fell into the hands of his enemy. Still maintaining his ostentatious affectation of magnanimity, the latter sent him away unharmed, giving him an escort as far as the nearest Democratic camp. He then returned to blockade the army of Norbanus. The Democrats complained, as Plutarch tells us, that "in contending with Sulla they had to fight at once with a lion and a fox, and the fox gave the more trouble of the two."

Sulla's first successes emboldened the surviving members of the Optimate party, who had escaped the sword of Marius, and had been lurking ever since in obscure hiding-places, to take arms. The senior in rank was the proconsul Q. Metellus Pius, but by far the most able were two young men, Gn. Pompeius and Marcus Crassus, each of whom had to avenge a father slain in the civil war, the one in a mutiny, the other in the great massacre of B.C. 87. Both were active, enterprising, and fortunate. Pompeius gathered in Picenum, where his family was popular, a tumultuary force that gradually swelled to three legions. Crassus levied a small army in the Marsian territory. These insurrections distracted the attention of the Democrats, who were forced to turn against them a considerable portion of their new levies, and had in consequence less men to oppose to Sulla.

It thus came to pass that the proconsul found himself strong enough to march on Rome when the spring of B.C. 82 came round. He planned a diversion on the east side of Italy, where Metellus and Pompey made such a bold advance that Carbo, with the main army of the Democrats, went off to hold them in check, leaving the younger Marius, with 40,000 men, to guard Latium and the Appian Way. When Sulla started for a sudden rush on Rome, he found only this latter army in his path. At Sacriportus, near Signia, he inflicted a crushing defeat on the young general, who was a brave soldier but no tactician. The Optimates were much outnumbered, but the slackness of the rank and file among their enemies gave them every advantage. In the thick of the fight five cohorts threw down their standards and went over to Sulla: this broke the line, the enemy fled, and Marius only succeeded in saving a fraction of his host within the walls of the fortress of Praeneste. The road to Rome was open, and Sulla marched hastily on the city: he occupied it without having to strike a blow, but found to his disgust that he was too late to prevent a fresh massacre. On getting news of the defeat at Sacriportus, the praetor L. Brutus Damasippus had laid violent hands on every person in the city who was suspected of sympathising with the Optimates. Mucius Scævola, the Pontifex Maximus, and many other respectable men, perished in this disgraceful slaughter.

After the fall of Rome Sulla's star was manifestly in the ascendant, and he possessed the obvious advantage of appearing to be the legal representative of the people, since he could compel the Senate and the Comitia to vote whatever he pleased. The war assumed a very confused and chaotic aspect, for fighting was now going on all

BATTLE OF THE COLLINE GATE

over Italy, and each side had dispersed its main force, in the endeavour to seize or to hold as many important districts as was possible. But the whole business came to a head on November 1, B.C. 82: while Sulla was facing Carbo in Etruria, and young Marius was still being besieged in Praeneste, the enemy made a vigorous attempt to seize Rome. A division detached by Carbo made a junction, behind Sulla's back, with the national levy of the Samnites, who were helping the Democrats more in the character of independent allies than in that of Roman citizens. Caius Pontius of Telesia, a namesake of the ancient hero of the Caudine Forks, led his countrymen to join Damasippus and Carrinas. The whole mass came rushing down from the Apennines upon the city, which the Samnites intended to sack rather than to save. Sulla received news of this concentration in his rear so late that he almost despaired of arriving in time. Rome was within an ace of destruction, for the vanguard of the Optimate cavalry arrived when the enemy were only two miles from the gates. If their generals had pushed forward a little farther on the preceding night (October 31st), instead of encamping close to the city, they would have found no one to oppose them. As it was, Sulla's legions had to be placed in line directly they arrived, after a fatiguing night march, and without being granted time to take a proper meal.

The battle that followed was far the fiercest of the whole civil war, for Sulla had to deal not with the lukewarm levies of Carbo, but with the sturdy Samnites. Pontius rode round his army crying, as Velleius tells us, that "Rome's last day had come; that the tyrant city must be destroyed to her foundations; that the Roman wolves, the bane of Italian liberty, would never be got rid of until their lair was laid waste." The armies met outside the Colline gate, on the northern side of the city, the Optimate legions being ranged with their back to the walls, and only a few hundred yards from them. Sulla had the left wing, his lieutenant, M. Crassus, the right. For some hours the fortune of the day was hardly contested: Crassus gained ground, but Sulla's own division was pressed backward, till some of the cohorts were crushed against the walls, and others vainly tried to re-enter the gates, which were closed against them by the citizens. The general himself was in imminent danger of death: those who were near him saw him draw from his breast the little golden figure of Apollo which he always wore, kiss it, and mutter to the god that it would be a scurvy trick if he allowed Sulla the lucky to fall at last on his own threshold by the hands of traitors.

Apollo was not unpropitious: the wreck of Sulla's wing held out at the foot of the walls till the night fell: soon after the news came that Crassus had completely routed the force opposed to him, which seems to have been mainly composed of the Democratic levies of Damasippus and Carrinas, not of Samnites. This caused the enemy to draw off from Sulla; their general, Pontius, had been mortally wounded, and it seems that there was no capable man to take his place. At dawn the two Optimate divisions joined and swept away the dislocated forces of their opponents: one Democratic legion came over to Sulla's side; the rest dispersed, but not so quickly but that 8000 of them were captured in their flight. The generals Damasippus, Marcius, and Carrinas suffered the same fate on the next day. Sulla cut off their heads and sent them to Praeneste, to be exhibited to young Marius and his famishing garrison. The dreadful sight had its effect: Marius committed suicide and Praeneste surrendered. The victor sorted out the Romans from among the prisoners, beheaded those of senatorial rank, but let the rest go free. The Italians were all put to death to the number of several thousands. The same fate had already befallen the captives taken at the Colline gate; 8000 of them—all save the Roman rank and file—were slain in the Circus Maximus, which had been utilised as their prison The Senate, sitting hard by in the Temple of Bellona, heard the groans and shrieks of the victims, and showed signs of terror. But Sulla bid them "stick to their business and not allow themselves to be distracted; it was only some malefactors who were suffering the reward of their crimes."

There was still much fighting to be done in Italy: Carbo deserted his army in Etruria and fled over-seas, but his partisans held out for some time in isolated bands. Norba and Nola stood long sieges, and Volaterrae held out for the incredible length of two years. But the main war in Italy practically came to an end with the victory of the Colline gate and the fall of Praeneste. The struggle after that date mainly consisted of the savage harrying of Samnium and Etruria, the two districts where the Democratic party had made itself most strong.

Leaving the completion of this guerilla warfare to his lieutenants, Sulla had set himself to the great work of his latter years, the remodelling of the Roman constitution on an oligarchical basis. With this object he had himself appointed dictator in November 82. But a dreadful preliminary to his political work was his great "Proscription," the formal revenge for what Marius and Cinna had done in B.C. 87-86. "Down to the moment of his victory," it was said, "he showed himself far more moderate and humane than could have been expected; after it was won, he was more cruel than could have been believed possible." He spared indeed the rank and file of the Roman Democrats, but he systematically cut off every man of note in their party. It seemed that he

K

was determined that not one leader should survive to rally the partisans of the lost cause. He started his operations by issuing three long lists of persons on whose heads a price was set; the first contained 80 names, the second and third 220 each. He then coolly gave notice that he had condemned every one whom he could remember, but that those whom he had forgotten should be put into supplementary catalogues. These dreadful appendices kept coming out for many weeks, and not till they ceased could any Roman who had not taken the Optimate side feel himself secure. Many comparatively obscure names crept into the lists, for the generals and favourites of Sulla often got him to insert their personal enemies among the executed. He himself seems to have been as impervious to corruption as to pity, but those about him were not, and all sorts of old grudges were paid off under a pretence of political vengeance. In all, some 50 senators, 1600 equites, and at least 2000 private persons were executed in the Sullan proscriptions.[1] The heads of the fallen were exhibited in the Forum, according to the disgusting custom which had begun at the death of Sulpicius. Their property was confiscated, and their children and grandchildren were declared of tainted blood and incapable of holding any public office. The "sons of the proscribed" formed a well-known group of malcontents during the next generation, on account of this disability which was now laid upon them.

But the Proscription was only, in Sulla's estimation, a necessary preliminary to the great work of reconstruction which he had taken in hand. He had resolved to rearrange the whole constitution, with the definite

[1] As Mommsen has clearly shown, the larger numbers given by Appian, i. 103, Eutropius, v. 9, and others, include all those who fell in the civil war, not those who were regularly proscribed and executed.

SULLA RECASTS THE CONSTITUTION 147

object of transferring the sovereignty of the state from the people to the Senate.

We have already pointed out that in the Roman politics of the last fifty years the main difficulty that lay at the bottom of all disputes was the quarrel for sovereignty. Should the Senate, according to recent usage, or the tribes, according to ancient constitutional theory, be the body that really ruled the city and the empire? *Senatus Populusque Romanus* was a sounding phrase, but neither Optimates nor Democrats had any love for the mutual interdependence which the words postulated.

Now Sulla thought that all the troubles of the time came from the fact that neither Senate nor people had full sovereignty; and, as a consistent oligarch and a conscientious party-man, he was determined to put the balance of power to an end, by conferring complete autocratic authority on his own senatorial order. The Optimates had, during the last fifty years, suffered from three different sorts of foes—from unruly tribunes galvanising into spasmodic life the cumbrous but all-powerful machinery of the Comitia; from over-great magistrates, like Marius or Cinna, who renewed their power from year to year and kept an army at their backs; and from the newly created Equestrian Order, the body of financiers, fighting for their own interests by the power of the purse, however sordid and anti-national these interests might be.

Sulla's laws, so far as they dealt with things political, resolve themselves into an ingenious and systematic attempt to break down the power of all these three enemies of the Senate—the Comitia Tributa and its tribunes, the great magistrates, and the equites. If all three were politically annihilated, there would be for the future no check on the omnipotence of the Senate. The dictator's object was to combine the maximum of real with the minimum of formal change; for though he was himself completely emancipated from that slavish respect for the letter of the constitution which swayed the average Roman, he knew that this was the case neither with his friends nor with his enemies.

The hardest blows were aimed at the most powerful enemies, the tribunes and the Comitia Tributa, whose power of issuing and repealing any laws that they pleased had been the greatest danger of the Senate. As long as any Democratic tribune could bring forward whatever bills he chose, and as long as such bills, when passed by the Plebeian assembly, became binding on the state, there was no security against a reaction that might annul the whole of the Cornelian Laws the moment that their author should have passed away.

Sulla's action against the Comitia was very ingenious. He made no pretence of abolishing it, or of abrogating the omnipotence of such bills as it might pass. He only determined that no dangerous bill should ever come before it. This was accomplished by reviving and making indisputably valid the old claim of the Senate that every law should of right be laid before them and receive their *auctoritas*, or certificate of legality, before the tribune introduced it to the assembly. Now, obviously, such bills as the Senate would pass on as harmless and useful, would be measures that did not cut short their own authority or clash with their ideas of expediency. Sulla therefore compelled the Comitia to pass a law which made the grant of a *senatus auctoritas* a necessary preliminary for the production of a law before the people. Henceforth, as he hoped, there would be no chance of tiresome and dangerous bills for land distributions, or corn-doles, or grants of abnormal powers to magistrates, being passed by the assembly. All such schemes, if broached in the Senate, would be stifled there and go no farther. No measure of a Democratic complexion would ever reach the Comitia. All that the people would be able to do would be to reject bills sent down to them with the senatorial sanction, if they had the pluck to contradict the governing power in the state. Their power of initiative would be gone. Thus reduced to impotence, the assembly was no longer an object of dread to Sulla; and for that reason he did not think it worth while to abolish it, or even to turn out from it the hordes of Italians whom Cinna had thrust into the midst of the old citizens. He made no attempt either to confine them to a few tribes or to suspend their franchise. Thus he kept to the letter the promise which he had made to the new citizens when he landed at Brundisium. Personally, as an old aristocrat, Sulla probably felt much less contempt for the Italians than for the original *Plebs Urbana*. What he thought of the freedmen, who were so prominent a feature in that body, may be guessed from the fact that he not only put them all back into the four city tribes, but actually foisted in among them in a single day no less than 10,000 voters of the lowest class, enfranchised slaves of those who had fallen in his own proscription. They all took him as their patron, and adopted his name of Cornelius, which was henceforth one of the commonest appellations in the slums.

To destroy completely the powers of the Plebeian assembly as an element in the constitution, it was necessary not merely to subordinate its legislative functions to those of the Senate, but to cut short the dangerous and anarchical privileges of its presiding magistrates, the tribunes. Some legislators would have abolished the tribunate altogether; and considering the way in which Tiberius Gracchus and Saturninus had used it, there would have been a fair excuse for so doing. Sulla, however, merely resolved that he would invent rules which should for the future keep tribunes out of mischief. It was not enough that a *senatus auctoritas* should be required for any bill that they might bring forward. He determined that they should for the future be nonentities, men unlikely to disturb the state by their personal ascendency or ambition.

This end was secured by the ingenious law which provided that for the future the acceptance of the tribunate should be a complete bar to the holding of any subsequent magistracy in the state. The man who chose to be a tribune would put himself out of the running for any further political promotion. But in spite of this disability, it was conceivable that an ambitious man might become tribune with the intention not of sacrificing any external career, but of being perpetually re-elected to this office like Caius Gracchus of old. Sulla provided against this possibility by repealing the law of B.C. 129, which had made it legal for a man to hold the tribunate in successive years. He enacted that tribunes (and, as we shall see, other magistrates also) should not be chosen again without an interval of ten years between their two tenures of the post. Thus it was secured that for the future no man of more than fifth-rate ambition would become a tribune, since by putting in for a nomination he cut himself off from all hope of a brilliant and continuous public career.

But even the nobodies who would now hold the office were not to be left shackled only by their own nothingness. Sulla gave the Senate a power of fining the tribunes for any conduct that it might consider illegal or unbecoming, so that they had to live in awe of the governing body all their days. If they held too many noisy public meetings or dared to use their veto freely, they might find themselves saddled with a crushing penalty and reduced to poverty. The only power, in short, which remained untouched among the tribune's privileges, was that which he had been given when the office was first invented in the days of the early Republic, the *jus auxilii ferendi*, or right to intervene in behalf of the individual Roman citizen who might be suffering oppression.

Having dealt thus with the tribunes and the assembly, Sulla had next to take in hand the second power in the state which was dangerous to the sovereignty of the Senate—that of the individual magistrates. According to the theory of the Roman constitution, the consul or praetor, deriving his authority directly from the people because he had been elected by them in the Comitia Centuriata, had a very independent position in face of the Senate. That body, indeed, had in early days been nothing more than the band of advisers chosen by the consul, whose monitions he was equally free to accept or to reject. Even in these latter times a headstrong consul could practically disregard the voice of the Senate for his whole term of office: and if he was chosen for several years in succession, he could go on administering thi gs much as he pleased, without being restrained to any appreciable extent. Such had been the position of Marius during the years of the Cimbric war, and of Cinna in B.C. 86-84.

Sulla therefore had to guard against the ambition of the magistrates of the future. His main weapon for this end was his *lex annalis*: this law provided that all the officers of the state must be taken in strict rotation—first the quaestorship, then the praetorship, and lastly the consulate. No one was to hold two offices in successive years; and the different limits of age prescribed for each secured that a considerable time must elapse between the tenure of them, otherwise, of course, an ambitious politician might, by taking aedileship, praetorship, and consulate in successive years, get a long spell of continuous power, and make himself permanently disagreeable to the Senate. Much less was it to be permitted that any magistrate should hold the same office continuously: one of Sulla's ordinances was to the effect that there must be a gap of no less than ten years before a man could be re-elected to the same post. We have already come across this provision when dealing with the tribunate. There would, therefore, no longer be any place in the constitution for a Marius or a Cinna: but, in the true oligarchic style, each man would get his turn, and no man more than his turn. Every politician would be able to calculate with precision when he ought to hold each office, without the danger arising that some interloper of genius might sweep down and monopolise the series of praetorships or consulships that ought to have been divided among half-a-dozen minor persons.

It is curious to note that Sulla, with all his acuteness, overlooked one fact—that an ambitious proconsul in a province, at the head of an army, might be quite as troublesome to the Senate as an ambitious consul at Rome proposing laws to the people. Yet his own career ought to have taught him that a governor in Greece or Gaul with half-a-dozen faithful legions was the greatest danger of all. He did realise the peril, as it would seem, but merely provided against it by enacting that any imperator who crossed the frontier of his province at the head of an army, or refused to quit it within a month of his successor's arrival, should become *ipso facto* a public enemy. This, no doubt, clearly defined high treason, but it gave no sufficient security against it. The Republic was ultimately to be overthrown by an adventurer of this kind—by a provincial governor who dared to cross the Rubicon, whatever might be the legal consequence, because he was well aware that his legions would follow him against any enemy whom he might choose to indicate to them. The real remedy against this peril would have been to separate the military from the civil command in each province—to have a governor who was merely an administrator, and a commander-in-chief who reported directly to the Senate. But this plan does not seem to have entered into the dictator's mind.

Sulla made a large increase in the number of the annual magistrates, raising the praetors to eight and the quaestors to twenty; but it is improbable that he intended, as some have supposed, to decrease the importance of each office by multiplying the numbers of those who held it. Incidentally this result might follow, but it is probable that the dictator was merely studying the convenience of the state, for till his day the administration was decidedly undermanned. Nor, again, does it seem to be true that he deliberately deprived the consuls of their military power for their year of office, by arranging that they should stay in Rome, where no legions would be at their disposal, and only utilise their *imperium* when they went out as proconsuls to their provinces in the succeeding year. The usage that the consul should remain at home, unless urgent military affairs drew him out of Italy, had already begun to grow up before Sulla's time. And on the other hand there are a few cases after his death in which the consul left the city and assumed command of an army before his year had expired—*e.g.*, this was certainly done by Cotta and Lucullus in the first year of the third Mithradatic war.

It would seem that Sulla made the quaestorship qualify its holder for a seat in the Senate, so that the governing body of the state was no longer filled up by the censors, but recruited automatically by the influx of young magistrates. In this way he abolished the necessity for a censorship, and made the Senate independent of the likes and dislikes of individual holders of that office.

Having thus muzzled the tribunes and curbed the consuls, Sulla had next to deal with the third enemy of the Senate, the Equestrian Order. It will be remembered that a disproportionate share of the massacre of the fourth proscription had fallen upon them—no less than 1600 had been put to death, so that the Democratic wing of the knighthood had been almost exterminated. At the other end of the line Sulla had promoted a very large number of Equites of Optimate views to a seat in the Senate, so that in legislating against the body he was not striking at his own friends. His object was to loosen the bonds which held together the rather heterogeneous classes which formed the Equestrian Order. These bonds were, firstly, their honorary privileges,—the *augusticlave* toga, the gold ring, and the rows of reserved seats in circus and theatre; secondly, their monopoly of the control of the Jury Courts, which they had used so unscrupulously as a weapon against the Senate and the provincial magistrates; thirdly, their tax-farming privileges, especially that most profitable enactment of Caius Gracchus, which handed over the collecting of the tithes of Asia to the *Societates*.

Sulla, therefore, launched a whole series of measures against the Equestrian Order. One bill took away the entire control of the law-courts from them, and restored it to the senators. Once more the latter became the only persons eligible as jurymen, as in the days before Caius Gracchus; they could look forward to being tried by a friendly instead of a hostile court if they incurred prosecution, and were able to audit their own accounts inside the family. The Equites suffered, but not the empire, for the previous state of things had been so bad that any change must have profited the provincials. A second bill put an end to the system of tax-farming in Asia, and imposed on each of its cities a fixed tribute, instead of the tithes. This was an enormous boon to the Asiatics; but probably the way in which the measure commended itself to Sulla's mind had nothing to do with their point of view. He made the change because it would be unpalatable to the knights, who lost an unparalleled source of money-making when the tax-farming disappeared. We may compare him to the Puritans of old, who abolished bear-baiting, not because it was cruel to the bear, but because it gave so much pleasure to the audience. Yet another bill, of which the details have unfortunately perished, would seem to have deprived the Equites of many of their honorary privileges, especially of their seats in the circus. These they did not recover till the law of Roscius Otho restored them in B.C. 67.

There were many other Cornelian Laws outside the three great groups with which we have been dealing One abolished the corn-dole, a most admirable measure, for which we should admire the dictator more if we could only suppose that he was acting on economic reasons, and not merely doing his best to disoblige the urban multitude. Others systematised the organisation of the Law Courts, which had hitherto been arranged in a very haphazard fashion. Very prominent among his innovations was the law which added new courts for the trial of criminal offences (*quaestiones perpetuae*) to those already existing, so that every form of offence had for the future its proper venue. But of these legal matters we have no leisure to speak. Nor need we say much concerning his colonial schemes: he settled many of his veterans in Etruria and Samnium, on the lands of the cities which he had destroyed for obstinate adherence to the Democratic cause. But he can hardly have expected his colonies to prove economic successes, considering the character of the settlers, who had long been estranged from the soil, and the indisputable fact that farming had long ceased to pay in Central Italy. They were, no doubt, merely intended to last out Sulla's own day, and to supply him for a time with compact blocks of adherents, accustomed to arms and cantoned in the close vicinity of Rome. It is a curious commentary on the wisdom of the step, that ruined Sullan veterans formed, sixteen years later, an appreciable element in the army of Catiline.

Sulla, as every one knows, laid down his dictatorship in January B.C. 79, after holding it for two years. When he had passed all his long code of constitutional enactments, and had seen the last embers of civil war die down, he laid aside the trappings of power and retired into private life. He had no personal ambition, and when his work was finished and the new constitution had been set going, he resolved to let it have the chance of a fair start, without the danger of overbalance caused by the perpetual presence of his own mighty personality. For the Sullan *régime* had in it no place for Sullas. The whole scheme of laws had been framed to keep down over-great men, and he was well aware that he was himself over-great. As a conscientious oligarch, it was his duty to remove himself from power, and to resign the abnormal office that he had held throughout B.C. 81 and 80. His function for the future was to stand by, outside the machine, to watch it work, and to step in to lend his aid if ever it showed signs of getting out of gear. His notion of how the new constitution could best be maintained may be gathered from the curious story of the death of Lucretius Ofella. That distinguished officer, the captor of Praeneste, so far presumed on his late services that he boldly proposed to break Sulla's *Lex Annalis* by standing for the consulate before he had held the praetorship. Sulla gave him fair

THE DEATH OF OFELLA 157

warning that he would not be allowed to take the office, but he refused to listen, and made a formal canvass in the Forum after the usual style. While Ofella was going his rounds with his white toga in the crowded market-place, his chief quietly told two centurions to cut him down. They did so; and when an uproar began, Sulla stepped forward to take all the blame and responsibility, and to offer to stand his trial for murder. No one dared to come forward as a prosecutor, and so he got off scot-free. The story has several morals; clearly the constitution was still so weak that an ambitious man could venture to attack it ere it was two years old; only Sulla himself could defend it, but as long as he survived it was safe. If he could have looked forward to twenty years of life, he might have dragooned the Roman people into an acceptance of it; but he was already elderly and ailing. Innovators should start young and live long, like the Emperor Augustus. What would have happened to the imperial system if Augustus had died at the age of forty, instead of living on till he was seventy-six?

No doubt Sulla's constitution was doomed from the first to failure. But, at any rate, the experiment of restoring the oligarchy was worth trying. The opposite political device of the Democrats, that of endeavouring to transact all the business of the city and the empire in the Comitia, had proved utterly impracticable. Under Cinna's domination such a *régime* had been working for nearly four years with the most deplorable results—the popular programme had been tried and found wanting—it had run to nothing more than corn-largesses and the repudiation of debts. At the touch of the sword the Democratic government had fallen to pieces, merely because it commanded neither respect nor affection from any quarter.

Sulla's scheme,—to set up a Senate unhampered by any other power in the state, and possessing full and complete

sovereignty, was at least equally worthy of a trial. It
failed no doubt, mainly from the want of men able and
willing to work the system when the old dictator had
passed away. For he left behind him a Senate most
unfitted to carry on his great plan—not a number of
men of good average ability, each ready to take his turn
of duty and power and not desirous of grasping at more,
but quite the opposite sort of assembly—a multitude of
nonentities and incapables mixed with a few ambitious
young generals. The heart and core of the old Optimate
party had perished in the Marian massacres; in spite
of all its faults, the Senate, down to the days of the civil
war, had always contained a certain number of men
of mark and respectability—persons such as Antonius the
orator; Catulus, the victor over the Cimbri; Crassus, the
father of the Triumvir; the consuls Octavius and Merula.
All these had been slain by Marius and Cinna. Of the
Optimate senators none survived, save those who had
been protected by their own insignificance, and the few
who had been absent with Sulla in Greece when the civil
war broke out. The reconstructed Senate of B.C. 81,
therefore, was mainly composed of a mass of trivial and
unimportant persons, whose nothingness had caused them
to escape Cinna's eye. But seated among them were the
military men who had come to the front during the
fighting, such as Ofella, Crassus, and Pompey. These
young generals—as was but natural—were not content to
take their single turn of power and office in company
with the herd of nobodies. They were ambitious, and
yearned for the *carrière ouverte aux talents*, in which
the able man could not only reach the front, but stay
there. The slow oligarchic rotation, which Sulla had
invented, was odious to them, and they were in the end
driven to overthrow the new constitution in order that
they might be able to assert themselves over the

mediocrities. There was no resisting power among the majority—no true heir of Sulla's breed survived to bind them together and to rally them to fight in behalf of the oligarchic system. So the great dictator's constitution fell, almost undefended, only ten years after it had been created.

This, at any rate, was not Sulla's fault. He did his best with the materials set before him. He constructed the first logical and well-planned constitution that Rome had ever known—a triumph of ingenuity, because it changed the essentials while leaving the external features still in existence. It was a thoroughly practical scheme for the governance of city and empire by a pure oligarchy. If it failed, it was because the machine was cleverly built, but its mainspring was not strong enough to keep the wheels moving, *i.e.* it demanded that the average senator should attain a certain moderate level of courage, capacity, and patriotism,—but the Fathers, as a body, were lacking in all these three essentials. In the hands of the senators of the third century before Christ the Sullan constitution could have been worked; but in B.C. 80 the motive power was too weak, through no fault of Sulla's, and the machine was bound to run down. As long as he stood beside it to give the pendulum an occasional swing, the clock continued to go. When he died, it ticked feebly for a short time and then stopped.

It was ruinous to the oligarchy that Sulla should have survived only a little more than a year after he laid down the dictatorship. For himself, his early death was probably not so unfortunate: it saved him from many disappointments. Even before he died he had suffered one at least, in seeing M. Lepidus elected to the consulship contrary to his expressed desire. But on the whole his last year was one of prosperity; for the first time for many a long day he was free from the cares of office and could live as he pleased. His powers of enjoyment do not seem to have been the least impaired by advancing years: he had still to make up for that youth spent in involuntary frugality. Just before he laid down the dictatorship he had married a young wife: the story of their first meeting, as told by Plutarch, gives an amazing picture of the light-heartedness of the man who had just waded through all the blood of the Proscription.

"The dictator was one day presenting the people with a show of gladiators, and it chanced that a lady of great beauty and good family sat close behind Sulla. Her name was Valeria, the daughter of Messala, and the sister of Hortensius the orator: she had lately divorced her first husband. This lady, coming gently behind Sulla, pinched off a thread from the edge of his toga, and then passed back to her seat. But he, much amazed at the familiarity, looked round at her, whereupon she said, 'Do not wonder, sir, at what I have done; I had only a mind to get a shred of your good luck.' Sulla was far from being displeased: on the contrary, it appeared that he was agreeably flattered, for he sent to ask her name, and to inquire into her family. Then followed, all through the games, an exchange of side looks and smiles, which ended ultimately in a contract of marriage. Now it seems to me that Sulla, though he got a wife of great beauty and accomplishments, came into the match on wrong principles, for, like a boy, he was caught with soft looks and languishing airs."

Sulla's last year was spent in his villa in Campania, near Puteoli, whither he retired and dwelt amid a court of clever and dissolute companions who kept him amused. He devoted his time partly to writing his memoirs—he finished the twenty-second book of them two days before he died—partly to pleasures (reputable and disreputable) of all sorts. The tale that his last months were vexed with a loathsome disease, which rendered life insupportable, is probably an invention of his enemies. It has been attributed to half-a-dozen well-hated tyrants, the last of whom was Philip II. of Spain. But it is certain that Sulla died from breaking a blood-vessel rather than from any lingering ailment. In the leisure of his last year he found time for business: he kept a keen eye on Roman affairs, and drafted a constitution for the neighbouring town of Puteoli at the request of its inhabitants. His last recorded act was a strange and violent interference in politics, which much recalls the story of Ofella. The Quaestor Granius was making himself notorious by embezzlements, and openly said that he should escape punishment because the ex-dictator was dying. Sulla lured him to his bedside by a polite message, and then had him seized and strangled in his very presence by his slaves. The excitement of the scene caused him to rupture a blood-vessel, and he died of exhaustion next day.

His party being still in power, he received the most magnificent funeral that Rome had ever seen. His monument was erected in the most conspicuous part of the Campus Martius, and two centuries later was still visible. Plutarch says that it bore a curious and characteristic epitaph, composed by the dictator himself, in which he said that "No friend ever did him so much good, or enemy so much harm, but that he had repaid him with full interest."

CHAPTER VI

CRASSUS

NAPOLEON, in one of his cynical moods, once asked his courtiers how the world would take the news of his sudden death, supposing that some chance bullet cut him off before his time. They hastened to give him all sorts of flattering versions of the dismay and regret that would fill all Europe. "No," said the Emperor, "that is not the sort of thing that would happen. All that would occur would be that every one would draw a long breath, and say with a sigh of relief, 'Well, *that's* all over.'" And so, it may be surmised, did things go at Sulla's death. When men knew that his iron hand would never interfere again in politics, they felt as if a long nightmare was over, and abandoning the assumed characters that they had enacted during his lifetime, dropped back into their real selves. Instead of the majestic and united Optimate party which seemed to stand so firm under his protection, there was now only a mass of slack senators, who wished to take life quietly, with the maximum of enjoyment, and a few ambitious men who felt at last that they could display their ambition without risking their necks. The Senate still contained some men of real ability who were loyal to the oligarchic constitution, such as the Epicurean general Lucullus, Quintus Metellus, who had made a good military reputation, the orator Hortensius, and Catulus, the son of that Catulus who had fought so well against the Cimbri—a somewhat duller reflection of his father's virtues. But the great majority were apathetic

UNREST AFTER SULLA'S DEATH

nobodies, while the two persons who were most important and influential among Sulla's lieutenants were men who disliked the Sullan constitution, simply because it gave them no scope for the display of the considerable abilities which they possessed, and for the satisfaction of their ambition. It is mainly on the doings of these two, Marcus Licinius Crassus and Gn. Pompeius, that the politics of the next twenty years were to turn. No two men could have been more unlike in character, but fate was always hurling them together, first as young soldiers in Sulla's camp with fathers to avenge, then later as consuls in the same year, lastly as members of the famous "First Triumvirate." Of the idiosyncrasies of each of them we must endeavour to gain a firm grasp.

At first, however, there were circumstances which kept the ambition and the rivalry of Crassus and Pompey from assuming the importance which they afterwards attained. In 78 B.C. men's attention was mainly occupied by certain evils, which, as long as Sulla lived, had given the government little concern, because they knew that, if things grew serious, one nod of Sulla's head would suffice to set them right. When he was removed, these problems suddenly began to cause alarm. First, there was suppressed unrest in Italy; the children of the Proscribed, deprived of all political rights; the citizens of the Etruscan towns, who had escaped massacre but had not escaped confiscation; the numerous population in the valley of the Po, who had obtained Latin rights from Pompeius Strabo, but wanted to become full citizens—were all discontented. The wrecks of the bands of Carbo and the younger Marius were not entirely dispersed: some were pirates on the high seas, others freebooters in Mauretania. In Spain their strongest man, the ex-praetor Sertorius, had raised a really dangerous insurrection—a peril to the state, not so much because it was a lingering remnant of the civil war between Roman and Roman, as because Sertorius was gradually de-Romanising himself, and becoming a Spanish national leader rather than a representative of the old party of the *populares*. Of him we shall have more to say when we deal with the life of Pompey. As long as Sulla lived, the Optimates talked of him as a tiresome survivor of a long-lost cause, much as we talk of Botha or De Wet. After the dictator's death it became clear that his insurrection, far from dying down, was distinctly spreading over a wider area, and threatening to tear away the whole of Spain from the Roman Empire. It had already been the death of several incapable Optimate generals, and the ruin of several small armies. The outlook in the West was gloomy.

But in the year that followed Sulla's decease it was not Sertorius who seemed the most dangerous foe of the senatorial government. Their main trouble was caused at home, by the vain and heady consul, M. Æmilius Lepidus, who tried in the most reckless fashion to pull down the whole of the new constitution almost before its founder's ashes were cold. Lepidus was "a rash, intruding fool," whose motive was nothing more than the ill-regulated ambition of a man who does not know his own mediocrity, and thirsts to be something great. He draped himself in the torn and soiled mantle of Saturninus and Cinna, and appeared in the character of a Democratic saviour of society. Now, the large majority of the people of Rome and of Italy disliked the senatorial *régime*, but disliked still more the idea of the recommencement of the civil war and all its horrors. The consul found little support, but contrived to gather in Etruria an army of political refugees, discontented politicians, liberated slaves, and even bankrupt Sullan veterans. The whole of this rising bears an astonishing resemblance to the doings of Cataline in the same district fifteen years later. It failed in much the same way.

THE INSURRECTION OF LEPIDUS

When Lepidus led his horde against the city, the Senate hastily fitted out an army against him under Catulus. These raw levies were just ready when the ex-consul reached the Tiber, and actually crossed it at the Mulvian Bridge and entered the Campus Martius. Here, among the monuments and polling booths, Catulus and his legions met him and gave him a severe defeat. He retreated into Etruria, took ship to escape his pursuers, and died immediately after in Sardinia, whither he had fled. The strongest body of his followers that held together was defeated by Pompey in Cisalpine Gaul, and its leader, M. Brutus, was captured and executed at Mutina. Only a small part of Lepidus's insurrectionary host, headed by the Praetor Perpenna, escaped by sea, and went to join Sertorius in Spain. There the insurgents were making marked progress; they carried all before them, and were not even checked when Pompey in the next year led a considerable army of reinforcements from Italy against them.

While the revolt of Sertorius was taxing all the energies of Rome, there were two other important struggles in progress. The first was the renewed war with Mithradates, an ill-managed and interminable struggle, in which the king of Pontus, whom Sulla had beaten with such ease and rapidity, baffled all the Roman generals for ten years, so that even the very capable L. Lucullus, the best general of really loyal mind whom the Senate possessed, could not entirely subdue him, though he beat him in battle often enough.

The third, and the most difficult and disgraceful of the three military problems with which the oligarchy had to deal in these troublous years, was the great slave-rising in Italy under the Thracian Spartacus, who beat ten Roman armies, and equipped forty thousand men from their spoils, though he had started as the leader of no more than seventy-eight runaway gladiators. Scandalous as it appeared, the Senate could not prevent the untrained hordes of Spartacus from ranging over the whole of Italy, from the Po to the straits of Rhegium. For several years he marched and countermarched among the Apennines like a second Hannibal, and won battles over the incapable Optimate generals that were in their way hardly less notable than Trebia or Trasimene.

The government whose weakness provoked, and whose incapacity protracted, the three disastrous wars with Sertorius, Mithradates, and Spartacus, deserved to fall. It only needed some one more able than the vain Lepidus to lead the attack on the Sullan state-system, and it was bound to crumble down. But the blow was to be given not by one man but by two. Pompey was returning from Spain on the one side, on the other Crassus was about to come to the front. Of him we have now to speak in detail; hitherto we have barely mentioned his name.

M. Licinus Crassus had been born in or about the year B.C. 107. We have already had occasion to tell how his father, Crassus the ex-consul, and his elder brother, Publius, fell in the great massacre of B.C. 87, hunted down by the gangs of Marius. But Marcus, the younger son, escaped through untold perils to Spain, where he lay hid for many months in a cave by the sea-shore. When he emerged from his lurking-place, it was to become a freebooter on the high seas. At last he heard that Sulla had returned to Italy, and sailed to join him at the head of his band of outlaws. He applied to the proconsul for a military command and a detachment of troops. "I can only," said Sulla, "give you as helpers the ghosts of your murdered father and brother." Crassus quite understood his chief's meaning; the Optimate army was so small that there was not a man to spare: the spur of revenge must serve him instead of regular resources. With no more than his

CHARACTER OF CRASSUS

original band of outlaws, he made a dash into the Marsian territory, and there succeeded in raising a considerable body of troops. When Sulla advanced into Central Italy, Crassus guarded his flank; after Rome fell, he was sent up into Etruria, where he did good service against Carbo and his crew. But his most striking exploit was that he saved the fortune of the day at the battle of the Colline gate; his wing, it will be remembered, was successful, while that of Sulla was broken and pushed back to the walls. It was only delivered in the end by the help of Crassus, who used his own victorious legions to save his leader from destruction.

At the end of the civil war, then, Crassus had achieved a brilliant military reputation. Of all the Optimate generals, there were none who were more esteemed, save Pompey and the ambitious and ill-fated Lucretius Ofella. The latter was soon cut off, but with the former Crassus had already started that rivalry which was to endure throughout both their lives. As the elder man, he bitterly resented the fact that Sulla always gave the higher place to Pompey, and honoured him with a distinction and a confidence that he accorded to no other of his subordinates.

Nevertheless Crassus might have gone far, and have been reckoned among the leading lights of his party, if he had not managed to offend the dictator, and to get himself marked down as a man who was not to be trusted. Hitherto his career reads like that of an adventurous soldier, but in his last campaign he was beginning to show the traits which were to be so prominent in his later life—that unscrupulous greed for money and that indifference as to the means by which it was to be got, which were to be alike his strength and his weakness during the rest of his life. Sulla's anger with Crassus arose from two sinister incidents. At the siege of Tuder in Umbria, Crassus had captured the military chest of the Democratic consuls; instead of handing over its contents to the treasury, he embezzled the whole for his private profit. Later in the war, being in command in Lucania and Bruttium, he committed the unpardonable offence of slaying some local magnates, whose names had never appeared in the proscription list, and seized their wealth for himself. Now Sulla, though he was ruthless in blood-shedding, had a system in all that he did, and objected to seeing his plans for weakening the Democratic party turned to the use of private greed. He was deeply incensed at Crassus for slaying men uncondemned by himself, and when his command ran out, sent him into private life with a bad mark against his name. He did not prosecute him, or drive him out of the Senate, but simply noted him down as a man not to be trusted or employed.

Having lost his military career, and being barred out of political advancement, Crassus turned his energies into money-making, and laid the foundation of the vast fortune which he was to accumulate by lucky speculations in the property of the proscribed. The Italian money-market was glutted with lands, houses, and investments belonging to the fallen Democrats. The man who had a little spare money to invest could, at this moment, buy up great masses of property, which would recover their value in a few years, when the glut and the panic was over, and Italy had settled down into quiet. Crassus had not very great paternal wealth; his own moderate fortune reached the competent but not startling total of three hundred talents —some £75,000 of our money—but he had amassed great sums by plunder during the war, and he boldly sunk every sesterce that he could scrape together in buying up depreciated lands and houses in and about Rome. He had his reward within a short time. When public confidence had been restored, and prices had risen to

CRASSUS AND HIS INVESTMENTS

their old level, he found himself a millionaire. What his wealth was at this period we cannot say, but at a later time it amounted—after a year of exceptional expense in all sorts of political corruption—to no less than seven thousand one hundred talents—one million seven hundred and seventy thousand pounds of our money.

While Sulla still lived, and while the oligarchy still hung together after his death, Crassus, excluded from public life, went on conquering and to conquer in the world of finance. Plutarch gives us most extraordinary details as to his ingenious and often undignified methods of money-making. Not only did he lend money at high rates of interest both to Roman senators and to provincial municipalities, but he invented strange devices of his own. One of them was his school for the education of slaves. He used to buy the raw material, and have them trained as readers, book-keepers, stewards, and cooks. It is said that he not only supervised the school, but often gave lectures himself—in the cooking of accounts, rather than of *entrées*, it is to be presumed. The slaves who had been through this academy sold at much enhanced prices. Still more astonishing was his amateur fire-brigade and the way in which he used it. He got together a body of five hundred workmen—carpenters, masons, and the like—provided them with ropes, buckets, ladders, and tools. Whenever there was a fire (and fires were as common as they were dangerous in the crowded city), he went down at the head of his gang and called on householders whose property was in the immediate neighbourhood of the conflagration. He then offered to buy their houses, as they stood, at a very low figure. If the terrified owner consented, the fire-brigade was turned on and the mansion generally preserved. If he refused, Crassus went away with his men and let the fire do its worst. Hence in time, says Plutarch, he became master of a very appreciable part of the house property of Rome. Historians have often written of this bold speculator as if money-making was his main purpose in life, and politics no more than a diversion to him. But he was no mere money-bag, no gatherer of wealth for its own sake, without any further end. Crassus was even more ambitious than greedy, and his huge accumulations of money were made for the definite end of raising himself to a high place in the state. They err who represent him merely as an ingenious and shameless financier. Crassus had felt bitterly the ostracism from public affairs to which Sulla had condemned him, and he was determined to win his way back to a prominent part in politics. Since the oligarchy had banished him from their ranks as a corrupt and untrustworthy member, he would get back to power by taking up the cause against which he had fought so strenuously in his youth.

Crassus had in reality nothing of the Democrat in him. The only point on which he touched the sympathies of the Democratic party was that by his enormous money-making, and the place to which he had risen in the world of finance, he had made himself the king and lord of the whole tribe of *publicani*, who, as members of the Equestrian Order, had been so badly maltreated by Sulla, and who were therefore constrained to fall back on their old alliance with the *populares*. Except in the fact that his interests were bound up with this class, he had no further connection in feeling or sympathy with the Democrats.

The basis of the influence which Crassus wielded was no doubt his importance as the leader of the Equestrian Order and the *publicani*, won by the fact that he was concerned in all their financial ventures. But it was not only in commercial circles that he had extended his influence; it was his object to make himself a power, by having as many persons as possible of all classes interested in his success and bound to him by obligations of one sort and another. Two of his methods are especially dwelt on by Plutarch; the first was his willingness to act as patron to any one who applied to him, and his constant appearance in the law-courts to defend all manner of clients. He was not a first-rate speaker, tending to be dull and prolix, but he always "got up his brief," and often beat better men, because he came prepared with facts, while they relied merely on eloquent declamation or personal abuse. Often when Hortensius or Cicero had refused to take up a case, he would undertake it, for he considered few persons too unimportant to be worth serving. An obliging, even an unctuous, manner and a real capacity for taking pains in small things gained him many dependants. "He never neglected to return a salutation, and could address an almost incredible number of citizens by their proper names." In this respect he was just the opposite of his opponent Pompey, who was *gauche* and ungracious.

His other method of winning influence was the more practical one of getting into his net any man who seemed likely to be useful, by offering to lend him money. Pushing young men who took to politics he was most eager to oblige, not charging too heavy interest, nor sometimes any interest at all. He lost enormous sums of money in this way, for, of course, he was frequently repaid neither the capital nor the interest; but he got instead what he cared for even more than money, a personal influence over all kinds of people in the most various walks of life, so that he could pull the wires in all manner of political circles without his hand appearing; for, of course, his debtors would do anything to keep him quiet. It is this personal consideration which explains the indulgence which the Senate showed him; there were so many individuals in it who owed him money that their collective influence prevented him from suffering at the hands of the whole

oligarchic party. Still these supporters were purely
interested and venal, and not to be relied upon; like
Richard III., as described by More, "With large gifts
he gat him unsteadfast friendship."

The reappearance of Crassus in politics came about
owing to the disasters which the Senate suffered in the
war with Spartacus. Several considerable armies, commanded by oligarchic nonentities, had been destroyed by
the brigand and his horde, who ranged all over Southern
Italy at their will. Resolved at last to look for a competent soldier of approved capacity, the Senate were
almost forced to use Crassus, who (as we have already
seen) had gained a reputation in the civil wars second
only to that of Pompey. The other two possible men
were unavailable: Pompey was in Spain fighting Sertorius, Lucullus in the East fighting Mithradates. When
appointed general, Crassus set to work at once to
discipline the beaten and demoralised legions which were
handed over to him by his predecessor in command. He
tried all methods with them, both those of persuasion and
those of punishment. On one occasion he is said to have
used, to a legion which had disbanded in the face of the
enemy, the terrible old punishment of decimation (if we
may use the word, for he took by lot one man in every
fifty, not in every ten, and put him to death). Whether
by fear, or by the good and regular pay and provisions
which he secured for his men, Crassus got them into
a better fighting mood than they had shown of late, and
gave Spartacus the first check that he had received.
At last he blocked him up by a circumvallation near
Rhegium in the tip of the Bruttian peninsula. The rebel
burst out, losing many men in the attempt, but was chased
north by Crassus, who at last caught him and his main
body in the open field, and slew them all in a battle in
Lucania. Only scattered bands got away to the north.

The war was practically settled when Pompey suddenly appeared upon the scene. The young general, who was to be Crassus's rival and yet his ally, had just put an end to the Spanish war, favoured, as we shall see, by the lucky chance that Sertorius had been murdered by his own jealous lieutenants. Returning with his army, he caught the last bands of the defeated rebels as they tried to escape across Northern Italy and cut them up. For this Pompey took over-great credit, remarking that Crassus had beaten Spartacus indeed, but that he himself had "torn up the war by the roots."

Two generals with two victorious armies were now approaching Rome from the north and the south respectively. Both were able and ambitious, and both detested the constitution of Sulla and the senatorial oligarchy, which stood in the way of their holding continued power. But they also hated each other as much as they hated the Senate, and were inspired with the bitterest jealousy. The all-important question was whether they would fight, or whether they would prefer to join their forces against the Optimates. It was the latter alternative that they chose. Pompey was too irresolute and conscientious, in his own way, to strike hard to win a tyranny. Crassus had the smaller army, and dreaded the military abilities of his rival. Hence it came to pass that they agreed to join in a campaign against the Senate and the Sullan constitution. They stood for the consulship for B.C. 70, keeping their legions outside the gates as a threat to people and Senate. The populace, indeed, did not need the threat, and was ready to do anything which would annoy the Fathers. So Pompey and Crassus were duly elected consuls, under the eyes, as it were, of their respective armies. It was a mere compromise, which satisfied neither of them, for each thought the other's presence very unnecessary. But since they were not prepared to fight, and neither of them had a real conception of a policy, nor a definite idea of what he himself really wanted, Pompey nor Crassus could not ask or receive any more.

So these two ambitious men, masquerading as Democrats, undid the constitution of Sulla at their leisure, meeting no opposition from the demoralised Senate. Without a man of genius to lead them, or an army to oppose to the two great hosts of Pompey and Crassus, the Optimates could do absolutely nothing. Their one great fighting man, Lucullus, was still in the East, and could not be called from thence to play the part of Sulla, firstly, because he had no wish to do so, being as careless as he was able, and secondly, because he could not have trusted his army to follow him. In spite of all his victories he was most unpopular with his soldiery.

When Pompey and Crassus had been installed in office, they proceeded to introduce a series of laws which destroyed all the main features of the Sullan constitution. But, as we shall see, they put nothing in the place of that which they were destroying, and the only result of their so-called reforms was to restore the constitutional chaos and the conflict of sovereignties which had prevailed in Rome from the rise of the Gracchi down to Sulla's legislation of B.C. 81. The fact is that they were bent, not on supplying Rome with a workable state system, nor even on harking back to the old Democratic projects of Saturninus and Cinna, but merely on smashing up those sections of the Cornelian Laws which stood in the way of their own ambitions. If they added some other measures to their legislative output, it was partly to achieve a little cheap popularity, partly to make a show of having a real constructive programme of their own— a thing which was, in fact, non-existent.

As a first measure, the various securities which Sulla

had provided to protect the Senate against disturbance were now done away with. Once more, as in old times, the tribunes were to be permitted to propose laws to the public assembly without having first obtained the Senate's leave. The other disability which had been imposed on them by Sulla, that of never being allowed to stand for any other office if once they had chosen to take the tribunate, seems already to have been removed by a law passed in B.C. 75 by Gaius Cotta. But this relief was a mere nothing to the boon now granted by Pompey and Crassus. The right to deal with the people without any *senatus auctoritas* was the real strength of the tribunate in all ages.

Secondly, and in this point Crassus was particularly interested, the Equestrian Order, of which he was the patron and lord, was restored to its old position in the state.[1] The knights were given back the privilege of farming the taxes of Asia, which Sulla had taken from them. Moreover, the *Lex Aurelia* restored to them once more a predominant share in the law-courts. They did not obtain, as in the days of Caius Gracchus, a monopoly of judicial power, for in future juries were to be made up of three classes of citizens. One-third were to be senators, one-third equites, one-third *tribuni aerarii*. But the knights seem to have secured something like their old control, because the third order, the *tribuni aerarii* were, from their fortune and tendencies, much more akin to them than to the senators: indeed, they were in a sense members of the *Equester Ordo*. This elaborate subdivision of classes in the courts does not seem, if we may trust Cicero and other witnesses, to have made any

[1] The law of Roscius Otho, which completed the rehabilitation of the Knights by giving them back their insignia and their seats in the theatre and circus, belongs to this same cycle of legislation, but was apparently not passed till B.C 67.

sensible improvement in the justice which Roman juries dispensed.

It was almost inevitable that Pompey and Crassus, seeking to ingratiate themselves with the Roman multitude, should hark back to the most popular and the most pernicious item of the old Democratic programme, by developing again the corn-dole, whose abolition had been by far the best of Sulla's measures. But to buy support from any class by lavish expenditure, whether from his own or from the public purse, was a regular part of Crassus's system. A moderate and limited amount of distribution had been restored as early as B.C. 78. But the consuls of B.C. 70 presented every citizen with corn for three months without exacting any payment. Crassus is also said to have given an enormous public dinner to the populace at the feast of Hercules, at which all comers were entertained at ten thousand tables laid down the streets.

Another political move of the consuls was the restoration of the Censorship, which had been practically in abeyance since Sulla's time. The first new censors, Cornelius Clodianus and Gellius Poplicola, celebrated their advent by a wholesale eviction of Sullan partisans from the Senate, which they could do all the more plausibly because many of the sufferers were men of blemished reputation. It will be remembered that the ex-consul Lentulus, the associate of Catiline, was one of the victims of this purging; he was expelled for what the censors called "luxury," *i.e.* notorious evil living.

It is most noteworthy that Pompey and Crassus did not include in their legislation two measures which any genuine Democrat would have been certain to insert in his programme. The first was the cancelling of the effect of the Sullan Proscription; it would have been natural to secure the return of the exiles, and to restore their status as citizens to the "Sons of the Proscribed," whom the dictator had deprived of so many rights. The second obvious measure would have been the institution of an inquiry into the awful deeds of murder and robbery which had been perpetrated, without any shadow of legality, during and previous to the dictatorship. The reason why these subjects were left untouched was that Crassus himself had been deeply implicated in the worst part of the Proscription. He had put men to death illegally, had seized on lands without any good title, and had bought up wholesale the property of the proscribed. Pompey, too, had some acts to his account which would not have looked well when investigated in a court of law, such as the executions of Carbo and M. Brutus. They had, no doubt, been declared outlaws by the Senate, but the officer who had put them to death would have felt some qualms in the days of a real Democratic reaction.

It was therefore impossible for the consuls of B.C. 70 to raise either of these questions, as it would have entailed inquiry into their own conduct, and in the case of Crassus the surrender of masses of ill-gotten property. It was not till a real Democratic programme was being brought forward, somewhat later, by Julius Cæsar, that the idea of the punishment of the people's enemies was mooted, by the celebrated trial of Rabirius for the murder of Saturninus. As to the rank and file of Sulla's assassins, the only person who ever took arms against them was one of their own party, the stern and rigid Cato, who, when he was quaestor, insisted on recovering from them the bloodmoney which the dictator had issued to them without legal warrant.

Though allied to overthrow the supremacy of the Senate, Pompey and Crassus did not learn to love each other any the better during their year of joint office. Their quarrels were unending; "they differed about every measure that came before them, and these disputes and altercations prevented each of them from doing many things on which he was set." It was this notorious enmity which led to a curious scene at the end of their year. When it came to be time for them to make their final orations to the people on quitting office, there stood forward a certain knight named C. Aurelius, a person of no note, who said that Jupiter had appeared to him in a vision, and commanded him to tell the Romans that it would not be lucky for them if they allowed their consuls to remain unreconciled. Wherefore he suggested that they should embrace in public. At this unpalatable proposal, the two magistrates were much disturbed: each stood lowering at his own corner of the rostra. But when the people continued shouting for a long space of time that the consuls must be reconciled, Crassus at last constrained himself—he was far the better hypocrite of the two—went up to Pompey and offered him his hand with a well-turned compliment. They embraced, parted, and hated each other rather more than before. The humorous Aurelius must have extracted huge enjoyment from the little comedy.

The two years that followed the resignation of the consuls on December 31, B.C. 70, are most difficult to understand. We should have expected that the enmity of Pompey and Crassus would have led them into some open outbreak against each other, the moment that they had ceased to be colleagues. But nothing of the kind happened; it seemed as if each had destroyed his rival's power of initiative. They remained watching each other and did nothing more. The Senate, which had thought that its last day had been at hand, was able to breathe again and to seek feebly to reassert itself. It had been generally expected that Pompey would choose some important province, and would provide himself with another army to replace that which he had disbanded after his Spanish triumph; but this was far from his thoughts; before his consulate expired he expressly disclaimed any such idea, and for the whole of 69–68 he remained quietly in Rome living the life of a private citizen. Probably the sight of his rival in retirement soothed down the anger of Crassus, who had half expected him to aim at a tyranny. For he too kept quiet, and relapsed into his normal round of money-making and wire-pulling on the back-stairs side of politics.

So things remained, the two great men keeping each other under close observation, but making no offensive move, till Pompey was at last called away by the Gabinian Law (B.C. 67), which gave him the command against the Pirates. In consequence of this commission, and of the subsequent Manilian Law, which transferred to him the command against Mithradates, he was absent from Rome for nearly seven years. Crassus had at first intrigued against the assignation of such important charges to his rival, yet, when he was gone, was glad to see the political stage left clear for his own action. While Pompey was away, he would have a better chance of convincing the Roman people that he was their true friend, and of carrying out his plans for his own personal aggrandisement. But, as we shall see, all the political intrigues of Crassus failed: while Pompey in the distant East was adding laurels to laurels in a way that kept his name perpetually before the citizens, and made it probable that when he should return, with his army at his back, he might ask for anything that he chose, with a perfect certainty of receiving it.

We seem to trace in the doings of Crassus during Pompey's absence in the East a progressive series of measures, by which he hoped to commend himself to the Democratic party, and to establish himself as their leader so firmly

that his position should be unassailable on his rival's
return. He had now bought himself a most able managing partner in the person of Julius Cæsar, whose first prominent appearance in politics belongs to these years.
The young man possessed the two gifts of eloquence and geniality, in which both Crassus and Pompey were so hopelessly lacking. But at this period of his career he was impecunious and a trifle disreputable; no one foresaw in him the future dictator and the founder of the monarchy. At this time he was absorbing Crassus's money at a preposterous rate, and flinging it about with both hands. Men looked upon him much as they looked upon Clodius ten years later, and never suspected that the lieutenant of Crassus was more than a splendid mob-orator and a skilled manager of "corner boys."

The chief landmarks of this period of Crassus's political career are a series of bids for popularity, which failed to produce the desired effect. As censor in B.C. 65 he tried to enrol as full citizens the entire population of Cisalpine Gaul, but his colleague Catulus refused to recognise the grant, and the Optimates continued to deny it right down to the Civil War. Another and more ambitious scheme was the bill to annex Egypt in the same year, the chief object of which seems to have been to find an excuse for giving Cæsar an army which might serve as a counterpoise to that of Pompey. But the Senate succeeded in stopping the design. A little later it would seem that the Democrats were growing more desperate. Cæsar's attack on Rabirius was a warning to the Optimates that extreme measures might be tried against them, if they stood in the way of his employer's road to power. But the bill of Servilius Rullus was far more startling: it styled itself an Agrarian Law, but was much more like a measure for suspending the constitution. With the ostensible object of relieving economic distress at Rome,

THE LAW OF RULLUS

it proposed to create a body of Decemvirs, with far greater powers than the *Triumviri agris dandis assignandis* of Tiberius Gracchus had ever held. These Land Commissioners, of whom Crassus and Cæsar were to be the chiefs, were to be granted the military *imperium* and the right to levy troops. They were to be permitted to select 200 subaltern officers from among the Equites, to have power to sell the public lands in Italy, and in the provinces, to plant colonies, to take out of the treasury whatever they wished, and to sit in judgment in all lawsuits which might arise from their own proceedings. Considering that the law was mainly levelled against Pompey (for it was of him rather than of the Senate that Crassus was in fear), it was adding insult to injury to place the public lands and revenues of Syria and the other newly annexed Eastern provinces at the disposition of the Land Commissioners. The immense machinery provided by Rullus was so disproportionate to the task which it had to serve, and the power given to the Decemvirs so inordinate (their very name recalled the old tyrannical ten of B.C. 451-450 and the misdoings of Appius Claudius), that the bill failed to pass. Cicero headed against it a combination of the Optimates and the friends of Pompey, who when allied proved able to triumph over the Democrats, in spite of all the bribes of Crassus and all the eloquence of Cæsar.

But the agrarian law of Rullus was not the strangest project that was attributed to the two Democratic leaders. There were many who accused them of being implicated also in the reckless plots of L. Sergius Catilina.

It is impossible to arrive at any certain conclusion concerning the character and scope of the so-called Catilinarian conspiracies. If we were to accept in its entirety the official narrative, which was composed by Cicero, and practically embodied wholesale in Sallust and most other historians, we should regard the participation of Crassus in the designs of Catiline as most improbable. We are told that the leader of the plot was a monster of depravity, a sort of malignant demon in human form, who, after spending his early years in murdering his relatives and debauching all the youth of Rome, wished in his middle age to inaugurate a reign of *cœdes* and *incendium*, to massacre the Senate, burn the city, and rule as a tyrant among the corpses and the smoking ruins. If there were any truth in all this, we should conclude that Crassus, as the largest householder in Rome, was not likely to be privy to a plan for wholesale incendiarism, and, as the greatest creditor in the city, would hardly wish to massacre a Senate in which a vast number of the members owed him large sums of money.

But Cicero himself furnishes us with much evidence for doubting his own narrative. If Catiline was such a notorious villain, it is odd that the orator should have proposed to run with him as a joint candidate for the consulship, and have offered to defend him when he was going to be indicted for extortion in his late province of Africa.[1] Still stranger are Cicero's statements in the *Pro Cœlio*, where (defending a friend of the conspirator) he remarks that he was always meeting Catiline in the best society: "I thought him a good citizen, and esteemed him for the many eminent virtues which he seemed to possess." If it was possible for Cicero to make such allegations with any show of good faith, it is clear that Catiline cannot have been the social pariah who is described in the orator's speeches of B.C. 63. Evidently the fluent consul, thinking his own neck in danger, had painted his foe and all concerned with him in very lurid colours.

[1] See *Ad Atticum*, i. 2 and i. 1.

It is impossible, on the other hand, to believe (with Professor Beesly) that Catiline was a respectable politician and the avowed head of the Democratic party at Rome during the years B.C. 65-63. If he had been beyond reproach, Sallust and other historians of the Cæsarian faction would have taken the opportunity to represent him as a martyr to the jealousy of the Optimates and a victim of Cicero's spiteful tongue. Since they did not dare to take this line, and reproduced the orator's account of him almost verbatim, we are driven to conclude that the insurgent chief was really a man of doubtful character and reckless designs. But at the same time we are forced to believe, from Cicero's own evidence already quoted, that he had not such a notoriously bad reputation as to make it impossible to use him as an associate or a tool in political schemes. If we look upon him as no more than an unscrupulous demagogue of the same type as Saturninus or Clodius—that is, as a desperate brawler and mob-leader rather than an anarchist—it does not seem so unlikely that Crassus and Cæsar may have had relations with him during the years of his activity. If their plan was to have a bold and reckless Democratic consul—a man who would not shrink from using violence when the crisis came—in power, when Pompey should return from the East, we can well understand that they may have taken Catiline into their pay. He and they, in short, may well have been aiming at a *coup d'état*, though it is most improbable that they intended either to massacre the whole Senate or to set the city on fire. These accusations are the embroidery with which Cicero adorned his orations, when he wished to enlist all the men of material interests on the side of the Optimates. Not only did he succeed at the moment, for even the Equites were seen with swords in their hands offering to kill Cæsar, but he has left for all ages a stain on the name of Catiline which is probably one or two shades deeper than that very unscrupulous politician really deserved.

The story of the Catilinarian plots, as we now have it, is too fragmentary and too obscure to bear complete unravelling. The version of the first plot, in which Cæsar and Catiline are said to have assembled a mob of assassins in order to murder the consuls of B.C. 65, Torquatus and Cotta, and then to have failed to give the signal for the onset, is most unconvincing. Concerning the conspiracy of B.C. 63 we have more details, but they are very contradictory. On the one hand, we know that there was a widespread rumour that Catiline was acting under the orders of Crassus. Sallust, no unfriendly witness, allows that a great part of the Senate suspected the great millionaire of being implicated in the plot. On the other hand, it is certain that Crassus volunteered some information to Cicero concerning the designs of the insurgents, though that information was tardy and practically useless. He is said to have come in a melodramatic manner, late at night and muffled in a cloak, and to have placed in the hands of Cicero an anonymous letter which had been delivered to him, warning him to be out of Rome on the day of the preconcerted outbreak. If this midnight visit really occurred, it is probable that Crassus was merely "hedging,"—that he told Cicero what he considered would be enough to protect him from a charge of complicity if the plot should fail, but not enough to do Catiline and his colleagues any harm if they were going to succeed.

One thing is clear—that Cicero did not consider it prudent to assail Crassus, and remained deaf to all the suggestions made to him with that object. Another public man, when incited to fall upon the millionaire, once answered with the proverb, "Fœnum habet in cornu" meaning that Crassus was too dangerous a sort of game for a hunter of his calibre to meddle with.¹ And so the consul of B.C. 63, with his usual prudence, refrained from accusing of high treason a man who could pull so many political strings, and had at his disposal such a command of money and influence. When the informer Tarquinius, in his examination before the Senate, began to give evidence incriminating Crassus, a curious scene occurred. Dozens of senators who owed Crassus money began to shout "False witness" with all the power of their lungs. Then Cicero, after glancing round the house and pondering on the situation, took the easiest way out of the position by remanding Tarquinius to prison, without permitting him to go on with his story. The charge was not allowed to be repeated, yet Sallust tells us that Crassus was so far from being grateful to Cicero that he ever afterwards regarded him as an enemy. Apparently he thought that the orator had been feeling the pulse of the Senate by producing such evidence, and had only drawn back from an open attack because he saw that he would not get the full support of his party if he persisted.

However much or however little Crassus had been implicated in the Catilinarian plot, this much is certain, that many people thought that he had known more about the business than he should, and that an additional stain was added in consequence to his already not unsmirched reputation. We are told that in the end of B.C. 63 he seriously thought of leaving Rome to preserve his personal safety, and provided ships to carry himself, his family, and his treasures out of Italy.

The reason why he did not actually depart was the unforeseen delay in the return of Pompey from the East. The conqueror of Mithradates had finished his military

¹ The Romans used to tie a wisp of straw to the horns of a dangerous bull to warn the passer-by against him.

work in B.C. 63 by the conquest of Syria. He was expected back early in 62, just when Cicero's consulship had expired, and while the embers of the Catilinarian conspiracy were still smouldering, after the main conflagration had been quenched. If he had presented himself at this moment, he would have found the Democratic leaders in the deepest discredit and dismay, and foiled in all their plans to raise up a power in Italy that should be able to oppose him. But Pompey chose to linger in the East for the whole summer of B.C. 62, pacifying and portioning out provinces, conciliating allied princes, and founding new cities. He showed no signs of coming home, and merely sent ahead his foolish and talkative partisan Metellus Nepos, the man whose pranks gave Cicero so much trouble. It will be remembered that his demands were so unreasonable, and at the same time so vague, that Cicero and the Optimates ventured to oppose them, and Crassus had time to recover from his panic and to reconsider his situation. There can be no doubt that the follies of Metellus, who certainly exceeded the commission that had been given him, did his employer much harm and lessened his popularity.

Yet when, in the autumn of B.C. 62, Pompey at last announced that he was returning to Italy with his army at his back, both Democrats and Optimates were seriously alarmed. Externally his position was so much like that of Sulla in 82 that both parties had a suspicion that he would be tempted to repeat Sulla's rôle. Neither Crassus and Cæsar on the one side, nor Catulus and Cato on the other, felt their heads quite safe upon their shoulders. For each party knew that they had been intriguing against the great general in his absence, and supposed that he might resent their action in a very drastic fashion.

Nothing of the kind happened. With rare civic virtue

Pompey dismissed his army, and returned as a private person to Rome, expecting to receive from his fellow-citizens the praise and gratitude that he had so well earned. Instead, he found the Optimates captious and critical, and the Democrats far more concerned in the Catilinarian conspiracy and its results than in the newly accomplished conquest of the East. His simple and moderate requests—the confirmation of his administrative work in Asia and the provision of the rewards due to his victorious soldiery—were refused him. When he put forward his friend the Tribune Flavius to pass a *plebiscitum* for the grant of lands to the army of the East, it was defeated by the unexpected and immoral combination of the Optimates and the *Populares*.

The great object of Crassus at this time was to prevent at all costs the conclusion of an alliance between Pompey and the Senate, lest the combination of the two should reduce himself and his party to entire impotence. How he did it we learn from Cicero's letters. When Pompey first returned to the city, it would have been quite natural that the orator and he should have agreed to work together; they had been old friends and allies in earlier days, their political views were not dissimilar, and if Cicero was now the most moderate of Optimates, Pompey was certainly the least democratic of Democrats. If the orator could have persuaded his friends to treat the great general with courtesy and ordinary consideration, and to grant his very reasonable demands, it is probable that matters would have settled down without any further trouble. But Cicero was still swelling over with pride at his successes in B.C. 63, and now thought himself quite as great a man as Pompey. His idea was to meet the proconsul with the phrase, "If you have saved the republic abroad, I have saved it at home." In his vanity he imagined that the crushing of Catiline's handful of desperadoes was quite as great an achievement as the conquest of the East. He was ready to assume an almost patronising attitude to his old chief.

The wily Crassus resolved to estrange the two by tempting Cicero into a display of foolish pride which should disgust Pompey. He carried out his shameless plan at the first appearance of the great general to take his seat in the Senate. The occasion ought to have been utilised to welcome and compliment Pompey according to his deserts. But when the proceedings had been commenced, Crassus rose and began a fulsome and interminable harangue in praise of Cicero's consulship. Not only was the subject-matter stale, for Catiline had been put down a whole year before, but Crassus was the last man who should have launched out on such topics. He was known to resent bitterly all that the orator had done, and to be his secret enemy. However he began to declaim to the effect that "the preservation of his own life and liberty, his name and his fatherland, his wife and children, had all been the work of Cicero; that Rome had been saved from fire and sword was due to this great man alone," and so forth. Cicero fell into the trap with the greatest simplicity. Instead of suspecting all compliments from this most doubtful source, he arose to continue the debate in his own self-laudation. The opportunity for conciliating Pompey, by turning the discussion on to his great deeds in the East, and paying him his due meed of praise, quite escaped him. Instead, he proceeded to sound his own trumpet in the most autolatrous fashion. Writing to Atticus in complete unconsciousness of his own folly, he says that "now was the time for my well-turned periods, my flowers of rhetoric, my antitheses and figures. You know my wonted thunders: this day they were so loud that I think that you must have heard them even where you are, in Epirus."[1] So having spoken at length of his own great doings, of the majesty of the Senate, the wickedness of the late conspiracy, and all his usual topics, he sat down, leaving Pompey unblessed. The general was not pleased: "*intellexi hominem moveri*," says Cicero, who had the best chance of knowing, for he was sitting next to him. He took the speech as a formal declaration that Cicero and his friends did not think much of his exertions in the East, and he was not far wrong.

Thus it came to pass that the shameless harangue of Crassus and the idiotic vanity of Cicero, which made him gorge the bait so greedily, began to destroy the chance that Pompey might enter into an alliance with the Optimate party, and become a defender of the constitution. His anger came to a head when at the instigation of his old enemy and rival, Lucullus, the Senate passed a decree that an elaborate inquiry should be made into all his doings in Asia before they were ratified. If anything was wanting to complete his discontent, it was the way in which his army was treated; the excuse made for denying its reward was that the treasury was empty—a manifest lie, for the enormous sums which had been paid in from his Asiatic spoils were still unexpended.

So the man who might, if he had been unscrupulous, have become tyrant of Rome, found himself flouted and set at nought, merely because he had behaved like a good citizen, and refrained from taking by violence that which was his due. He might have asked for anything that he liked while his army was still undisbanded. When he had dispersed it, Cicero's stupid friends refused to listen to his pleas and left him shamed before the eyes of his veterans.

While he stood involved in this bitter disappointment,

[1] *Ad Atticum*, i. 13.

Pompey received the offer which changed the whole face of affairs. Crassus and Cæsar and the whole Democratic party were still under a cloud, with a strong suspicion of complicity in the Catilinarian plot hanging about them. It would mean everything to them if Pompey, his respectability, and his veterans were placed on their side. Accordingly they offered him their assistance to secure the ratification of his Asiatic treaties and the grant of land for his legionaries, if he would join them against the Senate. It must have been a bitter moment for him when he was told that his desires might be gained, at the price of a second alliance with his old enemy Crassus, the man who had intrigued against him with such malevolent persistence all through the last ten years. But rather than break his word to his soldiers (whose interests he had promised to protect), and rather than endure more bullying from the Senate, he accepted the offer. The famous "First Triumvirate" was formed, Pompey contributing his great name, his respectability, and the potential aid of forty thousand veterans; Crassus, his inexhaustible money-bags and his power of intrigue; Cæsar, his unrivalled talent for mob-management and his cool and level brain. At the moment most men thought him little more than the agent and tool of the two elder triumvirs; the revelation of his greatness was yet to come.

When the triumvirate had been formed, and (in spite of the opposition of Cato and a few more irreconcilables) had shown that it could sweep the streets and clear the Forum, it remained to be seen how the victorious three would use their power. The first thing that strikes the observer is that while Pompey got something out of his bargain, and Cæsar a great deal, we can hardly trace any positive and tangible gain received by Crassus from his alliance with his old enemy. Pompey got his Asiatic

THE FIRST TRIUMVIRATE

doings confirmed; he was also enabled to give his veterans the land that he had promised them. Cæsar obtained his consulship, passed all the laws that he chose to bring forward, and had the pleasure (which to a man with his sense of humour must have been considerable) of seeing his colleague Bibulus shut up in his mansion and "inspecting the heavens" day by day without any effect. Moreover, at the end of his year of office Cæsar received the all-important provinces of Cisalpine and Transalpine Gaul, the district from which legions could best overawe Rome and all Italy.

But Crassus got neither consulship nor province, neither land nor ratified treaties. It is true that his position in politics was re-established; the slur that had been left upon him after the Catilinarian business was removed, and he could feel that he had pulled the strings of the whole intrigue. But of more definite profit we see nothing. The only satisfactory explanation of this curious fact is to remember that Crassus, all through his career, seems to have desired power as an end in itself rather than as a means to other objects. He was, to use a modern phrase, a man without a programme. He wanted to pull the wires of politics, rather than to carry out some definite policy when he had collected all the wires in his hand. If we must seek a modern parallel for him, we may think of that wonderful old Whig, the Duke of Newcastle, who allied himself with the elder Pitt on the terms that the latter should manage the whole imperial policy of Britain, while he himself should be permitted to conduct the parliamentary jobbery and intrigue. In short, when the opportunity came to him, Crassus had no particular set of measures that he wished to advocate. He was neither a true Democrat nor a true Oligarch. He had become the leader of the *populares* not because he had popular sympathies, but because he wanted at all costs to be the leader of some party. So the weakness of his position was, that having achieved his wish to obtain a share of supreme power, he had little that was definite to ask for. He merely wanted to be able to assert himself when he chose, to have his share in portioning out consulships and praetorships, to make money when and how he chose, and to use it by keeping dozens of minor political personages in dependence on him.

Hence it is that in the doings of the triumvirs during their day of power, it is hard to point out very much that can be ascribed to the personal initiative of Crassus. His main aim was to keep in check his ally Pompey, whom he hated no less than of old. That thereby he was helping a much more able man—Cæsar—on the road to supreme power he certainly did not realise. We may make a shrewd guess also that it was Crassus who really set upon Cicero and drove him into exile, Clodius being merely his tool, and not the originator of the orator's woes. We know from Sallust and Plutarch how bitter was the enmity that Crassus bore to the consul of B.C. 63, despite the flattery which he lavished on him when he was set on estranging him from Pompey. It is probable that the banishment of Cicero was his underhand revenge for seeing his old schemes frustrated; for both in the rejection of the law of Rullus and in the suppression of Catiline the orator had been the main cause of his defeat. On the other hand, it is hard to see that Clodius had really any adequate cause for the malignant persecution to which he subjected Cicero. The usual tale, that he had been angered by the way in which his ingenious *alibi* had been disproved, while he was being tried for the violation of the mysteries of the Bona Dea, does not seem to give a sufficient reason for his vindictive attacks on Cicero. If we imagine that he was spurred on by Crassus, the causes of whose enmity are so much more obvious, the matter becomes far more intelligible. If the triumvir simply delivered the blow at second-hand, it is quite in keeping with what we read concerning his feelings at this time. Plutarch tells us that he had conceived such a mortal hatred for the orator that he would have shown it by some act of personal violence, had he not been dissuaded by his son Publius, who chanced to be an old pupil and an admirer of Cicero.

Crassus was certainly closely connected with Clodius, whose acquittal at his trial for the violation of the Mysteries he had secured by his lavish bribery. He was the only one of the triumvirs who did not try to save Cicero from the worst extreme of exile, by pressing on him an honourable excuse for absence from Rome, in the shape of a legateship or a "free commission" to travel. That the orator himself suspected him of being at the bottom of his troubles may be judged from the fact that when writing from Thessalonica during his banishment, and estimating his chances of return, he speaks of Pompey as certain to be favourable—"Crassum tamen metuo." He had a fear that Crassus might not prove so accommodating. However, having learnt the lesson that it was not wise to cross the triumvirs, Cicero was ultimately allowed to return, and soon after was formally reconciled to the millionaire by means of the young Publius, his faithful friend.

We have, on the whole, extraordinarily little recorded of the doings of Crassus between B.C. 59 and B.C. 56, a time when he ought to have been able to ask and obtain whatever he chose from his colleagues. He had his share, no doubt, in the management of affairs by the triumvirs in that rather chaotic time, when, to the outward eye, Clodius rather than any one else seemed to be the real ruler of Rome. But apparently he was, as usual, more set on checking Pompey than on anything else. It is only in B.C. 56 that he again comes to the front.

By that time he had at last learnt, from the study of Cæsar's doings in Gaul, that any man who aspired to take his share in dominating Roman politics must have an army at his back. Hence it was that at the conference of Lucca he claimed not only the consulship for B.C. 55, but the command of the army of the East. He too must raise his legions, win his victories, and be in a position to meet Cæsar and Pompey on equal terms, if troubles should ever again break out. Those superficial writers who think that he chose the rich Eastern provinces out of mere greed and avarice are clearly wrong. All through his life money-making was to him the means and not the end. What he really wanted to secure was a loyal army, not a few more millions to add to his hoards. That military glory had turned his brain, and that he desired to emulate Alexander the Great, and "to penetrate to the Bactrians, the Indians, and the Erythraean Sea, so that in his hopes he swallowed up the whole East," we cannot readily believe. Clearly he wished to win a strong military position, such as could be secured by great conquests beyond the Euphrates, but it was needed mainly to help him to sway the balance between Cæsar and Pompey in the domestic affairs of Rome.

Nevertheless, when he had once been granted his desire and placed in command of an army, his spirits seem to have risen; his mind harked back to his old campaigns of 82 and 71 B.C., and he appears to have cast from him the memories of twenty years of finance and intrigue, and to have tried to become once more the enterprising soldier that he had been in Sulla's day. He showed a buoyancy of spirit that surprised every one, "indulging in vain boasts most inconsistent with his wonted demeanour, and most unsuitable to his age and his disposition — for in general he was far from being either self-assertive or conceited. But now he said that he would make the expedition of Lucullus against Tigranes and that of Pompey against Mithradates appear mere child's play. Yet he now counted sixty years, and looked even older than he really was."

The renewal of the triumvirate had so cowed the Optimate party that even Cato had to give up his attempt to struggle against the omnipotent three. It is, therefore, all the more curious to find that one man set himself to oppose Crassus's designs, and that from mere personal enmity. This abnormal personage was the tribune C. Ateius Capito, one of those strange characters who move for an instant across the political stage, and are then lost in obscurity. He ventured to place a veto on the levying of legions for Crassus: it was quietly disregarded. Then he announced awful hindrances of portents and prodigies, which were also met with derision rather than attention; indeed, he was fined by the censor Appius for fabricating false omens. But he reserved his great *coup* for the day on which Crassus passed out of the gates to take command of his army. After one final and futile attempt to interpose his tribunicial veto, he took refuge in strange incantations. " He placed a censer at the gate," we are told, "and threw incense upon it, uttering the most horrid imprecations and invoking strange and dreadful deities. The Romans say that these mysterious and ancient curses have such power that the man against whom they are directed never escapes ill-luck; nay, more, they add that the person who uses them is sure to bring misfortune on himself also."

Undaunted by these antiquated rites, and regardless of two or three other evil presages which Plutarch has carefully collected, Crassus set forth from Italy and arrived safely in Syria, where he found himself at the head of an army of seven legions. His first act on taking charge of his province was to plunder ruthlessly the temples of Hierapolis, Emesa, and Jerusalem, and to scrape together all the money that could be raised by taxation. But he was no doubt set on filling his military chest for a war that was certain to prove long and costly, rather than on gratifying the talent for extortion that was such a marked characteristic of all his life. His first strategical move was to bridge the Euphrates, and to establish a new base for himself in the Greek cities of Mesopotamia. This was easily accomplished, but his second advance was a much more serious matter. He had now to prove whether his old martial reputation won in the wars against Carbo and Pontius and Spartacus had been fairly earned.

Quite unconsciously, Crassus was going forth to solve a new and difficult military problem. Unlike Cæsar in Gaul, he had not to deal with an old enemy whose strength and tactics were well known. The Romans had met and defeated many an Asiatic army during the last century, but the Parthians were not like the other inhabitants of the Hellenized East, whom Scipio or Sulla or Pompey had so easily subdued. Their hosts did not consist of clumsy imitations of the Macedonian phalanx, but of masses of horse-bowmen. Some were the lightest of light cavalry; others bore helm and lance and breastplate, as well as the national bow. Of infantry the Parthians had none, save levies raised among their subject-races for operations in mountainous regions. When the fight was to be in the plains, they did not take a single foot-soldier with them. Of all the regions of the border, Mesopotamia, into which Crassus was now advancing, was most suitable for the tactics of the enemy: the battles would be fought among rolling sandy downs, destitute of trees, and crossed by rivers at very unfrequent intervals.

CRASSUS INVADES MESOPOTAMIA

Confident in his seven legions and his 4000 horse, the triumvir marched out from Carrhae and entered the desolate lands that lay between his base and the Parthian capital. He had resolved to take the shortest route to Seleucia, in spite of the advice of his Armenian allies, who had endeavoured to induce him to draw near to the Tigris and the Assyrian mountains, instead of plunging into the Mesopotamian sands, where the Parthians could use their horsemen to the best advantage. Tradition tells that he had been influenced in his resolve by the treacherous advice of an Arab sheikh named Ariamnes (or Abgarus), who had told him that speed was the essential thing in his advance. For, as he alleged, the Parthian king was not intending to fight so near the Roman frontier, and was sending his treasures eastward and preparing to evacuate Seleucia without any serious attempt to make a stand.

If Crassus was gulled by these stories, he was soon undeceived, for on the second day of his march his vedettes were driven in by the Parthian horse, and reported that the vizier Surena was close at hand with a mighty host. Eager to engage, the triumvir pressed on to meet the enemy, in full expectation of a victory that should eclipse all that Pompey had ever accomplished in the East. At first he drew up his men on a very long front, the legions deployed in line, with the cavalry in equal halves at each end of the array. But presently it struck him that this formation did not sufficiently cover his enormous baggage train, which was trailing along for many miles to the rear. Accordingly he changed his order to a great hollow square, and placed all his impedimenta in its centre. This would have been an excellent battle formation had he been about to contend with an enemy who employed "shock tactics," and intended to charge in upon the legions, but against horse-archers it was a mistake; it gave them a target which it would be impossible to miss, and at the same time made it hard for the Romans to charge without breaking their order of battle. The square is an essentially defensive formation, and useless against a light and evasive foe who has no wish to close.

When the Parthians appeared, at first in comparatively small numbers, but afterwards in huge hordes that seemed to cover the whole horizon, Crassus (in the usual Roman style) sent out his light troops to skirmish. But his slingers and archers were but a few thousand strong; after a short combat they were flung back upon the legions with heavy loss, absolutely overwhelmed by the concentric arrow-shower which was poured in upon them. The pursuing enemy then began to ride close up to the great square, and to take easy shots into the mass. They kept at a discreet distance, some 200 yards or so, and the legionaries were helpless against them, for the *pilum* had but a short range, and could not reach the horsemen. Nor was it any use to advance, for the enemy slowly retired, keeping always at the same distance from the legions, and continuing to pour in his long deadly shafts, which "nailed the shield to the arm that bore it, and the helmet to the head."

Crassus now began to see the difficulties of the situation. Since it was impossible to contend with missile weapons against the Parthians, it was necessary to close at all costs. Accordingly he gave his son Publius charge of 1300 cavalry—all Gallic veterans fresh from Cæsar's wars, 1500 archers, and eight picked cohorts of infantry, and bade him sally out from the square and charge desperately into the enclosing ring of bowmen. Before this sudden onset the Parthians gave way, retiring at full speed, and leaving a moment's respite to the harrassed legions. Young Crassus pursued them fiercely, his infantry pushing forward so rapidly that it almost kept pace with the horsemen. Apparently the young commander allowed himself to be carried away by the ardour of the charge, and entertained a vain hope of catching up the enemy, for he chased them for five or six miles, till he had got quite out of touch with his father's legions. Then he suddenly found himself face to face with the solid supports of the elusive horse-bowmen—heavy squadrons of mailed lancers, who met him in orderly array and offered battle. At the same moment the fugitives whom he had been chasing halted, and began to ply their bows from the flanks. Although his troops were much disordered by their long and reckless ride, Publius charged straight at the centre of the enemy. A furious *mêlée* followed, but the Romans were hopelessly outnumbered, and after a most gallant defence the whole detachment, horse and foot, was exterminated.

The triumvir, advancing slowly in his son's track, was horrified to meet the Parthians returning with shouts of triumph, and displaying the heads of Publius and the other fallen officers fixed on their pikes. But, with a resolution which shows that the old Roman spirit was not dead in him, he addressed his men, crying " that the loss of his son was his own private concern, and that the main army was intact, and might yet retrieve the day and avenge their fallen comrades. No campaign could be carried to a successful end without some casualties. It was not by her good fortune, but by her perseverance and fortitude in adversity that Rome had risen to be the mistress of the world." These words were not enough to stir the weary soldiery, who had thoroughly lost heart, and were already cursing the general who had led them into this snare in the desert. It was his ignorance and presumption, they complained, which were the causes of their present desperate condition. They held out sullenly till dusk came, but when the fall of night compelled the Parthians to withdraw, the whole army, officers and soldiers alike, demanded to be led back to the Euphrates. A deputation went to seek for the proconsul, who was found stretched on the ground, with his head wrapped in his cloak, mourning for his son. Since he seemed sunk in a dull apathy, and refused to issue any orders, the quaestor of Crassus took it upon himself to bid the army decamp under cover of the night, and make a forced march for Carrhae. The baggage and 4000 wounded were left to the mercy of the enemy.

A night retreat is always fatal to troops who have lost their nerve, and the Romans, dropping with fatigue and wearied by twelve hours spent under arms, had no longer the power to move rapidly or to keep their distances. When day broke, they were found straggling across the plains in half-a-dozen disjointed columns, each of which had to shift for itself. The Parthians came up a few hours later and beset the retreating army. Some of the more belated corps and multitudes of the stragglers were cut up, but the main body reached Carrhae in the afternoon.

Next night Crassus again commenced to retreat, for his troops were so demoralised that he felt sure that it was hopeless to make any stand east of the Euphrates. The second day of flight was as disastrous as the first, the troops lost all touch with each other, and the greater part of the horse, leaving the infantry in the lurch, never drew rein till they had saved themselves in the mountains. Crassus himself, with only four cohorts in his company, was worried all day by a swarm of horse-bowmen, who succeeded in intercepting his way to the hills, and finally compelled him to halt and stand at bay on an isolated eminence just outside the limit of safety. Then followed a miserable scene of treachery. The

THE DEATH OF CRASSUS

Parthian vizier came up, and seeing that it would be hard to storm the hill, proposed a conference, holding out prospects of granting a peace, on condition that Crassus should order the evacuation of the Mesopotamian cities and retire beyond the Euphrates. The soldiery hailed with joy a proposal that promised a relief from their present desperate condition, but the triumvir himself was not deluded, and warned all those about him that the only safe course was to hold out till night, and then make a dash for the hills through the lines of the enemy. His exhortations produced little effect, and seeing that his men were utterly demoralised and unwilling to fight any longer, he consented to go down and treat. It is said that he took his officers to witness that he went to his death with his eyes open, but that for the credit of Rome "it would be better to say that the general was deceived by the enemy rather than that he had been abandoned by his own men."

The sequel was exactly like the scene at Caubul in 1841, when the unfortunate Macnaughten went down to treat with Akbar Khan. Crassus and his escort were received at first with ostentatious respect, and a conference was begun. Presently a feigned scuffle was got up, and hands were laid upon the proconsul, whereupon one of his legates drew his sword. This acted as the necessary signal for open violence, and Surena's attendants fell upon the Romans and despatched them every one. Crassus's head was cut off and sent to Seleucia to be laid before the great king. Every one has read of the scene that followed the arrival of the ghastly trophy, a scene that illustrates accurately enough the curious admixture of savagery and civilisation at the court of the Arsacidae. King Orodes was witnessing the *Bacchae* of Euripides, wherein King Pentheus is torn to pieces by the frantic Theban women. The actor who was playing

Agave seized the head of Crassus, and used it instead of the mask that represented the head of Pentheus in the wild dance at the end of the play. Orodes was charmed with the idea and presented the tragedian with a talent of silver.

We must not blame Crassus too much for the disaster of Carrhae. Probably any other Roman general of the day, with the possible exception of Cæsar, would have suffered a defeat under the same circumstances. For the Parthian method of war was utterly unknown to the Romans, and the legion, a splendid weapon against any other foe, was useless here. In later campaigns, profiting by Crassus's experience, the generals of the West never attempted to attack the Parthian in the open with an army of the old Roman type. They took into the field large bodies of cavalry and tens of thousands of foot-archers. These last proved especially successful against the troops of the Arsacidae, for the Parthian bow, having to be used on horseback, was necessarily short, and was out-ranged by that of the foot-soldier. Hence the Orientals had the choice between being overmatched in archery and being forced to charge home. In both cases they usually fared ill when engaging with the Romans. There never was a second Carrhae, but it is hard to see how the first could have been avoided.

It was a strange and inappropriate end to the life of Crassus that he should go down to history with his name attached to an error in military tactics, rather than to some political or financial fiasco. But a certain inevitable futility attached to all that he undertook. He wanted power, and thrice in his life the power was placed within his hand. But when he had it, he could not use it, for he was equally destitute of an ideal and of a programme. Even if Pompey had not always been at his side to check his ambition, we see that he would never have achieved anything great. The story of his career shows just how much and how little mere wealth, ambition, and industry, without genius, an inspiring personality, or an honest enthusiasm could accomplish in Roman politics.

CHAPTER VII

CATO

AMONG all the statesmen with whom we have to deal in this last century of the Roman Republic, there were only two who were unselfish in their aims, looked for no personal profit, and devoted their lives to fighting for their party and their theory of the constitution. These were the two men who, among all the figures of this troubled time, bore the least similarity to each other— Lucius Cornelius Sulla and Marcus Porcius Cato. Save that each was a devoted and disinterested partisan of the Optimate faction, there is absolutely no resemblance between them. What Sulla was we have already seen —an Epicurean to the core, gay, fastidious, taking life easily save in the moments of actual crisis in war or politics,—but when the heat of the fray was upon him capable of systematic cruelty on the widest scale. In all save his reactionary politics and his contempt for monarchy and its trappings, he was a typical Hellenized Roman of the decadence. Cato, on the other hand, was consistent in his reaction; he looked back to old Roman ideals, not merely in politics, but in social manners, dress, bearing, and morals. He is the most complete instance in history of what we may call deliberate archaism,—the careful observance of the customs and views of an extinct generation by a man who was clever enough to see the strangeness of what he was doing, and yet persevered in it. For Cato was no mere Don Quixote, as Mommsen calls him; he did not spend his life in fighting monsters that were unreal, tilting at windmills or at flocks of sheep, or taking innkeepers and milkmaids for castellans and princesses. On the contrary, he knew precisely whom he was fighting with, and what he was fighting for, and used every means that an honourable man might, the most practical and positive no less than those mere constitutional figments in which the Roman mind delighted to deal. Unlike a Don Quixote, he was a thoroughly successful minister of finance, and an excellent and practical soldier. It was only because he fought for an impossible ideal, and because he was foiled by meaner and pettier souls, that he can possibly be called by the mocking name which Mommsen has imposed on him.

M. Cato was the great-grandson of old Cato the censor, a fact which was destined to colour his whole life, for it was his dearest wish to copy in everything, down to tricks of language and dress, a man who had already been noted as somewhat quaint and old-fashioned eighty years before. Hence came his reputation for eccentricity. It was in imitating his ancestor that Cato learnt to despise all fine raiment to such an extent that he habitually dressed in sombre colours. He would sit in the tribunal without his shoes, refused to ride when going about on public missions with his friends, and would not wear a hat even when he was marching across Africa in midsummer. It was probably the example of the elder Cato, too, that induced the younger to show the one concession to the spirit of the times of which he was ever guilty—to study Greek philosophy, and keep at home as a sort of private chaplain a tame philosopher named Athenodorus, whom he had picked up at Ephesus.

It is fortunate that Plutarch has preserved for us a long and detailed life of Cato. It is from anecdotes there related that we are able to make out how a man who was somewhat eccentric in his habits, and somewhat idealistic in his political views, was able to exercise so considerable a sway over the politics of his own day—the sway always exerted by the man who knows his own mind, is perfectly consistent, and is ready at any personal risk, however great, to act in accordance with his conscience. In a time when every one else was peculiarly slack and acquiescent, and given to the grossest opportunism, the man who refused to yield to the stress of affairs or the spirit of the times, and rigidly did his duty, got an influence far beyond that to which his merely intellectual powers entitled him.

Cato was born in B.C. 95. The earliest notices that we have of him show him displaying the same inflexible courage and the same adherence to old views, wrong as well as right, which distinguished him down to his death. His father died when he was very young, and he was brought up by his maternal uncle, the celebrated popular leader Drusus. The house of Drusus was haunted, during his agitation, by the prominent Italians for whom he was working, the men who afterwards led the revolt when he had been murdered. Q. Pompaedius Silo was staying with Drusus when he fell in with the boy Cato, aged five, and his younger half-brother, Servilius Caepio. "Come, my good children, you will help your uncle Drusus, will you not, to assist us poor Italians in getting our freedom," said the Marsian. Servilius lisped a polite assent; but Cato had already picked up political views, and did not love Italians. He said not a word, and appeared from his silence and his surly looks inclined to deny the request. Pompaedius, half irritated, half in jest, took him to the window and held him out of it by the scruff of his neck, threatening, if he would not promise, to let him drop. This he did in a harsh tone, and at the same time gave him several shakes, as if he were about to let go. But as the child bore this for some time without any marks of concern or fear, Pompaedius set him down, observing, "I verily believe that if this boy were a man, we should not get even one vote among the Roman people."

Nine years later, when Cato was fourteen, he was taken by his Optimate relatives to visit Sulla at the time of the proscriptions. While he was waiting with his pedagogue, Sarpedon, in the hall, he saw several *delators* bring the heads of democratic leaders to the dictator's house, and receive money for them. At this he was very wroth, and asked his tutor "why somebody does not kill this man." "Because," said Sarpedon, "men fear him more than they hate him!" "Then give me a sword," said Cato, "and I will go in and make away with him, for evidently he is enslaving his country!" So obviously in earnest was he, that he had to be hurried out of the house to prevent his doing something violent, and to be narrowly watched for some time.

Cato first appeared in public life some four or five years after this incident, attending the courts like other young Romans of his age; there he acquired a very good knowledge of law, and taught himself a kind of oratory which, as we are told, differed much from the florid style of Hortensius and the careful elaborateness of Cicero, for "there was neither heat nor artificiality in it—all was rough, strong, and sensible." Yet he had a turn for natural humour and a clear exposition which served him as well as the studied eloquence of others.

Besides attending in the law-courts, the young Roman had to serve his *stipendia* in the field. Cato saw his first service in the *cohors praetoria* of the proconsul Gellius, in the unhappy Servile War with Spartacus. He was noted as one of the few officers in the contemptible army of B.C. 72 who did his work punctually and intelligently. He was offered crowns and promotions by

Gellius, but refused them, saying that he had only done his duty and nothing that deserved honour.

When the Servile War ended, he went to Macedonia and served under the proconsul Rubrius in B.C. 68, with the office of military tribune, which gave him a turn in the command of a legion. His troops soon obtained a good name in the province, because, instead of caring for his own comfort like other officers, he insisted on living with the men and taking no better rations than they. On the march, though his freedmen rode on horses, he insisted on going on foot with his soldiers, and on carefully putting himself in the way of every fatigue that came to them. Yet he would not allow undue familiarity, was unhesitating in the application of punishments, and sternly repressed plundering; so that, as Plutarch says, "it was doubted whether his legion was more peaceable or more warlike—more valiant or more well-behaved." Having now passed twenty-four, the age at which it was possible to stand for the quaestorship, he came back to Rome, but refused to solicit the magistracy till he had spent many months in getting up all the duties and functions of a quaestor, so that he stood a year late for the office.

His year was notable in the history of the quaestorship for the thorough reformation which he made. He found the treasury almost entirely in the hands of the permanent under-secretaries, who had the routine of the business in their hands, and did practically what they liked with the young and inexperienced quaestors, who generally entered the office entirely ignorant of their functions, and were only just beginning to learn them when they found their twelve months at an end. But Cato started with his duties and powers at his finger-ends, and soon detected the permanent clerks committing all sorts of irregularities and illegalities, to their own private profit.

CATO REFORMS THE TREASURY

He turned out one chief clerk for embezzlement and another for forgery, though it set a hornets' nest of friends and patrons of the offenders about his ears. Having humbled the secretaries, he took the whole management of the *Aerarium* into his own hands, his lazy and indifferent colleagues gladly allowing him to bear all the burden. In a short time, it is said, he made the treasury much more respectable than the Senate, and his quaestorship more memorable than most consulates. For he recovered an immense amount of outstanding debts owed by men of mark, whom his predecessor had not dared to press, and at the same time paid off a number of bills owed by the state to poor men, which the unhappy creditors had long despaired of recovering. One extraordinary instance of his courage has been preserved. Finding a list of Sulla's *delators* and of the sums they had been paid for the murders they had committed, he compelled all the survivors to pay back the blood-money, because (as he said) it had been an illegal disbursement, never justified by any decree of the people.

When his year of office was running out, Cato had a complete chart and analysis of the public revenues for the last ten years made out, at the personal expense to himself of five talents. He kept it, and it proved invaluable to future quaestors, who always came to consult him when in difficulties, and to get his lights on the meaning of difficult points in the annual balance-sheet of the Republic. At thirty-one, then, Cato had a fair military record, and was acknowledged to be the best financial expert in the Senate, a reputation which he preserved till his death.

He would seem to have intended to spend some time in getting up the duties of the higher offices of state, but was suddenly called into activity by the Catilinarian conspiracy. He is generally remembered for the support that he gave to Cicero through all the troubles of B.C. 63

Yet curiously enough he was on one occasion brought into violent collision with the consul. He prosecuted Muraena, the Optimate consul-elect for B.C. 62, for bribery at the elections, and when he came into the court found Cicero opposing him as the defendant's advocate. The offence had been a gross one, and the consul had nothing better to do in the way of defence than to follow the good old forensic maxim, "If you have no case, abuse the plaintiff's attorney." Accordingly he grew offensively personal, jeering at Stoics, and hinting that Cato's love of purity and legality might be in place in some ideal republic, but not in Rome, till he set the jury in a roar. Cato was defeated, but contented himself with remarking that "Rome had a very facetious consul." He took no offence at the ridicule that had been poured on him, and remained a consistent supporter of Cicero.

The first occasion on which we find Cato exercising a really great influence on politics was at the celebrated debate on the execution of Lentulus and Cethegus and the other Catilinarian conspirators. Speaking as a very junior senator towards the end of the meeting, he completely undid Cæsar's feat of inclining the Senate to change the vote from death to banishment, though Cæsar had been so effective that he had actually induced Silanus (the proposer of the death penalty) to change round and accept the milder alternative. The speech which Cato actually uttered is certainly not that given by Sallust, who, after the manner of other ancient historians, has constructed an oration out of his inner consciousness. For the words which he puts in Cato's mouth do not at all agree with the notes in Plutarch, and the latter implies that he had seen the actual oration, which was taken down at the time by Cicero's shorthand writers. The chief point in Plutarch's version is that Cato attacked Cæsar by name, charged him with being concerned in Catiline's designs for subverting

THE CATILINARIAN CONSPIRACY 211

the Republic, and said that he might think himself fortunate for not being on trial along with Cethegus and his crew. The unscrupulous Sallust evades these points, being evidently set on keeping out of sight anything that might redound to the discredit of his patron Cæsar.

Cato's activity was strenuously displayed all through the year of the conspiracy, but in that which followed he was even more prominently before the eyes of the public. In the autumn, when he thought that he might snatch a moment's leisure, he had set out for his estates in Lucania. But on the way he met Metellus Nepos, who was coming to Rome from the East as Pompey's political agent. Hearing that Nepos was about to stand for the tribunate, in order that he might lay before the people his patron's demands, Cato grew excited. "This is no time for rural delights," he cried, and turned his face back towards the city. For, like so many other Romans of that day, he was firmly convinced that Pompey was aiming at a tyranny, and that his return to the city would be the signal for a *coup d'état*. Accordingly he conceived it his duty to endeavour to hold Metellus in check, and stood against him at the tribunicial elections. Both were successful, and the year B.C. 62 was made lively by their interminable quarrels.

Their main dispute was on the occasion when Metellus made his very unnecessary proposal that Pompey should be called home from the East, to quench the embers of the Catilinarian rising, a project which he must have made on his own inspiration and without his patron's knowledge. Since Antonius had crushed the insurgents at Pistoria, there was no serious work for Pompey to do. The proposal seemed to Cato entirely sinister; it confirmed the worst suspicions that he had nourished concerning Nepos and his employer. "The project was absurd," he said, " but Metellus's stupidity was so great that it sometimes became formidable." Accordingly, he determined to use his tribunicial veto to the uttermost. " While I live," he was heard to say, " Pompey shall never enter armed into the city." This determination led him into the first of those riotous scenes in the Assembly of which he was so often to be the centre during the next twelve years.

On the day on which Metellus proposed to introduce his bill, he packed the Forum with gladiators and hired bravos, and enlisted the support of Cæsar, whose talents for mob-management were considered to be unrivalled, till Clodius arose and carried the art one stage farther. It appears strange to find Cæsar aiding a partisan of Pompey at this date. Apparently he did so from sheer mischief, one of his reasons being that he was disgusted with Cato for foiling him at the trial of Lentulus and Cethegus; the other, that he wished to embroil Pompey with the Optimates. As a leader of the Democratic party, he did not really wish to see the army of the East and its general transferred to Italy. But it would profit the *populares* if the Pompeians could be induced to ask for over-great and unconstitutional powers for their chief; and it would be no less desirable to set Pompeians and Optimates at daggers drawn, by inducing the Senate to commit themselves to open antagonism to the measures proposed by Nepos. Accordingly Cæsar lent himself as a supporter to the unwise demands which the latter was making.

On the day of assembly the mob which Metellus and Cæsar had brought with them looked so threatening, that Cato's friends besought him not to risk himself among them. But the element of personal safety never entered into his calculations. He ploughed his way through the tumultuous crowd, and found Cæsar and Nepos seated side by side on the rostra. At once he plumped himself down between them; it looked rude, but it had the effectual result of preventing them from communicating easily with each other. When Nepos began to read his bill, Cato rose and interposed his veto. Encouraged by the shouts of his partisans, Pompey's friend ignored the interruption and continued to recite his preamble. Thereupon his colleague suddenly snatched the document from his hand and tore it up. Nothing daunted, Metellus went on with his clauses, speaking from memory. This was too much for Cato, who, assisted by another Optimate tribune, one Minucius Thermus, seized the orator, pulled him back to his seat, and laid his hands on his mouth. Nepos, as might have been expected, shouted to his friends that violence was being used against his sacrosanct person. The mob stormed the platform, and Cato was assailed with sticks and stones. His life was only saved by the consul Muraena, who covered him with his gown, and hurried him into a neighbouring temple. Seeing the coast clear and his adversary driven off, Nepos began once more to recite his bill; but he had not got far when Cato, much battered though he was, emerged from his place of shelter with a few friends at his heels, and charged the rostra from the rear. The whole meeting broke up into a riot, order could not be restored, and the bill was never carried. Probably Cæsar was as pleased at the fiasco as was Cato himself, for he can never have intended that Pompey should really be recalled. He had merely wished to provoke bad blood between Pompeians and Optimates, and in this he had certainly succeeded.

Metellus went back to the East to report his failure to his patron, after having denounced Cato as an enemy of his country and a conspirator against its most worthy son—accusations which not even the most fanatical democrat or Pompeian could take seriously.

When at last Pompey came home in person, Cato was still in the same mind concerning him; he was fully convinced that he was aiming at despotic power, and never attempted to separate the foolish projects of Nepos from the very reasonable requests which Pompey himself laid before the Senate and people. Considering the extreme moderation of the general's demands, there was no reason why he and the Senate should not have come to an agreement, and have united to keep down the Democrats. The two chief hindrances in the way were the foolish vanity of Cicero, whose conduct we have already had occasion to relate, and Cato's unconquerable suspicion of all that Pompey said and did. The general endeavoured to conciliate him by every means in his power, went out of his way to explain his harmless intentions, and even requested the hand of Cato's niece, Servilia, for his son Gnaeus, as a token of reconciliation. Cato was utterly unconvinced, imagined that an attempt was being made to bribe him with a great alliance, and sent away the friend who brought Pompey's message with the reply that "he was not to be caught with a female snare."

So far, indeed, was he from being conciliated, that it was undoubtedly he, more than any other single person, who made peace between Pompey and the Senate impossible, and ultimately drove the much-provoked general into the arms of Crassus and Cæsar. It was Cato who induced the Senate to refuse to ratify Pompey's treaties and grants in Asia: the plea which he used was that Lucullus had also made arrangements with the Asiatic states, some of which conflicted with those of his successor. In justice to Lucullus and those with whom he had negotiated, Cato declared that it was necessary not to ratify Pompey's doings *en bloc*, but to go through each document separately, after comparing it with the previous obligations contracted by his predecessor. This was rational enough in itself, but the result was unfortunate. Convinced at last that he would never get decent treatment from the Senate, the outraged general was forced into his alliance with the Democrats. There is something in Plutarch's conclusion that, judging by the event, Cato was in the wrong; though much was to be said in favour of discussing the treaties separately, yet the result was that, by forcing Pompey to league himself with Cæsar, he indirectly brought about the ruin of the Republic.

Cato at this time made himself no less odious to Cicero than to Pompey, by breaking up the *Concordia Ordinum*, —the alliance of Senate and Equites against the anarchic forces in the state,—which had been brought about by the Catilinarian insurrection. The consul of B.C. 63 had enlisted all men of property in defence of the existing constitution by the lurid account which he gave of the conspiracy and its ends. As long as the Equites were kept estranged from their old leader Crassus, by memories of the plot, the Democratic party was shorn of one of its strongest elements. But at last there arose a question on which the interest of the state and that of the Equestrian Order clashed. The great syndicate of capitalists which had contracted to raise the tithes of Asia found that it was making a worse bargain than it had expected, and came to the Senate with the request that the terms of the agreement might be varied in its favour. Cicero admitted in private [1] that such a demand was impudent; they had entered into the contract with their eyes open, and it was by no means proved that they were making an actual loss. But the whole Equestrian Order was directly or indirectly interested in the business, and the orator was so convinced of the necessity of keeping them allied to the Senate, that he was prepared to support them. Not so Cato: he had gone into the figures, and had come to the conclusion that there was no rational necessity for varying the contract. Why should

[1] *Ep. ad Atticum*, ii. 1, § 3.

disappointed speculators be compensated for receiving
a less percentage of profit than they had calculated upon
obtaining? He made out such a clear case against the
proposal that it was rejected. Cicero was disgusted.
" Cato," he complained, " speaks as if he was dealing with
the ideal commonwealth of Plato, not with our corrupt
and decadent Rome." Morally, he was right; practically,
he caused the resentful Equites to quit their alliance with
the Optimates, and to turn once more to their old friend
Crassus [June B.C. 60].

That by estranging the actual or possible allies of the
Senate he was dooming his party to destruction, was no
concern to Cato. His principle was that a loyal citizen
must not do evil that good may come, that anything is
better than opportunism, and that it is far more important
to have a clear conscience than to score a temporary political success. If evil days were at hand, he was perfectly
prepared to fight, by every device that an honest man
might use; but he would not buy support from any quarter
by what he considered corrupt concessions.

The crisis was not very long delayed; when Cæsar
came back from Spain in the summer of B.C. 60, and the
disheartened Pompey consented to join him and Crassus
in forming the " First Triumvirate," Cato took arms at
once. His first achievement was to " talk out " Cæsar's
demand for a triumph. In order to sue for the consulship
for the next year the returning general was bound to enter
Rome by a fixed day. In order to triumph he had to
obtain the Senate's approval before he passed the gates.
There happened to be only one meeting at which the
motion could be taken into consideration. When it came,
Cato beat the record of the ancient world by making a
speech which lasted the whole day. It was not a good
speech, as even his friends allowed, but it served the
desired purpose. Cæsar, more set on obtaining the con-

sulship than the triumph, was obliged to quit his legions and enter the city in order to begin his canvass. He was disgusted with the obstructionist orator, and never forgave him. Of all the opponents with whom he clashed during his stormy career, Cato was the only one for whom he nourished a real dislike. He showed it by publishing a very bitter and unfair satire, the "Anti-Cato," against his memory, after he had fallen in the civil war, a deed that contrasts strangely with his usual magnanimity to his adversaries.

After the turbulent consulship of Cæsar and Bibulus began, on 1st January B.C. 59, Cato had plenty of occupation provided for him. When the Julian Laws, which were to consolidate the triumvirate, began to be brought forward, he came down to the Forum to oppose every one of them. At the first great riot, when Cæsar illegally refused to listen to his colleague's veto, and went on with his legislative proposals in face of every constitutional hindrance, we find Cato at the side of Bibulus, enduring in his company the storm of stones and blows. When at last the Democrats drove them out of the assembly, it was Cato who brought up the rear, refusing to hurry as he went, and turning every now and then to tell the unheeding rabble of pursuers that they were lunatics as well as bad citizens. When Bibulus had retired to the safety of his house, and contented himself with putting up a daily notice that no legal meetings of the Comitia could be held, as he was intending to "observe the heavens," Cato sought no similar shelter. He came down to oppose the law for distributing the Campanian lands, and spoke so bitterly that Cæsar had him dragged from the rostrum and sent to prison, though he soon allowed him to be released by a friendly tribune. When the question of the Asiatic tax-farmers was brought up in the Senate, he tried to "talk out" the proposal, as he had talked out the question of Cæsar's triumph seven months before. But the consul had him stopped in the midst of his harangue, and no one dared to protest. At the most important assembly of the year, that in which the disreputable tribune Vatinius carried the law which made Cæsar governor of Gaul, Cato again came down to protest. He told the citizens that "they were voting a tyrant into the citadel" when they gave the triumvir the all-important Cisalpine province and the legions that lay in it. But it was to no purpose: Cato had liberated his conscience by making his protest, but he had no other consolation. All that he had succeeded in accomplishing was to make Cæsar use illegal violence in a way that in the eyes of strict constitutionalists vitiated all his legislation. But strict constitutionalists were a negligeable quantity at Rome in those unhappy days.

It may have been some consolation to Cato to find that he had at least succeeded in provoking his enemies to the point of expelling him from Rome. In B.C. 58 they let loose upon him the famous demagogue Clodius, then in the first energy of his tribunicial year. The annexation of Cyprus, a very unjust and disreputable piece of work, had just been determined upon. Clodius announced that as there were tempting opportunities for plunder in King Ptolemy's treasury, the most honest man in Rome had better be sent to conduct the business. Cato replied that he had no intention of touching such an iniquitous affair, and should not accept any such post. "It is not your pleasure to go," answered the tribune, "but it is my pleasure that you should be sent." Thereupon he procured a decree which appointed Cato to take charge of Cyprus and its annexation, and also to reconcile two factions at Byzantium which were engaged in civil war. He was to be kept out of Rome as long as the triumvirs and their agent thought necessary. To show that he was

CATO IN CYPRUS

in disgrace, he was given neither a single soldier, a ship, nor a supply of money, and he had assigned to help him only two secretaries, one of whom was a notorious thief, and the other a client of Clodius—which came to much the same thing.

When practical work had to be done, Cato was always at his best, and this unsought-for mission, which took him away from Rome during the time of Cicero's banishment, and of many other troubles, enabled him to do the state good service. He reconciled the Byzantines with no difficulty: the Cypriot matter turned out heart-rending to an honest man, but not otherwise difficult. The unfortunate king committed suicide when he heard that he was to be evicted, though Cato tried to smooth matters for him, by promising him a competent maintenance and the important post of high-priest of the Paphian temple, the chief sanctuary of the island. Ptolemy being removed, there was no hindrance to taking possession of his whole treasure, which amounted to the great sum of 7000 talents. The removal of such a mass of bullion to Rome was no light matter: fearing shipwreck, as we are told, Cato took the curious precaution of sealing up precisely two talents and 500 drachmae in each of several thousand vases. To the lid of each vase he fastened an immensely long cord, with a large cork buoy at the end, his idea being that if the ships miscarried the buoys would float on the surface of the sea, and guide salvage work. What was to be done if the misadventure took place in really deep water, Plutarch does not tell us.

Cato came back to Rome late in the summer of B.C. 56, in time to be involved in all the troubles which were caused by the renewal of the triumvirate at Lucca, and the determination of its members that Pompey and Crassus should be made consuls for 55. At first Cato had some personal troubles of his own to distract him. His old enemy Clodius was still reigning over the streets of Rome in all his glory, and thought that it would be a humorous and appropriate thing to indict Cato for embezzlement of some of that very Cypriot treasure over which the latter had taken so much trouble. The charge was too gross, and Cato easily got off, after making his famous *bon mot* that "what greater disgrace can the age see than Clodius as the accuser and Cato as the accused in a trial for embezzlement?" Yet, curiously enough, Cato was found at the same moment opposing a motion in the Senate to declare the acts of Clodius's tribunate illegal. It had occurred to Cicero, some time after his return from banishment, that the best way to get rid of the slur on himself caused by the decree that the demagogue had passed against him, would be to procure a declaration that the latter had never been legally elected tribune. To stand for the office Clodius had been forced to get himself adopted as a Plebeian, and his adoption had been carried out with the most flagrant disregard of legal formalities. Cato opposed this raking up of events now three years old, by pointing out that many accomplished facts depended for their legality on Clodius having been duly elected; among others, his own commission to Cyprus. If Clodius was no tribune, then he had been no commissioner, and all his doings in Cyprus and Byzantium were vitiated. This settled the matter, and Cicero's ingenious device was rejected—a result which made him as bitterly angry with Cato, as he had been once before over the breaking up of the *Concordia Ordinum*, and as he was to be once again over the matter of his triumph for his military exploits in Cilicia.

It is to the same year, B.C. 56, that belongs the most extraordinary, and to our eyes most objectionable, of the incidents of Cato's private life. Plutarch wrongly

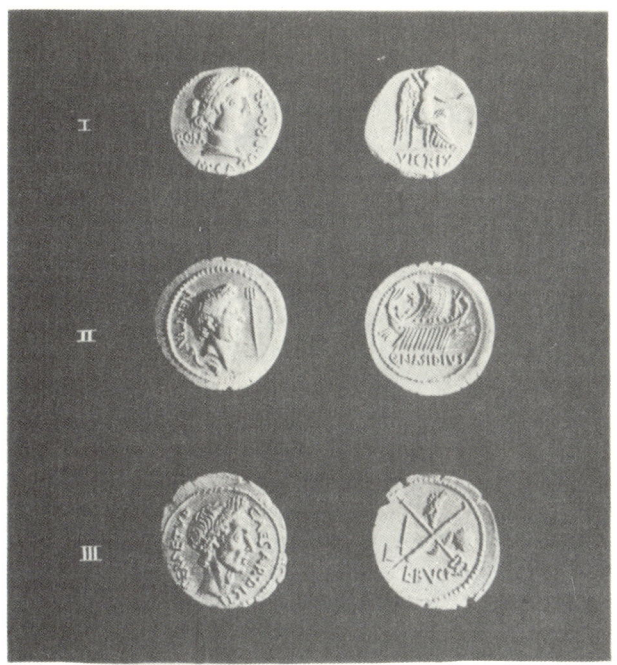

ROMAN COINS FROM THE BRITISH MUSEUM. (PLATE 3.)

    I. Denarius struck by Cato, during the Civil War.
    II. Aureus with portrait of Pompey, commemorating his naval exploits.
    III. Denarius with portrait of Cæsar, struck during his dictatorship.

gives it as having happened in 63, which the ages of the persons concerned makes impossible. He had married as his second wife Marcia, daughter of the consular Marcius Philippus; she was still a young woman, had borne him three children, and was a person of excellent character. Hortensius, a particular friend of Cato, came to him with the request, which he allowed was an unusual one, but which he trusted would not offend Cato, that he would kindly divorce his wife and allow himself (Hortensius) to marry her. For although Cato was quite satisfied with her, he thought that he himself was more interested in the lady. "Observing the vehemence of Hortensius," says Plutarch, "Cato did not absolutely refuse him, but said that it was necessary to consult his wife and her father Philippus. Finding them not unwilling, he said that his private inclination should not stand in the way." Accordingly he divorced Marcia, and she was married to Hortensius in his presence and with his consent—surely the most extraordinary instance of altruism known. For that, Cato was consulting in philosophic guise "the greatest happiness of the greatest number" is shown by the fact that when Hortensius died, six years later, he at once remarried Marcia, and lived with her again till death parted them. It was a strange example of Roman views and Roman morals in the aspect which appears most unlovely to us.

Cato's next field-day was during the consular elections of B.C. 55. The Optimates had been thoroughly cowed by the news of the conference at Lucca, and the assurance that Cæsar, Pompey, and Crassus were firm friends again. Accordingly, when Crassus and Pompey announced their intention of standing together for the consulship, no one had the courage to enter the field against them. Cato was much enraged at this, and went about trying to get one man after another to stand as an Optimate competitor.

At last he prevailed on Lucius Domitius, who had married his sister, to put himself in the way of honour and danger. Seeing Domitius canvassing assiduously, the friends of the triumvirs determined to use violence, and on the day of the election prepared gangs of Clodius's ruffians to block the polling-places at daybreak. But Cato and Domitius went down to the Campus Martius with torches at midnight to secure a good place. At dawn arrived the first gangs of the triumvirs' myrmidons, who killed Domitius' torch-bearer and chased away his and Cato's clients. The unwilling candidate would have fled, but Cato, though badly wounded by a dagger-thrust in the arm, "still kept Domitius on the spot, adjuring him not to desert the cause of the Republic as long as he had life in him." But his brother-in-law's firmness broke down; unable to stand the stress, he finally retired, and Pompey and Crassus were elected.

Cato then proclaimed that if other men fled he would not, and announced himself as a candidate for the praetorship, intending thus to secure himself thereby the sacrosanct position of a magistrate, and (as Plutarch quotes him) "a kind of fort from which he should be able to make sorties against the consuls." He failed, naturally, as he scorned to use either bribery or intimidation, both of which were lavishly employed against him. It was therefore only as a private person that he was able to speak against the Trebonian Law which gave Pompey Spain and an army, and Crassus Syria and an army. When the bill was brought forward, Cato got permission from a friendly tribune to speak, but when he had already talked for two hours, "with many repetitions and many predictions of evil," Trebonius got angry and bade his apparitors take him down from the rostrum. Yet, standing below among the people, he continued his speech, which so enraged Trebonius that he had him driven out of the

Forum. But in a few minutes Cato was back and climbing up the rostra again, whereupon Trebonius, thoroughly roused, had him haled to prison. He had wasted the day, but on the succeeding one the triumvirs' men blockaded the tribune Aquilius (who was going to veto the law) in the Senate-house by force of arms, cleared the partisans of the Optimates out of the Forum, and badly mauled Cato, who gravely kept asserting that he heard thunder on the left, and that the Comitia ought therefore to be broken up.

It was in the next year that Cato made his celebrated declaration that he intended to prosecute Cæsar, the moment that his proconsulate had run out, and he had become once more a private person. The cause was his treacherous dealing with the Usipetes and Tencteri. After concluding a peace with them, and seeing them start homewards to cross the Rhine, he had fallen upon them, alleging a breach of the convention on their part, and had slain more than 430,000 men, women, and children, according to his own version [B.C. 55]. Even as told in the *De Bello Gallico* the story has a very sinister look; there seems no doubt that Cæsar went very near the edge of treachery, if he did not cross it. Cato was so indignant at the transaction, that he gave notice that he would move that Cæsar should be put in chains at the expiration of his command, and surrendered to the surviving Usipetes, as Mancinus had been surrendered to the Numantines, or Poplilius to the Samnites after the Caudine Forks. Cæsar used this threat of Cato's to great effect as a reason why he must continue to hold perpetual office. To avoid such a danger he wished to be allowed to sue for the consulship of B.C. 48 in his absence, before his existing commission in Gaul should run out. Of course he was insincere in pretending that he would be in personal danger if he returned to Rome. There was not much chance that he would be condemned either by the Assembly or by a Special Commission. The former he commanded, the latter he would have bribed. Cato was alone, and it would have required a whole Senate like himself to have made such an attack upon Rome's greatest general.

In the following year, when Crassus had gone off to Syria, and Pompey was beginning to show some signs of slackening in his friendship for Cæsar, Cato stood for the praetorship again, and we learn to our surprise that he was successful. The lustre of an exemplary tenure of office was somewhat dimmed in the eyes of the public, we are told, by the fact that Cato showed his imitation of his great-grandfather rather too grotesquely, by often going to sit on the praetorial bench without his robe or his shoes, when he had to pass sentence on persons of high importance. We know little of his doings except that, as a testimony to his integrity, at the next praetorial elections all the candidates agreed to avoid bribery and to deposit 500 sertertia each with Cato, he undertaking to declare forfeit the deposit of any one of them whom he should consider to have acted unfairly in the canvass. One man was detected while distributing bribes: Cato therefore declared his deposit forfeited, and offered a share of it to each of the other candidates. But fellow-feeling, or the consciousness that their own private doings would not bear inspection, seems to have swayed them all, for each sent back what he had received to the convicted man. This curious transaction only took place after a very stormy scene in the Comitia: the mob disliked any attempt to put down corruption, and when they understood Cato's line of action pelted him with stones, so that all who were about him fled, and he was left alone on the rostra. "Yet, standing there unmoved, with a firm and steady aspect, he finally hushed the clamour of the mob, and demonstrated the righteousness of his proceedings" [B.C. 54].

Another curious incident from the year in which Cato enjoyed the praetorship has been preserved. He came down to support his friend Favonius, who was standing for the aedileship of the next year. When the votes were counted, it seemed that Favonius had been beaten; but Cato got permission to examine the tablets, and found so many obviously written by the same hand and foisted into the boxes by fraud, that he got the election quashed by the tribunes. At a second ballot his friend was returned; as a mark of his esteem he entrusted the management of the theatrical shows which he exhibited to the people to Cato—a strange choice considering his views and habits. Cato did not decline the task, but managed the details of the entertainment according to his own ideas of the becoming. He gave the actors crowns of wild olive instead of gold (one trusts that he remembered the difference when settling their salaries), and instead of showy and expensive presents distributed small and useful donatives. We are told that they included bundles of leeks, radishes, lettuce, and parsley, little bottles of wine, joints of pork, cucumbers, and faggots of wood. The theatre after the distribution must have looked like the shop of a general dealer; but we are told that the people were highly amused, and deserted a great show which Curio was giving on the same day, in order to see Cato acting as master of the ceremonies.

In the next year, when Pompey was obviously becoming estranged from Cæsar, and inclining towards the Optimates, Cato ventured to stand for the consulship. But his rivals, Sulpicius and Marcellus, bribed heavily, while he offered nothing, and did not even go out of his way to canvass. He expected to be beaten, and was not disappointed; on the day of the poll he was playing ball when the return was made. The messenger with the unfavourable news reached him in the middle of a game, which he quietly finished, and then took a walk round the Forum without shoes or toga to show his equanimity [B.C. 52].

In B.C. 52–51 we find Cato for the first time in friendly relations with Pompey. He had at last convinced himself that nothing was to be feared from that quarter, and that Cæsar was the real danger to the Republic. Accordingly he turned to exhorting Pompey to beware of his father-in-law. "You took him upon your shoulders eight years ago," he said, "and now you begin to find him heavy. You can neither support his weight nor cast him off; probably you will both fall together, and in your fall crush the Republic." In B.C. 50 Cato was the soul of the party which had made up its mind that war with Cæsar was inevitable, and that it was necessary to take the offensive against him. It was he who urged that the great proconsul should be given a successor in each of his provinces as soon as possible, and that all his many proposals for a compromise should be rejected. Pompey's vacillation drove him wild, and when at last the news came that Cæsar had crossed the Rubicon before any preparation to resist him had been made, he could not restrain himself. At the next meeting of the Senate he spoke in the character of a despised and neglected prophet, whose predictions had at last come true. If the Fathers had listened to him during the last ten years, he said, they would neither be living in deadly fear of the power of one man—Cæsar—nor putting their sole hope of defence in the strength of another man—Pompey. Nevertheless he supported the decree which placed the conduct of the war in the hands of the latter, using the scornful argument that "the authors of great evils should best know how they were to be cured."

When various senators were given charge of the different

regions of the empire, for the purpose of raising troops against Cæsar, Sicily was assigned to Cato. He went to Syracuse in deep despondency, but determined to do his duty. From the day when the war broke out he never cut his hair, nor shaved his beard, nor wore a garland; however the conflict might turn out, it was a grief to him that he had to contend with Roman citizens. In Sicily he had not long to stay, for Cæsar's general Pollio crossed into the island before he could assemble a respectable force, and he was forced to fly to Pompey in Epirus.

In the faction-ridden camp of the Optimates he was a useful if not a cheerful figure. It is true that he offended the more violent men by insisting that Roman citizens must not be put to death except in battle, and that there must be no proscription if they returned to Italy victorious. Nor did he conciliate Pompey when he bade him always to remember that he obeyed him as his military commander, not as his party chief. But he was so vigorous and untiring in his work of organising the new legions, and proved so capable of inspiring others with his own fire, that he was perhaps the most valuable officer in the army. His harangue to his own division before the battle of Dyrrhachium was long remembered. Abandoning his usual reserve, as Plutarch tells us, he spoke to them of liberty and virtue, of death and glory, with such impassioned eloquence, that they swore to follow wherever he would lead, and kept their promise. In the ensuing battle they did their best, drove back Cæsar's veterans, and broke the lines of investment. If Pompey had known how to utilise a success as well as he knew how to win it, the day might have been fatal to the enemy.

It is said that for a moment there had been a chance that Cato might have been given the command of the whole Optimate fleet, which Bibulus, who was made admiral in his stead, so grievously mismanaged. But Pompey on reflec-

tion came to the conclusion, that though he would be an
energetic lieutenant while the war lasted, he would be a
very uncomfortable colleague if it came to a successful
end, for he would certainly have used the naval force as a
counterpoise to the army. Cato's old suspicions of the ex-
triumvir would certainly have revived, and friction would
have been inevitable. Yet it would surely have been
better to have chanced future troubles, and to have utilised
for the present the services of a strenuous and capable
officer. To give Bibulus or Octavius the fleet was to risk
everything. Indeed, the failure of the whole campaign
may be traced back to the fact that the inefficient blockade
kept up by the Pompeian admirals allowed Cæsar's reinforcements to get across to Epirus. If they had never
been allowed to sail, the Optimates must have crushed
their opponents by mere force of numbers.

When Cæsar struck inland, and Pompey was compelled
to change the theatre of operations to Thessaly, he left
Cato in charge of his base-camp, his treasure, and his
naval stores at Dyrrhachium, giving him fifteen cohorts for
their guard. This important charge kept him from being
present at Pharsalus; if he had been there, it is probable
that he would not have survived the defeat, for it is
certain that he would not have been the man either to fly
or to surrender. As it was, he found himself at the head
of the only considerable fraction of the Optimate army
which had escaped destruction. He crossed over with his
fifteen cohorts to Corcyra, where he joined the fleet. A
powerful armament was thus at his disposal, but he would
not take up the supreme command, for he had discovered
that there was a senior magistrate on the spot. This was
Cicero, to whom he insisted on turning over the charge of
ships and men. The unfortunate orator was placed in a
most uncomfortable position, for he intended to do anything rather than fight, and was already meditating how

best he might make his peace with Cæsar. He refused to take over the command, with every sign of alarm, and so provoked the young Gnaeus Pompeius that he purposed to have him put to death as a traitor. Cato, though much disgusted with him, succeeded in preserving his life, and managed that he should escape by night to Brundisium, where he made his submission to the enemy.

Nothing now remained save to take the relics of the army of Epirus to the spot where they could be most useful. Cato resolved to join Metellus Scipio, and King Juba in Africa, the only province where a considerable force was still in arms for the Republic. Accordingly he crossed the sea, and landed at Cyrene with 10,000 men. He took them by a long march, around the head of the Syrtes, to place them at Scipio's disposition. Refusing either to use a horse or to shield his head by a hat from the African sun, he marched for seven days on foot through the Tripolitan sands at the head of his troops, and finally reached the African border.

The whole Optimate army, and Scipio himself, wished that Cato should take command of the province. But constitutional etiquette, as at Corcyra, was in the way. "We are fighting Cæsar," said he, "because he has broken the laws; it would not be right that I should break them too, by assuming superior authority over the head of a proconsul, when I am only a propraetor." So Scipio, though known by all to be rash and incapable, kept the charge of the army, while Cato was placed in command of the base-camp at Utica. He fortified the place with great care, and collected vast magazines in it for the use of the field-army. His advice to the proconsul was to avoid a pitched battle at all costs, and to wear down Cæsar's army by the African sun and the harassing assaults of Juba's Numidian cavalry.

But, as might have been foreseen, the stupid proconsul

soon allowed himself to be lured into a battle, and the disaster of Thapsus followed. Once more Cato found himself at the head of the mere wreck of an army, and encompassed with a campful of dispirited politicians who were thinking of making their submission to Cæsar. At first he resolved to resist to the end, and made every preparation to fight; but he found that the Roman residents of Utica were intriguing to surrender the place to the enemy, while the troops refused to shut themselves up in a city where there was a large population which might turn against them and admit Cæsar. Some of the soldiery informed Cato that they would only stand a siege if they were first allowed to put to death or expel every one whom they suspected of treachery within the walls. But he refused to listen to any proposals for a massacre, whereupon they told him that they should march off into the interior, and leave him to shift for himself.

Abandoned by his troops, and quite conscious that the Utican senate was prepared to admit Cæsar the moment that he appeared, Cato thought that he had reached the limits of his responsibility. It was still open to him to escape by sea, and join the last desperate levies which the two young Pompeys were collecting in Baetica. But it seemed to him that the cause of the Republic was so hopelessly lost that any further struggle was useless. He knew the two reckless and violent young men in Spain too well to believe that if, by some strange turn of luck, they were to beat off Cæsar, they would ever restore the old constitution of the state. Rome would merely get two tyrants instead of one; it was not for him to protract the war for such an end. All that remained was that he should seek the last refuge of the just man in the day of hopeless adversity, a voluntary death. The Stoic creed, of which he had always been such a firm adherent, supplied him with the advice which was necessary in such a crisis.

THE DEATH OF CATO

To fight was useless, perhaps even harmful; to surrender was dishonourable; it only remained to die.

There was still a day or more at his disposition before Cæsar could arrive, and this time he devoted to setting his house in order. He procured shipping for all those who chose to fly to Spain, and saw them quit the harbour. There remained with him none save his young son, his friend Statilius, and two philosophers, Apollonides the Stoic and Demetrius the Peripatetic, who had accompanied him from Cyprus. After bathing he went to dinner; he had invited the magistrates of Utica to join him, though he knew that they intended to surrender to Cæsar next day. Throughout the meal he showed himself cheerful beyond his wont, and led the conversation through many fields of philosophy. In particular, he dwelt long on the old Stoic paradox that "the good man only is free, the bad man, even in success, a slave." It was quite true, he maintained: he himself had done his duty, and was therefore happy. Cæsar had become the enemy of his country, and so was the most miserable of all men. He looked upon himself as the victor, and the dictator as the vanquished. To his son he left one legacy of advice—to keep clear of politics. In the Rome of the immediate future, he said, "you cannot fill any place in a way that would be worthy of your father; to do it otherwise would be unworthy of yourself."

After the dinner was over, he took a short walk in the dark with his son and his friends, and retired to his chamber. Then he said farewell to all in such words that none could fail to guess his purpose. When left alone, he lay down on his bed and began to read Plato concerning the Immortality of the Soul; but he had not gone far before he missed his sword from its usual peg at the head of his couch. His son had removed it when he guessed his father's intent. With some displeasure he summoned the young man, and asked him whether he desired to surrender him to Cæsar. If this was his wish, why had he not bound him and fettered his hands, for a brave man did not need a sword; if that was missing, there were other, if more painful, ways to die. Then, turning to the two philosophers, he inquired whether they thought it likely that they could convince him that it would be wise or honourable to submit to Cæsar. If not, what course did they intend to propose to him?

The son and the philosophers withdrew in tears, and seeing that nothing else was left, sent in the sword by the hands of a slave. Cato tried its edge. "Now, at least, I am master of myself," he said; and, lying down again, he twice read through the book on which he had been intent. Then he lay down for a short snatch of slumber; but at dawn he woke, and without further lingering stabbed himself as deeply as he could below the right breast. The noise of his fall roused his friends, who had been listening all night for some such noise. With cruel kindness they bandaged his wound, which was not necessarily mortal, and laid him on his couch again. But the moment that he came to himself he pulled away the bandages, tore open the hurt, and died in a few minutes.

Cæsar came up next day. At first he tried to play the magnanimous part: "How could Cato envy me the glory of pardoning him and saving his life?" he cried. But his real feelings for the one man whom he could not bend were shown when, not long afterwards, he published his satire, the "Anti-Cato." In this discreditable work he heaped together all the stories, true or untrue, which placed his enemy in a ludicrous light: he did not shrink from saying that Cato had passed the ashes of his brother's funeral pyre through a sieve, in search of melted gold, and that he had lent his wife to Hortensius for valuable consideration. But such slanders did more harm to the writer than to the subject of his libel.

Cæsar's pamphlet has long been forgotten, and Cato's life, in spite of the sneers of Mommsen and other blind worshippers of the dictator, will long continue to appeal to all who love an honest man. We no longer write tragedies to his glory; we grant that he was a little impracticable, a little grotesque—in short, a magnificent anachronism. Yet we feel that it is well with the state which has such men. Ten Catos might have saved the Roman Republic; one could only be a voice crying in the wilderness, prophesying the inevitable ill, which, unaided, he could not ward off. Like the Persian noble in Herodotus, he could exclaim, "What the gods have decreed it is not possible to avert, but surely the direst of all human ills is to abound in knowledge, yet to have no power to hold back the evil day."

CHAPTER VIII

POMPEY

IN Cato we have had to deal with a man who should have been born in an earlier age, who knew it, and who went through life with his eyes open, fighting against the inevitable, though he knew that it must come in spite of all his striving. Now we have to survey a still more unhappy and pathetic career, that of a man who did not even know the signs of the times, and went on blindly seeking he did not quite know what, and doing infinite mischief just because he did not know what he wanted.

There have been, alike in ancient and in modern history, great generals who were also great statesmen, for good or for evil, like Cæsar, or Frederick the Great, or Napoleon. There have also been great generals to whom all insight into the verities of contemporary politics was denied, and who yet insisted upon interfering in them, and found it easy to do so. For the multitude is always prone to credit great generals with universal genius in statecraft, just as it is equally prone to credit great orators with the same faculty. For it seems to be easy to forget that excellence in strategy and in oratory are about equally remote in character from excellence in statesmanship. Cicero or Burke, not to mention more modern names, cut poor figures as practical politicians, but even more pathetically futile are the great men of war who have been put at the head of the state by their admirers, and have gone astray in the Forum. The best example in modern times is probably our own Wellington, whose mismanagement had no mean part in bringing England to the edge of that revolution which she only escaped by the great Reform Bill of 1832. The best example in ancient history is undoubtedly Gnaeus Pompeius Magnus, three times the potential master of Rome, who thrice refused to lay firm hold of the helm that was thrust into his grasp, and yet could never quite keep his fingers from itching to handle it. Never did a man's virtues combine more fatally with his weaker qualities to bring about not only his own ruin, but the wreck of his country. A sternly stoical and self-repressing Pompey would have crushed down the ambition in his heart, and steeled himself to despise any misrepresentation and injustice that fell to his lot, like Phocion of old. He would have done the Republic no harm, though he might not have proved its saviour. On the other hand, a purely self-seeking and unscrupulous Pompey would have been able to seize the control of the state with ease, and might have tried whatsoever constitutional experiments he pleased. Perhaps the Republic might have fared none the worse if he had done so; he might have become its ruler without the civil war which Cæsar had to face. His opportunities were far better than those of Cæsar for gaining supreme power, without having to wade to the throne through oceans of Roman blood.

But Pompey was neither wholly unselfish nor wholly unscrupulous. Hence it came to pass that he took neither of the alternative paths, but fidgeted about between the two, sometimes obeying the impulse of ambition, sometimes that of loyalty, so that all his actions seem incoherent and inconsequent, and the general trend of his career appears both destructive to the constitution and disastrous to himself. Yet it is hard to grow very indignant with him; his personal virtues are too conspicuous, and his character too far above the level of the other Romans of his time. He was so ungratefully treated by those he fain would have served, and his final end was so piteous, that we are forced to shut our eyes to the mischief (mostly unintentional) which he did, and to view his whole life with sympathy rather than with impatience.

It is hardly necessary to say that Mommsen's estimate of Pompey is no more to be taken seriously than his estimates of Cicero, or Cato, or Cæsar. It is as misleading to treat him as a mere drill-sergeant, as to call Cicero a "fluent Consular," or Cato a "mere Don Quixote," or Cæsar a beneficent and unselfish saviour of society. He was in reality no military pedant but an excellent general and organiser. In war he fared well, save when he came in contact with the two men of first-rate military genius who crossed his path, Sertorius and Cæsar. Against them he fought not ingloriously, till the fatal day at Pharsalus, when he for the first time met with complete disaster, ruined not so much by his own fault as by the rashness of his officers and the inexperience of his men.

But it was not so much as a soldier that Pompey appeals to the student of those last troublous days. In that time of corrupt and degenerate Romans it is a relief to come upon a leading man who was neither a profligate nor an unscrupulous adventurer. Pompey's private life was worthy of the old times of the Republic for its modesty, honesty, and purity. No one ever accused him of greed, of debauchery, or of malevolence; "he was the slowest man at asking and the readiest at giving in Rome," says Plutarch. Nor was he merely honest and upright; he also possessed the virtue—rare above all others in that age—of humanity, shown not only to fellow-citizens, but even to foreigners and enemies. In all his Eastern and his Western campaigns, one of the most remarkable points is his habitual kindliness and moderation to the vanquished. Not only open foreign foes, but even outcasts, like the pirates of Cilicia, found in him a merciful conqueror. Any other man would have crucified those robbers along the coasts which they had plundered. Pompey turned them into colonists in his new cities in the Isaurian region, where, strangely enough, they repaid his confidence by turning out good settlers. Even the Jews, whose feelings he had outraged by forcing his way into the Holy of Holies at Jerusalem, speak nothing of him but good. Of all Roman conquerors he was undoubtedly the most just and merciful. He had not, like his rival Cæsar, huge stains of massacre upon his reputation, such as the execution of the senate of the Veneti or the treacherous slaughter of the 430,000 Usipetes and Tencteri. He would have been wholly incapable of that worst act of all, the saving in prison for six years of such a gallant enemy as Vercingetorix, in order that he might be duly led in chains and put to death in the Tullianum, when his callous victor's long-delayed triumph should take place. No one ever could accuse Pompey of deliberate and cold-blooded cruelty of such a cast as this. The only captives that Pompey ever slew were Romans and traitors, men whom it might have been profitable to spare, as Cæsar might very possibly have done, but whose crimes he thought too great for pardon. We shall have to tell the story of the deaths of Carbo, of Brutus, and of Perpenna in their proper places.

Gnaeus Pompeius was born in B.C. 106. He was the son of Gn. Pompeius Strabo, a man of equestrian rank, who had (first of his house) raised himself to consular office by his military achievements in the great Social war with the revolted Italians. Thus Pompey, though not a *novus homo* himself, was the son of one. Their family seems to have been for some time settled in Picenum, where we find both the father and his son after him exercising great local influence. Strabo, though a man of good abilities, had a sinister reputation. He played a rather equivocal part in the first year of the civil war between

the Optimates and the Marians. He was more than
suspected of having been privy to the murder of his rival,
Pompeius Rufus, in a military sedition. When he finally
espoused the side of the Senate, it was mainly because he
was forced to do so, since he could no longer play fast
and loose with both parties. He died in the middle of the
war [B.C. 87] while commanding for the Senate against
Marius and Cinna. We are told that his own soldiers
(who wished to join the Democrats) conspired against
him, and that his life was only saved by his son's
courage and vigilance. But a few days after he is said
to have been struck dead by lightning in his tent. Knowing
that his men were plotting against him, and that they
actually tore his body from the bier and dishonoured it,
we shall perhaps not be wrong in substituting " was
murdered " for " was killed by lightning." There are
other cases in Roman history of unpopular generals who
are said to have met their death from a thunderbolt, and
all are equally suspicious.

Strabo's son, Gnaeus the younger, was marked out for
slaughter by the Marians as his father's heir, though he
had only reached the age of nineteen. For some months
he concealed himself, but after Marius's death, when the
massacre was dying down, he was discovered and indicted
by the minions of Cinna, on a charge which might
have proved fatal, if the praetor Antistius, a powerful
man at the moment, had not protected him, and saved
him, on the condition that he should marry his daughter
Antistia. Thus preserved, the young man was able to
remain safe but obscure till the year B.C. 83, when Sulla
landed in Italy to attack the Democrats. It was then
that the future triumvir first showed the stuff that was
in him. Hastening to his father's native district of
Picenum, he raised a considerable body of followers, before
any one else in Italy had taken arms for the Optimate

POMPEY IN AFRICA

cause. He displayed extraordinary vigour and ability for one so young and so new to command. With very inferior forces he kept in check a large Marian corps, while Sulla was contending in Campania with the main body of the enemy. He defeated the praetors Brutus and Carrinas, and finally cut his way south, and joined Sulla at the head of an army which had swelled to no less than three legions. All the other Optimate refugees had come to Sulla empty-handed. Pompey brought 12,000 men already tried in war, and enthusiastically devoted to their commander. Italy had never before seen such a force raised by a private person, a young man who had but just reached the age of twenty-four. It was only natural that the Optimate chief honoured Pompey more than any other man of his party, saluted him as *Imperator*, and gave him precedence over all his other officers, though he was technically no more than a simple knight, and was barely qualified by his age to stand for the quaestorship. In the later years of the civil war Pompey won a reputation which was approached only by those of Crassus and of Ofella, and he was trusted far more than either of his rivals by Sulla. As a shrewd judge of character, the dictator could see that the young man, whatever his faults, was at least honest. Hence it came that when the flames had died down in Italy, he, rather than any other officer, was entrusted with the important task of rooting out the Democrats from Sicily and Africa. Though given but a small army, he accomplished his work with extraordinary vigour and skill, and a not less notable humanity. Sulla's legions did not always shine in the matter of consideration for provincials; they had been trained by their chief to regard anything as permissible. It is all the more creditable to Pompey that he kept them in such order that no town in Sicily was sacked nor any of the inhabitants harmed. He is said by Plutarch to have actually caused his soldiers' swords to be sealed down in their sheaths, after the fighting was over, that they might not use them against the Sicilians. But this odd statement looks like a translation into prosaic fact of some rhetorical flourish, which the simple old Bœotian had read in a panegyric of Pompey.

Crossing from Sicily to Africa, the young general easily routed Domitius and the large Democratic army which held that province. It a few weeks it was completely subdued. Only one man's life taken in cold blood marred the lustre of these triumphs. The single person whom Pompey executed was the leader of the whole Democratic party, Carbo, who fell into his hands in the isle of Pandataria, half-way between Sicily and Africa. On Carbo's head lay the responsibility for the whole of the late massacres in Rome, and Pompey owed him the personal grudge that in that slaughter had fallen his father-in-law, Antistius, the friendly praetor who had saved him in B.C. 87. Moreover the ex-consul was an outlaw by the decree of the people, and the chief of all Sulla's enemies. It was probably kinder in the end to slay him on the spot, than to send him to Rome to face Sulla's wrath and to suffer some elaborate punishment for his misdoings; but we may share with Pompey's friends of that day the regret that he took a part in the execution of even such an unpardonable enemy of the Optimate cause as Carbo.

On returning to Rome victorious in B.C. 81, Pompey was granted a triumph by Sulla though he was still technically a "private person," for he was an eques, not a senator, and held no office but that of *legatus* to the dictator. This is said to have been the only case in Roman history in which a triumph was granted to one who had never held any magistracy whatever. Sulla had not failed to note that his young lieutenant would be too much elated by his splendid position to bow readily to the new *régime*. It was a great thing to ask of one who had a victorious army at his back that he should step down from his triumphal car to take a modest place among the younger Optimates. But though Pompey was not destitute of ambition, he had from his earliest youth a singular dislike for violence and illegality. He duly disbanded his army and settled down in Rome as a private person without making much ado. This so much pleased the dictator that he saluted him by the name of "the great"—Magnus—the only cognomen which he ever bore, since he never took his father's unflattering name of Strabo—" the cross-eyed." Having once convinced himself that the young general could be trusted, Sulla allowed him liberties which he granted to no one else; not only did he concede him his abnormal triumph, but he even allowed him to support for the consulship of B.C. 78 the vain and heady M. Æmilius Lepidus, a man whom (rightly enough) he distrusted. He did not interfere with the canvass, but merely warned Pompey that he had acted with grave unwisdom. "You are proud of your victory," he said, as the train of the new consul swept through the Forum, " but be on your guard. You have used your influence and popularity to put a worthless man in power. Thereby you have raised up an adversary and made him stronger than yourself." Lepidus's subsequent conduct entirely justified the dictator's forecast. But it must be confessed that Pompey's political judgments all through life were invariably ill-advised : this support of Lepidus was but the first of a long series of mistakes.

After Sulla's death in 78 the new consul — freed from the wholesome restraint of fear which lay upon every ambitious man who remembered the fate of Ofella— broke out in open revolt against the constitution. He

came forward with a programme of public bankruptcy
(*novæ tabulæ*) combined with the restoration of the
Democratic constitution : to back his reckless schemes
he secretly raised an army of outlaws and swash-bucklers
in Etruria. Pompey had to take arms against the man
whom he had so unwisely placed in power. He was
given an army to clear the east coast of Italy and Cisalpine Gaul of the insurgents, while Catulus dealt with
the main body and the rebellious consul himself. How
the latter was routed in the Campus Martius when he
made his reckless assault on the capital we need not
again relate. Pompey was at the moment in the
north, dealing with Lepidus's lieutenant, M. Brutus (the
father of the tyrannicide of B.C. 44); after beating him
in the open field he shut him up in Mutina, and pressed
him so hard that he surrendered, in order to prevent his
own army from delivering him over to the besiegers. In
spite of this voluntary submission of the Democratic
chief, Pompey, after a day's hesitation, put him to death,
and with him Æmilianus, the son of Lepidus. This was
of all Pompey's doings, the one that was most criticised
during his lifetime. He had accepted the surrender of
Brutus, spared his life, and sent him away in custody.
Then, on mature reflection, and after composing a despatch to the Senate in which he announced the capture
of Mutina, he put to death his prisoners in cold blood.
No one could dispute that Lepidus and all his crew were
public enemies, so that there was no formal illegality
in the act. But it was felt that if Pompey had intended
to slay the Democratic leaders, he ought not to have
received them to surrender : it would have been better
for his reputation if he had sent them to Rome and
allowed the Senate to do its own killing. It was true
that the prisoners were factious traitors, who had stirred
up a wholly unnecessary civil war, but, if Pompey felt

POMPEY GOES TO SPAIN

such righteous indignation against them, that he was constrained to put them to death, it was unfortunate that only seven years later he should himself introduce and carry through several of these same Democratic reforms which Lepidus and his followers suffered for supporting [B.C. 77].

For the second time Pompey now stood victorious in Italy with a large army at his back. In spite of the unswerving loyalty to the Optimate cause which he had hitherto displayed, the Senate felt uncomfortable with such a stirring and capable general at their gates. It was with considerable relief, therefore, that they heard that he was not unwilling to undertake a new military commission, which would remove him far from the capital. He wished to be given the charge of the difficult and dangerous war against Sertorius in Spain, which had been in progress ever since Sulla drove the Democrats out of Italy five years before. Metellus, the best general of the old Optimate ring, had been striving against the great guerilla chief with indifferent success, if without actual disaster. There was no one else to send against him, least of all did the consuls of the year show any wish to set out upon such an uninviting errand. "We must despatch Pompey to Spain," said the witty L. Philippus, "*non pro consule, sed pro consulibus.*" Doubtless the more suspicious members of the oligarchy muttered to each other that if Pompey slew Sertorius, the state was freed from a great public danger, while if Sertorius slew or foiled Pompey, there was at least a dangerous pretender removed from the political stage. So the young general was duly assigned the province of Hither Spain, and permitted to march forth from Italy, taking with him the army which had subdued the Cisalpine rebels and captured Mutina. Troubles in Gaul delayed his march, and it was not till the spring of B.C. 76 that he reached the Pyrenees, there to find that

Sertorius was in possession of the greater part of the Iberian Peninsula. The tribes of the north-east were still faithful, as were most of the coast cities on the Mediterranean. But Metellus was fighting an uphill battle in Baetica, and over the whole of the interior, and the western parts of the two provinces, Sertorius reigned supreme.

The fact was that the Spanish war was no longer a struggle between the two Roman parties, nor a prolongation of the old contest in Italy between Democrat and Optimate. It was much more like a national rising of the greater number of the Iberian tribes to recover their ancient independence. The old programme of Marius and Cinna had nothing in it to attract the Spaniards, and Sertorius was not fighting for that outworn creed; he was sustained by his personal ambition and his determination not to submit to the oligarchy. It was as a Spanish chief, not as a Roman propraetor, that he was now strong; the Italian element in his host was daily growing less, the native element more preponderant. The war was becoming an attempt, led by a man of genius, to found a new Romano-Spanish national state. If Sertorius was not yet wholly successful, it was because the ancestral feuds of the Celtiberian tribes always supplied his enemies with a considerable following of native supporters. Yet their number was daily growing less, as the loyal states of the interior, unsuccoured by the arms of Metellus, fell one after another into the hands of the great guerilla chief.

Spain was already the land in which, to quote the epigram of a great general of the modern world, "large armies starve and small armies get beaten." Pompey found that he had undertaken no easy task, when he looked on the boundless arid plains and the rugged sierras over which the bands of Sertorius were roving. How was he to deal with an enemy who moved twice as fast as the heavily loaded legion, who knew every pass and ravine, who dispersed when beaten, yet assembled within a few days to fall upon the victor's flanks and rear. The army of the rebels, it was said, was like one of their own rivers. At one moment Sertorius would be wandering lost in the plains with a handful of followers, like a meagre July stream; at the next, like the same stream after rain, he would be dashing along swollen by countless fierce affluents from the mountains, almost irresistible, with 150,000 spears at his back.

For five years the weary struggle with the Spaniards continued [B.C. 76-72] amid many alternations of fortune. If Pompey had hoped to win an easy triumph over enemies no more formidable than those he had encountered in Italy and Africa, he must have been disappointed. Many times he was foiled, once he was defeated in open fight: on another occasion he owed it to the arrival of his colleague Metellus that he ended the day with a drawn battle instead of a defeat. But his spirit never failed, nor did his legions waver from their belief in him. The Senate supported him badly, as might have been expected: there was a moment when the pay of his soldiers was two years in arrear, and when he had used up the greater part of his private fortune in making advances to his loyal followers. But in spite of the neglect of the home government, the difficulty of the country, and the unrivalled mixture of craft and courage displayed by his adversary, he worked on slowly towards his end. Many historians have sneered at Pompey's management of the war, and have hinted that a general of ordinary capacity would have brought it to a much earlier end, without any of the "unfortunate incidents" that chequered its earlier years. We, who have learnt of late what guerilla warfare means, shall be loth to condemn him when we reflect on the superior numbers of his enemies, on the character of

his troops, almost entirely infantry, and on the slack way
in which he was supported from home. He never despaired, even when the struggle had dragged on for four
years: he slowly drove back Sertorius into the inland:
when at last that great man fell by the hands of his own
discontented followers, he brought the war to a sudden
end in a few months. It would have ceased long before,
if the rebels had not possessed such a splendid leader.
Perpenna, the double traitor who had murdered Sertorius,
fell into Pompey's hands in the last decisive battle. To
save his life even for a few days he offered to place in his
captor's hands the private correspondence of his late chief,
containing many letters of the most compromising sort
from prominent men at Rome. Pompey burnt the papers
unread and consigned Perpenna to the headsman. He
might have crushed the malcontents by producing their
treasonable correspondence, or have made them his humble
servants by threatening to divulge the documents if they
thwarted him. But such methods were far from his
honest mind.

Leaving Spain at last pacified, Pompey set out for Italy
in the spring of B.C. 71. On his return journey he was
fortunate enough to run into the midst of the wrecks of
the army of Spartacus. After their defeat by Crassus,
and the death of their leader, the rebels were flying
towards the Alps, but met the Spanish legions in
Liguria and there were cut to pieces.

It was now for the third time that Pompey came
victorious to the gates of Rome, with a loyal army of
veterans who would have followed him on any enterprise.
Sulla's troops, who came over from Greece in B.C. 83,
were not more devoted to their leader or more ready to
attack any enemy that he might point out to them. The
Senate might well tremble, for they had done their best
to provoke Pompey, by their culpable neglect of the

Spanish war and their persistent refusal to grant money and reinforcements to him for the last five years. They had no force to oppose him, for Metellus, the other commander in Spain, had disbanded his legions, and Crassus, who had put down the Servile revolt, was known to be even worse disposed toward the Senate than Pompey himself. There were only three possible ways out of the situation. The two generals—old personal enemies, as we have seen when dealing with the life of Crassus—might fall to blows and fight for the sovereignty of Italy; or one of them, in jealousy of the other, might espouse the cause of the Senate; or they might agree to sink their private enmity and join in an attack on the Optimates and the constitution of Sulla.

As we have already had to relate, it was the last and the least likely of these three alternatives that came to pass. Pompey did not attempt to fight his way to supreme power across the body of his rival Crassus, but joined with him to overthrow the Senate. He had long seen that the Sullan constitution was too narrow and cramping for a man of his own ability and ambition. He was flattered by the almost universal applause which he had won by ending the lingering war in Spain; flattered all the more, perhaps, because it must be confessed that Perpenna's dagger had given him the final triumph almost as much as his own sword. He owed the Senate no gratitude; a great body of the enemies of the Optimates—the rural knights and municipal Italy in general—were ready to welcome him as their natural leader. Hence came his definitive acceptance of the place of leader of the anti-senatorial party, and his alliance with Crassus. Probably he was in the end unwise to make their cause his own; he was reopening the floodgates of Democracy, when a Democratic constitution was really more unsuited to him than the rule of an oligarchy. He was, in truth, by virtue of his orderly mind, his rather stolid virtue, his practical ability, uninspired by any spark of erratic genius, much more fitted to be the trusted general of the aristocracy than to be the leader of the turbulent mob of Rome. His reserved manners and his slow and uninspiring speech were enough in themselves to handicap him for the career of a Democratic politician. But since the Fathers, much as they feared him, showed no wish to enlist him as their champion, while their opponents were eagerly imploring him to become their chief, he finally made the plunge and stood for the consulship along with Crassus in the character of "the friend of the people."

How he and his colleague abolished the laws of Sulla, and how they quarrelled from the first day to the last of their joint magistracy, we have already told in another place. When their office ran out, both appear somewhat stranded on the shore of politics. The position of an extemporised party leader when he has carried out his programme is always uncomfortable. It is often forgotten that Pompey sat quiet for two whole years [B.C. 69-68] after laying down his consular fasces. If any further proof had been needed to convince his friends and his enemies that he aspired to be the first general of the Republic, but not its master, this voluntary retirement should have sufficed. A would-be tyrant would not have spent so long a time without meddling in politics. Pompey was seldom seen in the Forum, or indeed in any public place. When he did appear, it was always with a considerable train of friends and clients who kept off from him the attentions of the populace, "for he hated the familiarity of the many, and thought that true dignity is soiled by their touch." Instead of playing the demagogue and keeping himself perpetually in evidence, he lived quietly at home with his wife Mucia[1] and the three children that she had borne him. We need not say with Dr. Mommsen that he was playing at this time "the empty part of a pretender who had resigned his claims to a throne." Clearly he had never wished for that throne, and was contented to dwell in Rome as her greatest citizen, till a crisis should again arise which might call him once more into the field as her greatest general. In B.C. 69–68 no such crisis existed; the second Mithradatic war seemed to be going well in the capable hands of Lucullus, and there was no other trouble on hand which was important enough to call forth Pompey from his retirement.

In B.C. 67 things began to change. The exploits of Lucullus ended miserably in the revolt of his legions and the loss of all his conquests. The army of Triarius was cut to pieces at Ziela, and the light horsemen of Mithradates once more appeared on the border of the Roman provinces. At the same time a famine began to rage in Rome, caused partly by a bad season, but much more by the depredations of the pirates, who at this moment were playing a more prominent part than ever before in Mediterranean politics. Purporting to act as the allies of the King of Pontus, but really plundering for their own profit, they were making every sea unsafe, and even daring to make flying descents on Italy, where Spartacus had first invited their presence and made them welcome. Though their base of operations lay far to the east, in Crete and Cilicia, they were habitually to be found cruising off Spain and Narbonese Gaul. Since the incapable M. Antonius Creticus had failed in his attempt to put them

[1] She was his third wife. He had divorced Antistia in B.C. 80 and married Æmilia, the niece of Sulla. She died after only six months of wedlock. Pompey then married Mucia, daughter of Scævola, the consul of B.C. 95. By her he had three children, Sextus and Gnaeus. the generals in the Civil War, and a daughter, Pompeia, who married Faustus Sulla, son of the dictator.

down in B.C. 74, they had been practically left unmolested by the Roman state, and the boldness caused by this impunity was making them almost as daring as those Algerine rovers of the seventeenth century, whose voyages extended as far as Kinsale and Reikjavik. The Senate might yet have remained torpid, had it not been that the non-arrival of the African and Egyptian corn-fleets in a year of dearth drove the people to riots and outbreaks which could not be disregarded.

Something had to be done, but this something might have been nothing more than the appointment of one more aristocratic incapable to raise a fleet, if public opinion had not intervened. The moment that an expedition against the pirates was mooted, there was a general cry for Pompey, the one available commander whose efforts were always crowned with success. The Democratic leaders of the day, Quinctius, Gabinius, and the young C. Julius Cæsar, were quick to grasp the spirit of the times, and saw that an attack on the Senate for its maladministration must be accompanied by a proposal to place the charge of the Pirate war in the hands of the man whom the people trusted. Hence came the sudden and vehement agitation for the appointment of Pompey to a special command against the pirates, which took shape in the Gabinian Law of B.C. 67. He himself is said to have shown no great enthusiasm for the proposal, and to have required much pressure before he lent it his support. There is no reason to accuse him, as does Dr. Mommsen, of hypocrisy. He had no great knowledge of naval affairs, and may have doubted his own capacity to deal with a maritime problem. Moreover, the pirates must have seemed a despicable enemy to one who had contended with Sertorius. Nor is it to be forgotten that Gabinius and Cæsar were no friends of Pompey, and that they were both regarded as rather reckless and disreputable politicians. It may have displeased him to receive a boon from such hands, and to feel that his popularity was being exploited for the benefit of a pair of demagogues. It is at all events certain that he studiously kept out of the agitation, and even withdrew from Rome on the day when the Gabinian Law was put before the assembly. Evidently he wished to show that the command was unsolicited by him, and that if he accepted it he only did so in deference to the strongly expressed wish of the people.

The bill, indeed, was somewhat startling in its details. There had been previous grants of a special commission to various generals, and the imbecile Antonius had seven years before been given a command of this same sort against the pirates. But the Gabinian Law was on a much larger scale than anything of the kind that had been seen before. Pompey was to be given the *aequum imperium* over all Roman territory that lay within fifty miles of the sea—*i.e.* he was to possess equal power with all other provincial governors in their own spheres throughout the greater part of the empire. For there was not a province whose larger half was not situated within the prescribed distance from the shore: the Roman empire was still essentially a domination over the Mediterranean littoral, and the broad inland was for the most part still unconquered. To control such a wide-spreading field of action, Pompey was to be granted twenty-four lieutenants of senatorial rank, whom he might select for himself: each of them was to be given praetorian power and insignia. A magnificent grant of money, no less than 144,000,000 sesterces, or £1,350,000, was set aside for his military chest. He was authorised to raise men and ships up to any amount that he chose— as far as the enormous figures of 120,000 men and 500 galleys. As a matter of fact, he did not find it necessary to levy anything like so large a force. The term of his command was to be for no less than three years. For a man who wished to be king, all the essentials of a military monarchy were thus provided. But Pompey had no desire for throne or diadem, and this (we cannot doubt) was well known to shrewd observers of his character like Cæsar and Gabinius, or they would not have put the temptation in his way. It was not so obvious to the Optimates, who made as loud and frantic a protest as if a tyrant was being openly voted into the Capitol. They urged that the command was too extensive for one man, and that a colleague should be appointed to take some of the burden off the great general's shoulders. We are invited to believe that when Roscius Otho urged that Pompey should be given a colleague, the roar of "No!" was so loud that a bird flying above fell down stunned upon the heads of the citizens. Nor was it to any effect that the oligarchic tribune Trebellius was induced to interpose his veto. Gabinius scared him by threatening to deal with him as Tiberius Gracchus had dealt with Octavius sixty-six years before, and when he saw the tribes actually called upon to vote for his deposition, Trebellius collapsed and withdrew his proposed veto. As a last move the Optimates strove in vain to get Pompey given lieutenants nominated by the Senate instead of by himself—an ingenious way of seeing that his orders should not be too zealously carried out. The proposal was rejected with scorn.

The Gabinian Law, therefore, was passed, and Pompey received *carte blanche* to deal with the pirates as might seem best to him. It is easy to detract from the credit which he received for the very thorough way in which he executed his commission. His enemies have taken care to point out that the fighting power of the corsairs was insignificant compared with that of the Roman empire, and that they had only survived so long because they had hitherto been opposed by commanders of approved incapacity. "The suppression of the pirates was a great relief to the state, but not a great achievement," writes Dr. Mommsen; "it was a naïve proceeding to celebrate such a *razzia* as a victory." But this is not the true way to look at the campaign; a war is not easy merely because the enemy is not able to face the assailant in a pitched battle. To make an end of a swarm of guerillas is no light matter, and the guerilla at sea is even more hard to catch than the guerilla on land. Pompey's suppression of the corsairs was a triumph of organisation and ingenuity. He mapped out the Mediterranean into districts, and set moving at the same moment thirteen separate squadrons, which all worked together and played into each other's hands. In forty days the whole of the seas west of Sicily had been completely cleared, and corn was so cheap in the Roman market that it was said that the very name of Pompey had finished the war. Then the commander-in-chief went eastward with the best of his fleet, and swept the Ægean and Levant. There was no want of fighting: no less than 400 pirate ships, of which ninety were fully equipped wargalleys, were captured. Ten thousand of the corsairs were slain in battle; twice as many were captured. The fastnesses of the Cilician coast were one and all destroyed. Tens of thousands of prisoners were set free; immense quantities of plunder recaptured. The sea was freed from robbers as it had seldom been before since the beginning of authentic history. These are not achievements at which it is reasonable to scoff; but perhaps the most creditable item of the whole campaign is the fact that Pompey did not massacre his prisoners, but turned them into successful colonists in the maritime towns which he restored to life, Mallus, Adana, Dyme, and his new foundation of Pompeiopolis-Soli. No Roman commander before him had

done the like: even Cæsar in the succeeding decade used
the axe and the rods with cruel severity upon many a
conquered foe. He knew no mercy save for Romans and
citizens, while Pompey spared even the corsairs, whom
any other general would have doomed to the cross.

The Gabinian Law had allotted three years as the term
of office of the great High Commissioner; but no more than
seven months had elapsed when he was able to report
that his task was complete, and that piracy was suppressed throughout the Mediterranean. In the winter of
67–66 he was finishing up his work by restoring the Cilician
cities, and organising a system of coastguards to preserve
the peace of the seas for the future. There is no reason
to doubt that he intended to come home in the following
spring to surrender his command, according to his invariable fashion: but he was not yet destined to leave the
East. A bill was brought in by the tribune C. Manilius, to
transfer to him the charge of the war against Mithradates
and the care of all the provinces of the East. The genesis
and object of the Manilian Law is rather obscure: its
author was not one of the acknowledged heads of the
Democratic party, but a rather obscure personage, who
had just failed in some small political plans of his own,
and was apparently making a bid for renewed popularity
by devising a scheme which should please the multitude.
He was neither a friend nor a partisan of Pompey, and
certainly was not acting as his agent. But he saw that at
this moment Pompey's name was the one to conjure
with, and that a certain amount of importance would
accrue to himself if he could gain credit with the
people as the advocate of their idol. His proposal was
reasonable in itself: the war with the Pontic king had
proved a failure: Lucullus was in disgrace: Glabrio
and Marcius Rex, who were to take up the command,
had done nothing that made it probable that they would

succeed where their able predecessor had failed. On the other hand, there was a general belief that to make over the war to Pompey would secure its prompt and successful conclusion. So clear was this, that neither the leading Democrats nor the moderate Optimates dared to say a word against the project. Cicero, whose main aim at this moment was always to make himself the mouthpiece of public opinion, gave the bill his warm support. Cæsar also granted it his approval. Indeed no one save a handful of irreconcilable Conservatives ventured to oppose it, so popular was the scheme from the first moment that it was broached. It became law almost by acclamation, though there was hardly a prominent man in Rome who would really have supported it had he been free to speak his mind without fear of the multitude. Yet, as a mere measure of foreign policy, it was the best thing that could have been devised. There was no other man in Rome whose reputation would have justified him in asking for the Asiatic command. The one fortunate general of tried ability was the proper person to send against the Pontic king.

Pompey is reported to have received the news of the passing of the Manilian Law without any signs of elation, and to have replied to the congratulations of his friends by complaining that the state gave him no time of leisure, that he was hurried on from one task to another, and hardly was suffered to get a glimpse of his home, his wife and children. "It would be better to be one of the undistinguished many," he is said to have murmured, "than to be the one Roman who was never granted a holiday." Of course, his adversaries could see nothing but the most contemptible hypocrisy in such a speech. It is not necessary to think so badly of the man. That Pompey loved power, we cannot deny; he felt (like Lord Carteret) that it was his special avocation "to go about knocking the heads of kings and princes together for the benefit of his country." But it is equally certain that he loved his home, and after finishing off a heavy task like the suppression of the pirates, he might reasonably repine at being sent forth without a moment's respite to take in hand another, which might lead him to the Caucasus and the Caspian, perhaps even to the Tanais or the Erythræan Sea.

The Oriental campaigns of Pompey occupied him for very nearly five years (B.C. 66–62). It is as easy to belittle his achievements in the East as his achievements against the pirates; but to call his battles farces and his conquests military promenades is wholly unjust. The enemy who had baffled Lucullus was not to be despised; the wild tribes of Albania and Iberia were not "effeminate Orientals;" the marches through the bleak Armenian uplands and passes, or across the burning sands of the Arabian border were not simple or easy. Remembering all that Pompey did, and the apparent ease of his unending successes, the reader is prone to forget how Rome had failed before in these regions, and how she was destined to fail again. The army which he took with him was of no great strength—little greater, indeed, than that with which Sulla had conquered Greece: he never seems to have had more than 40,000 or 45,000 men. He was operating across utterly unknown country; each successive enemy whom he had to face had different methods of fighting; the devices that were useful against one were futile against another. Yet Pompey went on in an absolutely unchequered series of successes. He was as cautious as he was enterprising, as untiring as he was prudent. He never desisted from a task that he had taken in hand, but he never took in hand any task that was rash or unnecessary. When he first marched against Mithradates, the old king was in posses-

MITHRADATES EXPELLED FROM ASIA

sion of his whole kingdom, and had an army that he had at last trained to face the methods of Roman warfare by endless guerilla tactics. Within a year he was not only beaten, but expelled from his Pontic realm; his host had been not only scattered, but annihilated, by a sudden and brilliant night surprise, which formed the unexpected termination of a cautious and careful campaign. When Mithradates had thought that he had been facing Fabius, he suddenly found that he had to do with Hannibal. All that was left to him was to fly over-seas to his distant dependency in the Crimea. With Tigranes Pompey did not have to fight at all: he encouraged the Parthians to assault Armenia, while he was himself engaged with the Pontic king. When he turned towards Artaxata after expelling Mithradates, the Armenian monarch, vexed by foreign war and internal rebellion, refused to fight, did homage to Rome, paid a large war indemnity, and resigned all his claims to his late conquests in Syria and Cilicia. It does not detract in the least from Pompey's merit that this adversary was so much impressed by his mere approach, that he surrendered without a contest all that could have been asked from him after the most complete victory. Then came the turn of the wild tribes under Caucasus, who had been the vassals and the allies of Mithradates. In B.C. 65 the Roman army was pushed forward along the northern edge of Armenia, and scoured the valley of the Kur, and then by a backward sweep that of the Phasis. The Albanians and Iberians came out against the invaders in full force; they staked the fords and barricaded the passes, tried to cut off the convoys, and fell upon outlying detachments. But it was to no effect. On every occasion, and even on the most favourable ground, they were repulsed. At last they made their submission, surrendered to Pompey the golden table and bed of their king, disowned

Mithradates as overlord, and swore allegiance to Rome.

Asia Minor and the lands behind it were now disposed of. Mithradates, it is true, still held out in the Crimea; but though overflowing with wrath against the Romans, he was practically powerless. It was in vain that he crushed his few remaining subjects with taxes and requisitions to raise a new army. He enrolled, it is true, some thousands of slaves and Scythians, and spoke of trying the fortune of war once more. But there was nothing to be feared from his menaces, for his troops were untrustworthy. He spoke of a wild plan of marching by land from the Tauric Chersonese to Italy, across the steppes of the Dnieper and the valley of the Danube. But this was a vain imagining; his mercenaries would not listen to the plan, and the tribes of the steppe would neither have followed him nor allowed him to pass. He was eating out his heart in impotent wrath, slaying his sons and his generals for suspected treason, and earning the bloody end that was soon to come upon him.

The Pontic king having become a negligible quantity, Pompey was able to turn his attention southward to Cilicia[1] and Syria. These regions had been ceded to him by Tigranes, their last owner, but the king's rule had always been disputed by the late subjects of the Seleucidæ. When the last Armenian viceroy withdrew, anarchy set in; two princes, both claiming to represent the old Greek dynasty, half-a-dozen Arab emirs, a local tyrant or two, and the Jewish king from Jerusalem were filling the land with their futile strife. The Phœnician cities had declared themselves independent republics, and the tribes of Amanus were devastating every valley that was within reach of their fastnesses. Pompey saw no way out of the

---

[1] Eastern Cilicia and Tarsus had been in Tigranes' hands. Western Cilicia was already partly Roman.

POMPEY ANNEXES SYRIA

chaos but annexation to Rome. It would have been absurd to set up again some representative of the Seleucidæ, whose fratricidal civil wars had been the ruin of Syria in the previous generation.

Marching down from Asia Minor, the great general occupied Antioch and proclaimed the incorporation of Syria and Cilicia with the Roman empire. Almost everywhere the change was welcomed as a happy deliverance from anarchy. The cities and dynasts made their submission, and little fighting was needed. A mountain tribe or two had to be chastised, the Arabs were thrust back into their deserts, and a handful of fanatical Jewish patriots, who shut themselves up in the temple of Jerusalem, were beleaguered and annihilated. It was after storming this stronghold that Pompey made his entrance, sword in hand, into the Holy of Holies, and marvelled (as Josephus relates) at the strange sanctuary of the Jews, where a bare room without an image, and now even without an ark, was set aside for the earthly abode of the invisible God of Zion. The Roman proved a not ungenerous conqueror: but the rabbis of the next generation, and after them many a mediæval chronicler, loved to tell how he lost his good luck from the moment that he dared to draw aside the curtain and step across the fatal threshold. Hitherto all had gone well with him; from B.C. 63 onwards all was to be disillusion and disappointment.

It was while lying in his camp at Jericho, planning an expedition against the Nabatæan Arabs of Petra, that Pompey received the news that Mithradates was dead. The old king had tried too long the patience of his sons and his soldiers. Wearied of his wholesale executions and his wild plans for directing impossible expeditions against Italy, they had risen against him, and he had been forced to save himself from murder by committing suicide. His son and successor, Pharnaces, sent his embalmed body to Pompey, who, shocked at the unfilial act, ordered it to be laid in the family sepulchre of the kings of Pontus at Sinope.

The next year, B.C. 62, when all opposition in the East had been beaten down, was devoted to the delimitation and organisation of the new provinces which Pompey had added to the Empire—Syria, Cilicia, and Bithynia-Pontus. It is universally agreed that the settlement was carried out in a wise, generous, and statesmanlike way. Even Dr. Mommsen acknowledges that "though conducted primarily in the interest of Rome, secondarily in that of the provincials, it was comparatively commendable. The conversion of the chief states into provinces, the better regulation of the eastern frontier, the establishment of a single and a strong government, were full of blessings alike for the rulers and the ruled." The name of Pompey always remained popular in the East; fifteen years later, when he was engaged in his great civil war with Cæsar, he found the Asiatic provinces perfectly loyal, and drew from them his most important resources. His dealings alike with the petty princes and the Hellenized cities were wise and upright. But he set his mark most notably on the land by the great number of towns which he founded or restored. Almost without exception his new colonies proved successful; their sites were well chosen, their constitutions wisely framed; they grew and flourished. Indeed, to Pompey more than to any other single person must the first beginnings of civil life in many parts of Eastern Asia Minor be ascribed; before him towns in the Pontic inland and certain other districts were almost non-existent. Even the places in Cilicia peopled with reclaimed pirates did well. In short, he was in the East almost as great a founder and organiser as Cæsar in the West, though his work in this direction has been well-nigh forgotten.

POMPEY RETURNS TO ITALY

In the winter of 62 Pompey had at last completed his long and laborious task, and set out on his homeward way, bearing his enormous spoils, and with his victorious legions at his back. Of the stir and disquiet that his approach produced we have already written, while dealing with Crassus and Cato; but when the "New Sulla," as his disloyal critics chose to call him, landed at Brundisium, he showed no intention of marching on the city or starting a proscription; he behaved like a victorious general of the good old days, duly disbanded his soldiery, and came up to Rome unarmed, to receive, as he supposed, the thanks and the credit that were most certainly due to him.

It was an astonishing piece of civic virtue, if we consider the temptations to a man of ambition. If he had chosen to stretch forth his hand and ask for supreme power, it would undoubtedly have been within his grasp. The Democrats were cowed by the failure of the Catilinian conspiracy; the Optimates had no army to oppose to the victorious legions of the East. But the crown and the sceptre were not his desire. He had no notion of upsetting the Republic, in which he only desired to be the first citizen. It is absurd to say with Mommsen that "fortune never did more for any mortal than for Pompey, but on those who lack courage the gods lavish all things in vain." Is it the duty of every capable man to snatch at a tyranny? And why should Pompey be called a coward for refusing to subvert the immemorial constitution of Rome? He had no political schemes to work out, no great programme of reform to broach. All that he asked was to be the first servant of the state, the man to whom practical tasks of first-rate importance should be assigned in times of difficulty, and who in times of peace should live in dignity and quiet, enjoying the honours that he had earned. He demanded no more at present than the ratification of his arrangement in Asia, and a liberal provision of land or money for his faithful legions.

Expecting to find the people grateful for all his splendid successes in the East, Pompey came confidently before them to give an account of his doings of the last five years. To his surprise, he found that the Roman public was only half-informed as to his achievements, and rather disposed to be indifferent to them. "His first oration," says Cicero, "promised nothing to the poor; it gave no encouragement to the Democrats; to the wealthy it was unsympathetic; to the Optimates it seemed trivial." Instead of meeting with a brilliant reception, he was pestered with a hail of questions on domestic politics from the spokesmen of the rival parties in the state. Did he or did he not approve of the execution of the Catilinian conspirators? Was Cicero *pater patriæ* or guilty of judicial murder? Pompey was surprised and gave no certain sound: *itaque frigebat*, says Cicero—he was coldly received by every one.

The Senate, nevertheless, might have made him their good friend by a little courtesy and encouragement, for he disliked Crassus far more than any of the leaders of the Optimates, and he quite realised the way in which the Democratic party had been worked against him in his absence. Cicero hoped for a time to secure the alliance, but there were insuperable difficulties in the way. In the first place, the orator could not speak for his party or conclude any bargain in its behalf, for the short-sighted oligarchs, whose leader he imagined that he was, declined to follow him. When Lucullus and Cato declared that Pompey was not a safe ally, the majority of the senatorial party trusted them rather than Cicero. They adopted an attitude of covert hostility to the great general, and when the critical day came round, would not vote that his requests should be conceded. If anything more was needed to estrange Pompey from the Optimates it was the personal character of Cicero. The orator wished to be friendly with him; he loved to go about in his company and to hear him called in jest "Gnaeus Cicero;" but this was merely because it gratified his vanity to be able to treat as an equal the man to whom he had once looked up as a leader. The two were not really suited to be friends. Pompey was stolid and solid and wholly uninterested in literature or society; Cicero was a literary man to the finger tips, with all the self-consciousness and vanity of the "artistic temperament." It is certain that they bored each other, and that their friendship was a hollow and lukewarm affair.

Pompey might have continued to tolerate Cicero, if the latter had been able to carry out his share in the projected alliance—to induce the Optimate party to grant the ratification of the Asiatic treaties, and the provision of land and money for the disbanded veterans. But this Cicero proved utterly unable to do: meanwhile he irritated his would-be friend by his ludicrous vanity and his oratorical airs and graces. We have already seen, while dealing with the life of Crassus, how he succeeded in offending Pompey by his autolatrous harangues in the Senate, and his frank assumption of equality with his former chief.

As the year B.C. 60 wore on, Pompey came gradually to see that he would never get his very moderate demands conceded by the Senate. His disgust was complete when Cato, at the instigation of Lucullus, proposed, and carried, a motion to the effect that his Asiatic *acta* should not be ratified, but that the Senate should go through and criticise every treaty and edict that he had made, confirming or rejecting each as it might think proper. The proposal to provide land for the veterans was also taken into consideration, but it came to nothing, on the excuse that the treasury was empty, a manifest evasion, since the enormous Asiatic spoils had been very recently paid into the public chest. When Pompey set up his friend the tribune L. Flavius to propose a *plebiscitum* giving a competent grant of land to the soldiers, Democrats and Optimates combined against him, and the bill had to be dropped.

It is impossible not to regret the unwisdom of Cicero and the suspicious hostility of Cato, which frustrated the chance that Pompey might settle down once more into an honourable retirement. But his present position was unbearable. Because he had neither armed cohorts at his back, nor bands of hired rioters to sweep the streets he was impotent. He might still have got what he wanted by raising his hand and bidding his old legions reassemble: forty thousand angry and disappointed men would have rallied around him in a moment. But however much provoked, he shrank from open treason and from civil war. Before all things he was a good citizen, and now, as in B.C. 71, he made no unconstitutional move.

But when he received the offer of the Democratic chiefs to do for him what the Senate had refused, and to obtain for him complete legal satisfaction for his desires, he did not now hold back. Cæsar had shown his willingness for an alliance by supporting Metellus Nepos in B.C. 62; Crassus also now came forward with proffers of friendship though he had almost fled from before Pompey's face when first he returned to Italy, and though he had been doing his best to thwart him ever since. Seeing no other way out of his difficulties, the Conqueror of the East reluctantly accepted their advances, and the "First Triumvirate" came into being.

Once before, in B.C. 71, Pompey had leagued himself with his rival; then the alliance had been a passing phase in politics, and no permanent results had followed from it. But the "First Triumvirate" was a very different matter: it was the dominating fact of the next ten years, and marked a new stage in the decadence of the Roman Republic. The state had experienced before the tyrannical domination of a party, under Cinna and Sulla; but the triumvirs were not a party: it would be ridiculous to call their success a triumph of the Democratic faction. They were three men of very different character and aims, who had combined to secure their personal ends, and not to carry out any party programme.

Pompey received all that he had asked in the matter of grants and laws, and was, no doubt, satisfied for the moment; but it must very soon have been borne in upon him that he had now made himself a mere partner in a firm. The days when his personal influence could be exerted for any end that he chose were over: in all his doings he would have for the future to consult his partners. He was no longer responsible to himself only, but had to consider the wishes of Cæsar and Crassus.

Meanwhile there was no crisis either at home or abroad which seemed likely to provide work for Pompey. In such times of peace he had been wont to relapse into a dignified retirement till he should again be wanted. This was once more the line that he took in B.C. 59 forgetting that his whole position had now been altered by the fact that he had accepted a place in the triumvirate. It is a different thing to be a general taking holiday on furlough, and to be a sleeping partner in a great firm. The soldier, liable to be called back to the field at any moment, has no responsibilities save to his country, and may do much as he pleases; but the partner who does not take his share in everyday business, and prefers dignity and leisure to the incessant work of supervising details, gradually loses his controlling power. When he does, on occasion, sally forth from his retirement, he finds that he has got out of touch with the affairs of the firm. He may resent the situation, but he will find it difficult to reassert himself.

This is more or less what happened to Pompey during his long alliance with Cæsar and Crassus. No sooner had he seen the bills in which he was interested safely passed through the Comitia, than he withdrew for a space into private life. As one of the pledges of the alliance, he had married Julia, the young and charming daughter of Cæsar. He retired with her to his Alban villa, seldom came down into Rome, and took no important part in public business. Of his colleagues, Crassus seems to have relapsed once more into his obscure wire-pulling behind the scenes. Cæsar had gone off to Gaul, there to build up the army which was one day to make him the master of the world. There was no doubt that the triumvirs could, when they pleased, make their power felt, and do anything that they might choose: but for a space they did not assert themselves, and allowed the local politics of the streets and the Senate-house to drift on in their old fashion. The fact had yet to be realised that those who have taken responsibility upon themselves must interfere in small matters as well as in great, if they wish their power to be remembered and respected. While Pompey lived the life of the Aristotelian $\mu\epsilon\gamma\alpha\lambda\delta\psi\nu\chi o\varsigma$ and kept aloof from the dirty details of politics, while Crassus jobbed and intrigued, and Cæsar slew Germans and Helvetii in Eastern Gaul, the city was disturbed by all manner of unnecessary riots and tumults, the work of that irresponsible and absurd personage, the demagogue Clodius.

Since the downfall of the *Concordia Ordinum* and the triumph of the triumvirs, the Senate was wholly incapable of keeping order in the streets. On the other hand, the new triple alliance did not choose to undertake the task; indeed, there was no legal machinery by which they could have done so. So while the fortunes of the world were really being settled in Gaul, the city was at the mercy of the noisy young aristocrat who wished to be taken for the heir of the Gracchi and of Saturninus. Clodius was an accurate copy of Cæsar, so far as debts, debauchery, and a talent for mob-oratory could go; he called himself the last of the great Democratic tribunes, but he was really nothing more than an exuberant rowdy who loved rioting for rioting's sake. His only redeeming qualities were a sense of humour and a love of practical jokes. It is impossible to take him seriously; if we did, we should have to denounce him as the worst example of the decadent Roman. He was of no real political importance; his programme was a patchcloth of flimsy odds and ends from the rag-bag of the practically defunct Democratic party. Any one that had the command of half-a-dozen cohorts could have disposed of him in ten minutes: the days were past in which the city mob was a factor of serious importance in Roman politics. But as long as the triumvirs let him alone, he could do much as he pleased in the Forum, and he made himself an intolerable nuisance for seven long years.

The proper way to have dealt with this pestilent fellow would have been to borrow half a legion from Cæsar and clear him and his myrmidons out of the city. The Senate could not do this, and Pompey and Crassus would not. At first he had been their tool. When he set up in business for himself, they suffered him for a long time to deal with the Optimates as he chose. Pompey would not even intervene to save Cicero from banishment, in spite of all the orator's appeals. He considered that he had been badly treated by him in B.C. 60, and was not unwilling that he should have a lesson which would show him the vanity of his belief in his own political importance.

After no very long time of waiting the orator was avenged, for Clodius, intoxicated with his long series of successes in the Forum, took to treating Pompey himself with less respect than was his due. He began with releasing, contrary to the triumvir's wishes, the captive son of Tigranes, the Armenian king, who was being kept at Rome to prevent him from raising trouble in the East. Then he prosecuted some of Pompey's dependents, and when their patron came down to give evidence in their behalf, assailed him with ribald insults and set a carefully selected mob to hoot at him. Pompey's dignity was hurt. He had often been the object of hate and fear in his earlier years, but it was a new thing to be the butt of vulgar jokes—to be called in one breath the tyrant of Rome and "the man who scratches his head with one finger."

It may be hard to say what is the right course for a respectable politician of first-rate importance to take, when he has been mocked and flouted by a vulgar demagogue. It is clear, however, that Pompey's reply to Clodius was a hideous mistake. He summoned clients and pugilists about him, and replied by violence to the violence of the tribune. This was undignified, unwise, and unprofitable. It was honouring the rowdy overmuch to copy his methods. But the worst thing of all was that Pompey was not even successful. His bands were amateurs in rioting compared with the partisans of Clodius: they were several times out of the field, and he himself was beleaguered in his house.

This wretched interlude lasted throughout the later months of the tribunate of Clodius, and it was not till he had gone out of office that things righted themselves a little, and Pompey was able to reassert himself. In the next year he took his revenge on the demagogue, by assisting the leading Optimates to recall Cicero from exile, The orator had learnt his lesson, and no longer over-esti-

BUST OF POMPEY.
From the Museum at Naples.

mated his own power and authority. He never forgave Pompey for having allowed him to be expelled in B.C. 58. However, he was constrained to behave as if gratitude for his tardy return was his only sentiment. Shortly after reaching Rome he is found supporting an important proposal for the creation of a new special commission for Pompey's benefit.

Some five years had now passed since the great general had held any office, and he seems to have thought that it was high time that he should again come forward. Something must be done to make the Senate and People forget the ignominious contest with Clodius, in which he had cut such a poor figure. No war was raging at the moment, save indeed the Belgic campaign, in which Cæsar was winning new laurels; but if Pompey could not ask for military work, there was a tiresome administrative problem on hand, with which he thought himself competent to deal. The year B.C. 57 was a time of dearth and famine all over the Mediterranean lands, and even Rome itself was suffering from scarcity. There was no regular machinery in the constitution for dealing with such troubles, and in earlier years famines had been met by special decrees of the Senate appointing persons to buy corn. At a hint from Pompey, his friends (led by the tribune Messius) brought forward the proposal that a special commissionership should be assigned to him, empowering him not only to deal with the existing dearth, but to reorganise the corn-supply of Italy on a permanent basis. Remembering the times of plenty which had followed on his campaign against the pirates, the people eagerly took up the cry, even though Clodius tried to persuade them that the famine had been brought about by a deliberate "corner in wheat" got up by Pompey's friends. The accusation was a little too absurd to deceive even the denizens of the Suburra. In spite of the dema-

gogue's noisy opposition, and the secret intrigues of the
irreconcilable Optimates, a commission was granted to
Pompey, which gave him charge of the corn-supply for
five years, placed a large sum of money at his disposal,
and granted him proconsular authority, concurrent with
that of the governors, in the provinces. A very unnecessary addition, to the effect that he should also be
empowered to raise a war fleet and a land force, if he
found it necessary, was rejected. It does not seem that
Pompey himself asked for such a grant. It was probably
the invention of some of those over-zealous friends with
whom most statesmen are cursed.

The famine was daily growing worse, and the high
commissioner did not delay his departure. He announced
that he himself would visit Sicily, Africa, and Sardinia,
while his legates should deal with the remoter provinces.
He set sail in the midst of a fearful tempest early in
November B.C. 57. The captain of his vessel made much
ado as to starting, and asked him to wait for a few days
till the gale should have blown over. "It is necessary to
sail, it is not necessary to live," replied Pompey, and
put to sea in the face of the tempest.

In this commission, as in every other administrative
work that he took in hand, Pompey acquitted himself in
the most satisfactory way. His winter voyage to Sicily
and Africa turned out most prosperously. When he
sought for corn he found it: apparently the dearth had
been due as much to maladministration by the local
governors as to a real shortness of supply. He insisted
that, in spite of the season, ships should be sent out at
once to carry the grain that he had collected to Italy.
"In short, his success was answerable to his energy. He
covered the sea with vessels and filled the markets with
wheat, insomuch that there was soon an overplus in Rome
to feed the provinces, and plenty, as if from a fountain,

flowed over the world from the city." Nor was it only the needs of the moment that were provided for: Pompey made permanent arrangements for the improvement of the corn-supply, which worked perfectly well during the short remainder of the Republican *régime*.

While he was still absent in Sicily there was a complicated interlude at Rome. The worthless King of Egypt, Ptolemy Auletes, who had just been expelled from his realm by the Alexandrines, came to Italy to ask for help. There was considerable competition among the leading men at Rome for the commission to restore him to his throne, for such jobs were always profitable to the commander to whom they were intrusted. Lentulus Spinther and several others intrigued for the post, and while they were wrangling Pompey's friends proposed that he should be sent to Egypt as soon as his present task was completed. The Optimates hunted up a Sibylline oracle, to the effect that "the king must not be restored by an army." But when the news reached Pompey, he sent back a message that he was prepared to restore Ptolemy without asking for a single cohort: it would merely be a matter for negotiations. In accordance with this hint, the tribune Caninius brought forward a bill providing that Pompey should be sent to Alexandria with no more retinue than two lictors, in order to reconcile the king to his subjects. But the Optimates used all their influence against the proposal, employing the hypocritical plea that so valuable a life must not be risked among the turbulent Egyptians. The Caninian bill was rejected, and Ptolemy went back to the East; in the next year he got himself restored by a private bargain with Gabinius, the proconsul of Syria — a simpler if not a cheaper method than that of making a formal appeal to the Senate and People.

In spite of the fact that he had stopped the famine,

Pompey found that he was in a more unenviable position than ever when he returned to Rome. The Optimates, elated by the rejection of the Caninian bill, raised their heads and dared openly to oppose him: Clodius began once more to make him the mark of the foulest abuse and to raise mobs against him: Crassus, in spite of the fact that the alliance of B.C. 60 was still ostensibly in existence, intrigued against him, and even (so Pompey complained) became privy to a plot for his assassination. So helpless did he feel, that he resolved at last to appeal to Cæsar, the one man who was able, if he chose, both to make Clodius keep silence and to frighten the Optimates. This must have been a bitter humiliation to him; he had to confess that he had proved totally unable to manage domestic affairs, and to ask for the second time for his father-in-law's help. Cæsar was now a very different personage from the mere Democratic politician of B.C. 59. His Helvetian, German, and Belgic campaigns had raised him to the highest rank as a general, and he already had a numerous and devoted army at his back. Pompey must have felt that their relative importance was much changed since they had last met each other on the eve of Cæsar's departure for Gaul. Then he had been Rome's only general, and his colleague a clever demagogue with a doubtful past: now he was a notorious political failure and Cæsar the idol of the soldiery. But the Gallic wars were only half over, and it is probable that the elder man did not even yet realise his ally's full genius. It was to Cæsar, the manager of Rome's politics, not to Cæsar, the master of many legions, that he was appealing.

Pompey's visit to his father-in-law's province was made in the guise of a mere side-excursion. While purporting to be on his way to Corsica and Sardinia, to reorganise the corn-supply, he turned aside to Lucca, where Cæsar had fixed his quarters for the winter of B.C. 57-56. He was not the only visitor whom the proconsul of Gaul had received. Crassus had been with Cæsar at Ravenna a few weeks before, bent on the opposite design. He thought that he at last saw his opportunity for edging Pompey entirely out of his political position. If Cæsar refused him help, he would sink into insignificance, and become a mere negligible quantity. But it was not the intention of the conqueror of Gaul to break with either of his colleagues. He preferred that during his absence there should be a balance of power at Rome. It would not suit him that either Pompey or Crassus should be reduced to impotence; still less was it his game that the Optimates should be allowed to seize the reins of power. The more distracted were home politics, the more important would be his own position. Some day he would come back to Rome to work his will; and when that day should come, he would prefer to find the city masterless and ill-governed. Meanwhile, there was still much work to be done in Gaul; the province was but half subdued, and his own army was not as yet so large or so devoted to himself as he hoped to make it.

Hence it came to pass that the conference at Lucca ended in a way that must have been unexpected to many of the onlookers. Cæsar insisted that Pompey and Crassus should both remain his allies, and once more (as in B.C. 70) they went through a solemn farce of reconciliation, and professed to put away their old quarrels. The next step was to draw up the political programme for the ensuing year. Cæsar claimed nothing more for himself than the renewal of his proconsulship in Gaul for another five years, and the right to raise more legions. In return for this concession he undertook not only to get Pompey and Crassus made consuls for B.C. 55, but to allow each of them to take a province and an army when their year of consulship should have expired. Pompey was to receive Spain, Crassus Syria. These were astoundingly liberal terms! Cæsar seemed to be arming his colleagues against himself, and to be making them the present of a position which they could not have obtained by their own exertions. For it was he, and not they, who managed the whole business; he had but to give the signal and pull the wires, and immediately Clodius relapsed into silence, and the Optimates drew in their horns and stood still. It is not till we mark the consequences of the conference of Lucca that we realise how predominant was the position that Cæsar had already acquired. To his ancient power of intrigue and mob-management he now added the command of an ample provincial treasury and a large army. Absent though he was from Rome, he could secure that his desires should be carried out. If he now assigned provinces and legions to his confederates, it was because he knew their characters well, and did not fear them. They would always be at secret enmity with each other, and would practically cancel each other as factors in the political situation. Meanwhile they would, as he calculated, keep the Optimates quiet; each of them had suffered too much from the senatorial party to be willing to conclude an alliance with it.

In making this political forecast Cæsar committed an error. Pompey and Crassus duly received their consulships and provinces, and the Optimates were duly repressed. Cicero, as their representative, was forced to make that apology for his late attempts to kick against the triumvirs which he called his "recantation" [παλινῳδία]. So far things went well for Cæsar, but he had not allowed for two possibilities. The first was the death of Crassus, who lost his life and his army at Carrhae in B.C. 53. By his removal from the scene the counterweight which kept Pompey in check ceased to exist. The second factor in the new situation was the growth of an overmastering jealousy in Pompey's mind, which led him into paths where it had seemed unlikely that he would ever stray. The elder general did not want to be king or dictator of Rome; this he had proved half-a-dozen times already. But he was also entirely resolved that no one else should aspire to such a position, and month by month it grew more clear that Cæsar might do so. This Pompey was determined to prevent; he had given himself a colleague, but he did not intend that his colleague should become his master. Such was the secret at the bottom of that gradual estrangement between the two men which grew more and more evident as the years B.C. 53-50 rolled on. Both morally and legally Pompey's suspicions of Cæsar were entirely justifiable. But unfortunately he had placed himself under great obligations to his colleague; his conduct was bound to wear an invidious aspect when he began first to take measures of precaution against the man who had helped him out of his difficulties, and then openly to oppose him. Of this he was himself well aware; it was the main reason for his long hesitation and hanging back, before he finally declared himself the foe of his benefactor. When Cato, not long before hostilities commenced, taunted him with having allowed Cæsar to grow to his present greatness unopposed, Pompey replied that the man had been his friend and his father-in-law.

Those who, with Mommsen, attribute to Pompey nothing but the meanest impulses, call personal jealousy alone the cause of his breach with Cæsar. And that feeling was undoubtedly a powerful element among the mixed motives which swayed his mind; but there was something more: there was the honest political conviction that Rome did not want a despot. He himself, whose opportunities in the past had been so great, had not chosen to be king; why should another be allowed to snatch at the crown? The literary partisans of Cæsar justify their hero by replying that he turned out to be a heaven-sent saviour of society. But even granting that this is true, how could any Roman of B.C. 51 have known it? Cæsar was naturally judged by his dubious past, not by the glorious present in Gaul; his future no man could have foreseen.

It is clear, then, that the steady growth of Cæsar's fame, wealth, and political influence gradually frightened Pompey into precautionary measures, which could not be justified according to the strict letter of Roman constitutional law. After his consulship of B.C. 55 had expired, he ought to have raised the legions which had been granted to him and to have gone off to take up his province of Spain, just as Crassus had departed to take up his province of Syria. Instead of doing so, Pompey lingered behind in Rome, and only sent his legates, Afranius and Petreius, to Spain. Moreover, after mustering his legions, he despatched some to his province, but dismissed others on furlough, so that (though disembodied) they could be called out when he needed them. This practically amounted to keeping an army in Italy, a most unconstitutional step: it gave Pompey the power of overawing the Senate, but had obvious military disadvantages, for troops left long on furlough lose their efficiency and *esprit de corps*. That he did not really aim at absolute power is sufficiently shown by the fact that he never employed his army against the state; but what could be a worse precedent than to keep it in Italy? After committing such a breach of constitutional usage as retaining his Spanish proconsulship and his legions, while he still remained at home, Pompey could not plausibly complain of any acts of doubtful legality on Cæsar's part.

It is curious to find that even while Pompey and his

legions were looking on, Rome remained as turbulent as ever. The years B.C. 54–53 were the most anarchic time that had been seen since Catiline's day, and the perpetual riots and affrays stirred up by Clodius and his rival Milo made the city almost uninhabitable. The very consular elections could not be held in 54; so that in the early months of B.C. 53 the state had no existing supreme magistrate! It was not till the middle of the year that Domitius Calvinus and Valerius Messalla were elected and installed. Things only grew worse in the autumn: again the consular Comitia were broken up by violence, without any new magistrate having been elected. At the moment when Milo murdered Clodius, on January 18, B.C. 52, Rome was again destitute of consuls; and there was no one whose office it was to repress the fearful riots that followed, when the Senate-house was burnt, and the streets were for some days in the possession of an armed mob, which only failed to carry out a revolution because it lacked able leaders. Such phenomena hardly justified Pompey's policy of remaining in Italy. While he pretended to be the first man in the state, and had military force at his back, it was absurd that anarchy should be allowed to prevail in the city.

It is true that when the Senate at last made a definite appeal to him to act, and allowed him to be given the strange office of sole consul, Pompey promptly restored order. He mobilised many of his cohorts, brought them within the city, stopped the rioting, and caused both Milo, the slayer of Clodius, on the one side, and Plancus and Rufus—the leaders of the Democratic mob—on the other, to be tried and sent into exile. But if he was able to do this with such ease in the spring of B.C. 52, it is clear that he might have stopped the anarchy eighteen months before. A statesman who let matters drift so long before he intervened was not one fitted to

deal with the hopeless constitutional problems of the
degenerate Republic. But his honesty, at least, was
made more evident than ever, when, after the suppression
of the urban disorders, he took a colleague in the consulship, dismissed his troops, and finally dropped back
into his old position.

By this time it was practically certain that the open
breach between the two surviving triumvirs could not be
long delayed. Julia, the strongest bond between them—
for both loved her well—had died in B.C. 54. The last
act of undoubted friendship that ever linked them—the
loan of a legion by Pompey to Cæsar to repair the loss
of the cohorts which perished with Sabinus and Cotta—
took place in 53. After 52 the war might have broken
out at any moment; but Pompey, jealous and suspicious
as he felt, shrank from striking the first blow, while
Cæsar's hands were completely tied by the great revolt
in Gaul under Vercingetorix, which was not wholly
suppressed till the autumn of B.C. 51. By that time
Pompey's attitude could not be mistaken: he had given
his aid to the Optimates for the renewal of the celebrated
law which declared that all candidates for office must
come to Rome and sue in person—a direct challenge to
his colleague, who had let it be known that he intended
to stand for the consulship of B.C. 48, but did not intend
to leave Gaul till he had been safely elected. Such a
move seemed to show that the long-delayed rupture
between the two great men was at last about to take
place. Cæsar was determined to see exactly how matters stood, and wrote to demand an explanation. But
when he made formal complaints to Pompey as to his
hostile action, the latter, with inexplicable feeble-
ness, allowed a clause to be added to the law which
exempted Cæsar by name from its operation; but as
this supplement was never even submitted to the

THE OPEN BREACH WITH CÆSAR

Comitia, it was of more than doubtful legality. Either Pompey was trying to pacify his ally by a concession which could be afterwards denounced as invalid, or he was strangely ignorant of legislative technicalities. His personal character and reputation for honesty tell against the former supposition. We can but hope that jealousy and suspicion had not degraded him into unworthy double-dealing; but the general effect of the incident is dubious.

Into the miserable wrangle over the constitutional technicalities which filled the year B.C. 50 we need not inquire in detail. The legal pettifogging on both sides could not conceal the main facts. Cæsar was resolved to have the consulship for B.C. 48, and to rule as supreme magistrate at Rome for that year, and probably for many a year to follow. On the other hand, Cato and his friends were honestly convinced that the installation of Cæsar as consul would mean the establishment of monarchy—of a monarchy half military, half Democratic—which would probably be inaugurated with a proscription and a general confiscation of the property of the monarch's political opponents. What else could be expected from a tyrant who had conspired with Catiline, and who had employed and encouraged Clodius? Pompey may not have thought so badly of his late father-in-law; but he was as fully convinced as the Optimates themselves that Cæsar aimed at supreme power, and while he lived he did not intend to suffer a master to be placed over his head. He had not refused half-a-dozen times to make himself tyrant of Rome, in order that another man should be given the chance and should accept it.

The struggle was inevitable, and it was to no purpose that the weaker men in the Senate, who failed to grasp the meaning of the situation, continued to cry for peace and to pass idle votes calling on both Cæsar and Pompey to lay down their official positions and disband their armies. Cæsar would not disarm unless Pompey did the same: Pompey refused to do so, because he was fully convinced that if he had not an army at his back when Cæsar came home from Gaul, he would find himself helpless. He had at last realised the fact that he was utterly unable to control domestic politics, while Cæsar was an adept at managing a mob or raising a riot. If neither side were armed, it was certain that his rival would sweep the streets and get control of the Comitia. Even while absent in his province, Cæsar had been able to intervene with effect whenever he chose, and he had now enlisted as his political lieutenants all the promising young demagogues of Rome—all that gang of which Antony, Curio, Cælius, and Dolabella were the most prominent members. They were not a very reputable set of followers, but there was not one of them who could not have given Pompey lessons in the art of mob-management.

So Pompey, with the full approval of Cato and the Optimates, refused either to depart to Spain or to lay down his province and to disband his legions. This being so, Cæsar could do no more than search for the best technical *casus belli* on which to cross the Rubicon and march on Rome. His adversaries were obliging enough to provide him with a very fair plea of the kind that he wanted, by mishandling and expelling his satellites, the tribunes Antony and Cassius. It was with the fine old Democratic cry that the tribunicial authority, the palladium of the constitution, must at all costs be protected, that Cæsar launched his legions into Central Italy, much earlier than his enemies had expected him to take the decisive step.

The winter campaign of B.C. 49 is one of the best

CÆSAR CROSSES THE RUBICON

examples in history of the all-importance of time in war. Pompey's military merits were many, but rapidity was not one of them. He was a good organiser, a sure and steady leader, a capable strategist; but he was not one of those generals who fly from point to point with lightning speed, and win by swift marching as much as by hard fighting. Cæsar's sudden move across the Rubicon had caught him with his army still unmobilised. To those who had questioned him about his preparations he had replied that "he had but to stamp his foot in any part of Italy and legions would at once spring up." The boast was not unfounded, for his name had still the greatest influence with the military classes, and if he had been allowed a few weeks of preparation he would have taken the field at the head of an imposing force. But Cæsar knew the fact, and was determined that those few weeks should not be granted him. It was this knowledge that made him strike so early, and advance into Picenum with a mere vanguard, while the main body of his legions was still trailing through the Alpine passes. This sudden irruption disarranged all Pompey's plans; instead of being able to mobilise at leisure and to face the invader on the frontier, he was forced to abandon Rome in the first days of the war, and to order his recruits to collect far to the south in Apulia. He had no force actually under arms and capable of taking the field, save two legions at Capua, which could not lightly be trusted. For they had been under Cæsar's orders till the preceding year, and had been borrowed from him for the ostensible purpose of being sent to the Parthian war. If Pompey risked opposing them to their old leader, it was possible, or even probable, that they would desert to him *en masse*. They were not given the chance, but were marched off at once to the south, out of harm's way. The levies of Northern Italy were never raised by the Republicans—

Cæsar had been too quick for them. But those of the central regions ought to have been led in safety to the camp at Luceria, the great centre of mobilisation, if Pompey's orders had been properly carried out. If they had arrived, it might yet have been possible to maintain a hold on Southern Italy. But the plan of campaign was ruined by the strange mixture of presumption and cowardice displayed by L. Domitius Ahenobarbus, one of the many officers of tried Optimate principles and equally tried incapacity whom Pompey had been forced to put in high command. With 20,000 newly embodied men, not wholly armed nor even told off into legions, Domitius ventured to oppose himself to Cæsar, in spite of orders that bade him march for Luceria without risking the smallest skirmish. He was promptly surrounded, driven into Corfinium and blockaded. Seven days later the undisciplined horde of conscripts surrendered to Cæsar, when they saw that there was no relief at hand, and that their general was preparing to abscond by night and to leave them in the lurch.

Deprived of half the army which he had hoped to concentrate at Luceria, and left alone with two untrustworthy legions and the not over numerous levies of Apulia and Lucania, Pompey dared not fight. In spite of the complaints and criticisms of his Optimate allies—even Cicero dared to taunt him with want of military skill—he resolved to evacuate Italy and retire to Epirus, where, under cover of his fleet, he might drill and organise his recruits in safety. The whole army was shipped off from Brundisium, in spite of Cæsar's efforts to prevent its retreat. When pressed by his opponent, Pompey showed that his old reputation was not undeserved, by foiling the attack of the Gallic legions and bringing off his whole force without any appreciable loss.

It was now only the 17th of March, and the whole

campaigning season lay at the disposal of the two adversaries. But Pompey could not use it for active operations. He had to form his masses of conscripts into a fighting machine, and to wait for the distant reinforcements that could be raised in the East. There were two old legions in Syria—the wrecks of Crassus' host—and one other in Cilicia. More could undoubtedly be raised among the numerous Roman citizens residing in Greece and Asia, but it would take months to bring these distant resources into working order. Meanwhile Pompey could do nothing but order his fleet to blockade Italy, and to prevent the Cæsarians from taking ship to follow him across the Ionian Sea.

Cæsar, on the other hand, was in a very different position; his old army was entirely at his disposition, and he had already raised many new legions from Italy. Secure against any interruption from Pompey for many months, he could strike at the one region where the Republican party was really strong—Spain. In that province lay seven old legions devoted to Pompey, if not to the Senate; they were in charge of Afranius and Petreius, two commonplace veterans, willing and courageous enough, but destitute of any spark of military genius. Cæsar resolved to destroy this dangerous force in his rear, before paying any further attention to Pompey's disorganised host. "I march," he said, "to deal with the army that has no general; I shall then come back to deal with the general who has no army." He carried out his project; in a campaign of three short months he defeated, surrounded, and captured five of the Pompeian legions at Ilerda: the other two surrendered a few weeks later. Long ere the army of Epirus was ready to move, Cæsar was back again in Italy and planning out his second task, the destruction of Pompey's main body.

When Pompey and Cæsar were once face to face, we

note that the younger general found that his task was far harder than he had supposed. It was the best-contested campaign that he ever conducted; hazardous it was bound to be, since the Republicans were in very superior force, but Cæsar endeavoured to reduce the hazard to a minimum, and in especial made his troops entrench and stockade themselves in the most laborious fashion. He could have paid no greater compliment to his adversary's generalship, for he knew that man for man his soldiers were each worth two of Pompey's recruits. Pompey, on the other hand, was bound to show an even greater caution; if once his active and vigilant enemy could force a battle upon him on anything like equal ground, the result (in spite of their relative numbers) would be more than doubtful. It was his object to contain and check Cæsar rather than to endeavour to destroy him; his strategy had to be defensive, and for ultimate success he relied on his power to starve out his adversary by confining him to a narrow space of barren coastland and cutting off his supplies that came by sea. In all of this he was successful; Cæsar's attempts to bring on a battle were foiled; the war stood still for four months in the long lines which both parties had constructed outside Dyrrhachium. This delay was all in Pompey's favour, for he had far more reinforcements to expect and resources to draw upon than had his opponent. When Cæsar tried the desperate game of trying to cast a complete circumvallation round the Republican camp he was utterly foiled. Waiting till the line—some twenty miles long—grew over-thin, Pompey burst out one morning, broke through the entrenchments, drove off the legions opposed to him, and inflicted on the Cæsarians a loss which their leader himself confesses to have amounted to over 1000 men.

The prospects of the great adventurer looked dark: his food was giving out, his ranks were growing thin, even his hardy veterans were somewhat dashed in spirits by their first defeat. The prolongation of the present situation was impossible, and Cæsar tried his last move. It was skilful and daring, but hazardous in the extreme. Abandoning his lines, he marched off southward, and then struck inland, up the valley of the Aöus, across the Epirot mountains, as if he were meditating a blow at his opponent's base at Thessalonica. Pompey would probably have done well to have let Cæsar march whither he pleased, and to have thrown his whole army on to Italy. His fleet could have taken him over in a few days, and the Peninsula was practically undefended. There was nothing but a legion or two of recruits to defend the Cæsarian cause, and the country-side would probably have received the return of Pompey with enthusiasm.

But Pompey preferred to consider Cæsar and his army, not Rome, as his objective, and marched off inland in pursuit of the enemy. He came up with them at Pharsalus, and there at last risked battle. There was much to encourage him: his legions were improving in value every day; during the last combats round Dyrrhachium they had behaved admirably. He had nearly double his adversary's numbers, including a force of cavalry to which Cæsar had hardly anything to oppose. His officers were set on fighting: the Optimates thought that they had their enemy in a trap, and were only anxious to make an end of him. Their constant appeals, which grew into taunts and angry recriminations, finally drove their commander into risking the general engagement which he had so long avoided.

He was, as it turned out, misled when he yielded to the murmurs of his officers and the prayers of his legionaries. The great battle in the plain of Pharsalus turned out a complete disaster, not from any want of tactical skill in Pompey, but mainly from the inferior quality of his men.

He had determined to win by a desperate cavalry assault upon the enemy's flank. It failed, simply because the horsemen—mainly Asiatic auxiliaries—did not press the charge home, and allowed themselves to be beaten back by the band of indomitable veterans whom Cæsar had told off as his flank-guard. The cavalry rode off the field, and the flank of the Pompeian legions, who had so far held their ground with commendable steadiness, was left exposed to the enemy. Cæsar used his reserve to strike in upon the undefended point, and suddenly the hitherto unbroken line of the Republican infantry crumpled up, and the whole force rolled back in confusion into their camp, and then, after a short attempt to defend the *vallum*, retreated in utter disorder into the hills. The day was lost, the army scattered to the winds, and Pompey, broken-hearted at the sudden and disastrous end of his hitherto successful campaign, rode off the field, not following the main mass of the fugitives, but seeking the sea. "When he saw that he was not pursued, he went softly on, wrapped up in such thoughts as we may suppose a man to have who had been used for thirty-four years to conquer and to carry all before him, and now, on the verge of old age, first came to know what it was to be a vanquished fugitive. In one short hour he had lost the glory and power which had grown up among so many wars and conflicts; and he, who was lately guarded with so many armies and fleets, rode on with such a scanty train that the enemies who were in search of him passed over the little party without noticing them."[1]

At the mouth of the Peneius Pompey was taken up by a casual trading vessel; putting into Mytilene, he picked up his wife and some other Roman refugees. He collected a few ships in the Asiatic waters, and when his depression had passed away, began to think once more of reorganising

[1] Plutarch.

POMPEY MURDERED IN EGYPT

resistance in the East. For that purpose he sailed for the Nile, where he wished to prevail on the Egyptian government to lend him the considerable mercenary army—largely composed of Italians—of which it could dispose The boy-king, the son of Ptolemy Auletes, was only ten years old, and the control of the state was in the hands of a camarilla of obscure courtiers, the eunuch Pothinus, the rhetorician Theodotus of Chios, and the *condottiere* Achillas. The miserable Levantines were scared at the news of Pompey's approach; they did not for a moment think of lending him assistance, but at first they had no further purpose than that of getting rid as quickly as possible of their unwelcome guest. But a thought struck the rhetorician. "If we receive Pompey," he said, "we make Cæsar our enemy. If we reject Pompey, we earn his undying hatred: and it is quite possible that he and his cause may yet triumph in the end. But if we lure him ashore and kill him, we do Cæsar a favour, and have nothing to fear from Pompey. For," he added, with a smile, "dead men do not bite."

The argument seemed unanswerable to the Egyptian privy council, and the plan was carried out with complete, success. The great general was invited to land, and promised an audience with the young king. Achillas rowed out to his galley, taking with him Septimius and Salvius two centurions who had once served under Pompey in the East, but were now holding high rank in the Egyptian army. Reassured by the sight of these Roman faces, and by the smooth words of Achillas, Pompey descended into their barge and was rowed ashore. Just as he stepped on to the beach, the three traitors drew their swords and stabbed him from behind. He fell dead almost before he realised that he had been betrayed, and without uttering a single word.

So ended an honest man and an able general, the victim

partly of his own unwise persistence in trying to pose as a great statesman, partly of the incurable rottenness of decadent Rome. He should have been born two hundred years before, when the ancient Roman virtues still met their reward, and when it was possible to be the first soldier of the Republic without being also required to become an autocrat or a "saviour of society." Military greatness he had won with his sword; political importance was thrust upon him by the inevitable tendency of the times. He yielded, unhappily for himself, to the temptation of playing a part in politics, of overturning constitutions and dictating laws. Tyrant of Rome he never wished to be, yet he was led into doing many things tyrannical. All his life shows that he aspired to nothing more than the place of first citizen in the Republic. Yet he helped to make the Republic impossible, by setting precedents and examples of fatal encroachment on the free constitution. The Gabinian and Manilian Laws, and the sole consulship of B.C. 52, were landmarks in the history of the growth of the imperial idea. Pompey neither reigned nor wished to reign himself, but he did much to make monarchy possible for his rival and successor.

CHAPTER IX

CÆSAR

MANY and diverse have been the views taken of Cæsar and his career during the nineteen hundred and forty-six years that have elapsed since his death. He did much to shape the future destinies of the world, more perhaps than any other single man that has ever lived, and even in the darkest times of the Middle Ages his story was not forgotten. It may be said that when we have ascertained the way in which Cæsar was regarded in any particular century, we know at once the general character of that century's outlook on history. From the days of Charlemagne down to the Renaissance the Holy Roman Empire was the great political ideal of Christendom. Cæsar, as the founder of that empire, was regarded as a semi-divine figure; he lacked but Christianity to make him the patron saint of Europe. Certainly the nimbus would have sat upon his head with as good a grace as on that of Constantine, whose tardy baptism hid a multitude of sins and crimes from the eyes of the Middle Ages. But, pagan though he was, Cæsar commanded the unquestioning respect of thirty generations of Christians. The best proof, perhaps, of the aspect that he presented to the men of mediæval Europe is that Dante, in his vision of the midmost hell, where the worst of all sinners suffer the direst of all punishments, saw three figures only in the mouth of the arch-fiend—Judas Iscariot, Brutus, and Cassius. The traitors who murdered their master in the Senate-house found only one fit companion, the traitor who betrayed his Master in the Garden of Gethsemane. Astounding as such a view appears to us, we must recognise that it was entertained by the best minds of the Middle Ages. Dante was no ignorant chronicler, but a much-read man, a great political thinker, who looked out on a broad field of historical knowledge before he drew his conclusions.

Ere three centuries more had gone by, Brutus and Cæsar had changed places in popular estimation. The scholars of the Renaissance, with their Plato and their Plutarch before them, had reconstructed the old republican ideas of the elder world. To them Brutus was the "last of the Romans," the martyr of freedom, and Cæsar's murder was "tyrannicide," the righteous slaughter of the enemy of the state. Instead of being the revered founder of the sacred empire, the dictator had become the splendid criminal who made an end of laws and liberty. His greatness could not be impeached, but he served as the type of reckless ambition which strides through battle and ruin to a bloody grave. This was the Cæsar that Shakespeare knew; it needs but a glance through his tragedy to see that Brutus is the hero. Cæsar, in spite of all his genius and his magnanimity, is at bottom the man in love with power, who cannot be happy till he has added the sceptre and the crown to the imperator's purple robe. There is no hint that he desired to rule for others' benefit, to reform the world, to reconstitute an empire that was falling into hopeless rottenness.

Yet another four hundred years have gone by, and now a third reading of Cæsar's career is presented to us. We are told to recognise in him the great "saviour of society"; the man who saw that the Republic had gone too far on the way to decay to be capable of restoration, and who resolved to save the citizens in spite of themselves, even if it were necessary in the process to sweep away all the old constitutional landmarks and to introduce autocracy. Mommsen, the most extreme advocate of this school, goes so far as to praise in Cæsar the man who felt within his breast "true kingly greatness," and therefore rightly felt that he must make himself a king. The doctrine seems dangerous. Of a thousand able and pushing young men who fancy themselves the chosen instruments of fate, nine hundred and ninety-nine turn out to be of the type of Alcibiades or Clodius or Rienzi, and only the thousandth is a Cæsar. It does not seem wise to encourage the man of ability to regard laws and constitutions as trifles, which he may sweep away in the justifiable endeavour to assert his personality and live his life.

Every one must grant that the Roman Republic, with its absurd and antiquated state machinery, had gradually sunk into a hopeless slough, from which it seemed impossible that it could ever be dragged out. There was even less hope of salvation from the Democratic party than from the Optimates; both factions, their ideals and their programmes, were hopelessly played out. But in spite of all, we refuse our moral sympathy to the affable, versatile, unscrupulous man of genius who made an end of the old order of things. Cæsar had many aspects: as the manager of mobs and the puller of political wires—as the general—as the legislator—as the organiser of provinces, colonies, and municipalities—as the litterateur and the man of fashion, we know him well. But Cæsar the altruist is a fiction of the nineteenth century. To read into his many-sided activity the ideals of a benevolent prophet, who wished to restore the Golden Age, is absurd. Rather was he a brilliant opportunist, dealing sanely and practically in turn with each problem that came before him. Enlightened ambition and the love of doing work well, if it has to be done at all, explain his career. Of real unselfishness or idealism there is not a trace; if he ever denied himself anything that he desired, it was because he saw that the result of indulgence would be dangerous to his political schemes. His self-restraint was strong enough to enable him to refuse even the crown itself, the dearest object of all his wishes, when he saw that the move would be unpopular. But it was policy and not conscience that kept him back on this and on many another occasion.

To represent Cæsar, even in his later years, as a kind of saint and benefactor who had lived down his earlier foibles, is wholly untrue to the facts of his life. The man is consistent all through his career; the dictator of B.C. 45 was but the debauched young demagogue of B.C. 70 grown older, riper, and more wary. Those who represent him as a staid and divine figure replete with schemes for the benefit of humanity, need to be reminded that at the age of fifty-four, in the year of the victory of Pharsalus, he was ready to lapse into undignified amours with a clever and worthless little Egyptian princess. It is worse still that two years later, aged fifty-six, he could condescend to write and publish his "Anti-Cato." To pen a satire—and a poor satire at that—on an honest and worthy enemy, whose ashes were hardly yet cold, was worthy of a second-rate society journalist. The monarch of the world was at bottom the same man as the clever young scamp whose epigrams and adulteries had scandalised Rome thirty years back.

To understand Cæsar as a whole, we must look not merely at the wonderful military and administrative achievements of the last fifteen years of his life, but at the record of his chequered and turbulent political career from B.C. 70 to B.C. 58, when he was posing as the hereditary chief of the Democratic party, and winning his first start in political importance by his talent for self-advertisement and the management of mobs.

THE FAMILY OF THE JULII

The Julii were among the most ancient—by their own showing they were far the most ancient—of all the old patrician houses. There had been consuls of their name in the first century of the Republic, and when it grew fashionable to construct an elaborate family-tree going back to the days before Romulus, the Julii connected themselves with Æneas, asserting that Iulus was an *alias* of Ascanius, the eldest son of the Trojan hero. They worshipped as their family patroness Venus Genetrix—a circumstance which may either have been the cause or the result of their claim to descend from Æneas and his divine mother. Remembering that Virgil's Æneid was one of the remote consequences of the construction of this ambitious pedigree, we must be grateful to the domestic mythographer of the Julii. The name Cæsar crops up for the first time in the third century before Christ: from B.C. 208 onward there had been a long and not undistinguished succession of consuls and praetors in the house. None of them won a reputation of the first class, but many had been well-known figures in their day: we may especially note Caius Cæsar the orator, a contemporary of Sulla, and Lucius Cæsar, who gave his name to the famous law which enfranchised the Italians in B.C. 90. The greatest of the house did not descend from either of these men, but came from a younger branch. His father was by no means a notable personage, though he attained the praetorship: of his grandfather nothing is known but his name. The Julii had for the most part adhered to the Optimate faction, as befitted a family of such ancient descent; three of them had perished in the massacres of Cinna, but Caius, the father of the dictator, would seem not to have shared the family views: we find him living quietly under the Democratic *régime* of B.C. 87–84, and his sister Julia had been married to no less a person than Marius himself, a fact which may have gone far to determine her brother's politics.

The connection had, at any rate, a lasting influence on the career of Cæsar himself. His fierce old uncle-by-marriage took an interest in the lad, and caused him to be made *flamen dialis* in the year of the great massacre, although (having been born in B.C. 102) he was at that time only fifteen years of age. The flamen's cap came to him from the brows of the virtuous Cornelius Merula, one of the countless victims of Marius's reign of terror. It should surely have brought ill-luck to the boy; but Cæsar, till he came to the fatal Ides of March, was the child of fortune. He escaped in the evil day when Sulla came back from Greece in B.C. 83 to avenge the murdered Optimates. His youth saved him: he was but nineteen, and though he was the nephew of Marius and had married the daughter of Cinna, Sulla let him live. This was all the more astounding because the lad had refused to divorce his wife, a course which had been dictated to him as necessary to propitiate the conqueror. Indeed, Cæsar had to go into hiding for some time, till influential relatives begged him off. But we may probably dismiss as a fiction the tale that Sulla, while he spared him, muttered to his friends that "in this loose boy there were the makings of many Marii." The story bears on its face every mark of having been forged long after, when Cæsar had already grown to greatness. If Sulla had really supposed that the lad was dangerous, he was far too conscientious a party man to have spared him. All that Cæsar suffered at the hands of the Reaction was the loss of his priesthood, and that of his wife's large fortune;

---

[1] Merula was long remembered for his punctilious discharge of his duties of flamen. When forced to commit suicide, he carefully laid aside his official head-dress (apex) and wrote out a certificate that he had not defiled it with his blood

for the property of Cinna, like that of the other Democratic leaders, was forfeited to the treasury.

We know little of Cæsar's life for the next few years. He was still very young, and politics in the earlier days of the Sullan *régime* were dangerous. Indeed, he would seem to have left Rome in order to keep out of the dictator's notice. We find him serving in B.C. 80–79 under Minucius Thermus at the siege of Mytilene, where he gained distinction by saving the life of one of his comrades, and was rewarded by a civic crown. If Suetonius, ever greedy after scandals, is to be believed, he also won attention in Asia, in another and a less creditable way, by his licentious private life. When Sulla died, Cæsar returned to Rome; but it is noteworthy that he is not said to have taken any part in the agitation set on foot after the dictator's death by the heady and incapable Lepidus. The rising was fatal to all of the surviving Democrats who were rash enough to entrust their fate to such an imbecile leader; but Cæsar was not found among them.

We hear of him as taking his first steps in political life in the year after the fall of Lepidus, when he prosecuted the pro-consul Gnaeus Dolabella—one of the old Sullan gang—for maladministration in Macedonia. But the senatorial judges acquitted him, as they also did C. Antonius Hybrida, another and a more disreputable member of the same ring, when Cæsar impeached him in the following year. This notorious ruffian was destined to survive, and to take a prominent part thirteen years later, first as the associate and then as the betrayer of Catiline. It was a good advertisement for a young man of decidedly Democratic antecedents to be able to accuse such persons, even if he could not get them convicted. In B.C. 77–76 the Optimates were still so much in the ascendant that it was something even to dare to attack them.

After the trial of Antonius, his young accuser went off again to the East. It is said that he had not been satisfied with his own speeches, and that he was determined, before resuming his political career, to learn all the tricks of the orator's trade. With this object he sailed for Rhodes, where he intended to study under the celebrated rhetorician Apollonius Molon, who had also been one of the instructors of Cicero. But these years were the golden age of piracy in the Levant, and as Cæsar sailed by the island of Pharmacusa, off the Ionian coast, his galley was captured by a Cilician corsair. The whole tale of his captivity, as told by Plutarch and Suetonius, is too full of characteristic traits of the young man to be omitted. The pirates, who were business-like persons, bent on ransom and not on massacre, took stock of their prisoner, and rated him at twenty talents—about £5000 of our money. Cæsar professed to be deeply hurt at being valued at such a small sum, and said that he was well worth fifty talents. This was a kind of captive to whom the Cilicians were unaccustomed; they eagerly accepted him at his own valuation, and let his companions and freedmen depart to Miletus to raise the money. Cæsar remained alone at their headquarters, accompanied only by his physician and two valets. "He lived among the pirates for thirty-eight days," says Plutarch, "treating them as if they had been his bodyguard instead of his gaolers. He used to send out, whenever he wished to take his *siesta*, and order them to keep quiet. Fearless and secure, he joined in their diversions, and took his exercise among them. He wrote poems and orations, and rehearsed them to the gang, and when they expressed too little admiration, he called them blockheads and barbarians." He would often tell them, in a jesting manner, that when he should be liberated, he intended to come back and crucify them all, a threat which they took as a piece of playful humour on the part of this affable young gentleman. But he was speaking in perfect candour. The moment that the fifty talents of ransom money had been paid, he hired a few galleys at Miletus and ran out to look for his late captors. He found them still at Pharmacusa, celebrating their stroke of luck by a great carouse. He surprised them, captured the whole gang, and recovered his money intact. He then took them to Pergamus, to hand them over for execution to Junius, the governor of Asia. But learning that the worthy magistrate had an itching palm, and would probably let off the Cilicians for a bribe, he proceeded to put them to death on his own responsibility. He crucified the whole of the late audience of his poems and orations, after having first, as a special favour, cut their throats before he affixed them to the cross.

Cæsar then resumed his interrupted voyage to Rhodes, and studied rhetoric with Apollonius for some months. His stay in the island was brought to an end by the news that one of the generals of Mithradates had invaded proconsular Asia. He sailed to the mainland, raised some levies at his own expense, and soon expelled from the province the raiding cavalry of the Pontic king (B.C. 74). At this moment he received letters from Italy informing him that he had been elected a *pontifex*, in the place of his deceased uncle, C. Aurelius Cotta. He returned at once to Rome to take up this not unimportant religious office; how such a comparatively unknown young man came to be elected to it, and that too in his absence, our authorities do not tell us.

From his return to Rome (B.C. 73) down to the time of his praetorship in B.C. 62, Cæsar was gradually working himself up from a position of comparative insignificance to that of the managing director of the Democratic party. How popularity with the urban multitude was achieved in the last days of the Roman Republic we know only too well. The days were long past when the favour of the citizens could be won by fluent oratory and noble sentiments alone. The would-be demagogue had not only to tickle the ear of the sovereign people with his harangues; he had to be continually slipping bribes into its eager palm, and filling its insatiable belly with doles and distributions of corn. The age of Tiberius Gracchus was long past; Saturninus and Sulpicius were the heroes and martyrs whom the Democratic party regretted. Clodius was looming in the not far distant future.

Dazzled by the magnificent career of Cæsar in his middle age, many writers have striven to represent him as an enlightened statesman and a true lover of Rome (even of the world at large!) in his youth. It is difficult to support any such theory from the facts of his early years of political activity. It must be confessed that he appears as a demagogue of the usual type. If he had died in B.C. 62, he would be dimly remembered in history as a second Glaucia, whose wit was less vulgar than that of his model, as the legitimate successor of Sulpicius and the natural predecessor of Clodius. He fought with the common weapons and with the usual methods of other popular leaders of his day. We perpetually hear of him as organising and leading down to the Forum or the Campus Martius gangs of armed rabble. He broke up assemblies, or overawed them with the stones and bludgeons of his satellites. He swept the streets, and fought on equal terms with the hired bands of the Optimates. He was the ally and assistant of Gabinius and Manilius in all their turbulent proceedings in 67 and B.C. 66; it was his gangs which supported the stupid Metellus Nepos in B.C. 62, and bruised and battered the bellicose Cato. Worst of all, he was more than suspected of having been deeply engaged in the Catilinarian conspiracy, at least in its earlier stages. Not one, but many authors tell us that in the plot of B.C. 66 Cæsar and Catiline had joined their hands for the *coup d'état* which was to make Crassus Dictator and Cæsar his Master of the Horse. Why the outbreak never took place is explained to us in half-a-dozen different versions, one of which says that it was Cæsar, not Catiline, who failed at the critical moment to give the signal for the rioting to commence. Whatever may have been the exact truth at the bottom of the many floating rumours which have survived, it is certain that, rightly or wrongly, Cæsar was regarded as having been even more deeply implicated than Crassus in the obscure plots of B.C. 66–63. We may guess that he ceased to be an active mover in them only when he discovered the full scope of Catiline's designs, and realised that he was too reckless and violent to make a safe coadjutor. Those modern writers who urge that it is improbable that the two men could ever have acted in concert, use as their main arguments two very weak pleas. The first is that Cæsar was too magnanimous and patriotic to have joined in a conspiracy which involved treason and massacre. The second is that Catiline was such a notorious criminal and ruffian, that no sensible man, with a career before him, would have compromised himself by taking such a partner. But the first argument is wanting in historical perspective. Cæsar, the demagogue of B.C. 66, was a very different person from Cæsar the dictator of B.C. 48. We must not argue back from his last stage to his first; an ambitious young man, with his way to make in the world, may well have contemplated things which would not have commended themselves to the statesman who, twenty years later, had fought his way to supreme power. The second argument—that Catiline was frankly impossible as a colleague—falls to the ground before the fact that the respectable Cicero was in B.C. 64 only too eager to secure him as a friend and ally. What Cicero desired may well have commended itself to the more adventurous Cæsar. Evidence as to good or bad character is as useless in the one case as in the other. Cæsar, as a popular demagogue, must have rubbed elbows with so many strange people between B.C. 73 and 60, that we shall not easily believe that he drew the line above Catiline's name.

Indeed, it would be useless to pretend that Cæsar paid any particular attention during his early years to the reputation of his associates, or indeed to his own. His way of life did not resemble that of the blameless Tiberius Gracchus or the priggish Livius Drusus. He had rather borrowed his manners and morals from Sulla. He was anything rather than an austere fanatic or a model of all the virtues. Romans of the old school detested him for his absurd fastidiousness in dress; the long fringes of his toga, the breadth of his purple stripe, and the peculiar loose style in which he girt himself displeased them. They sneered at his exquisite care over his toilet; his barber not only shaved him, but finished him off with tongs and tweezers. When an early baldness came upon him, every art of the hairdresser was employed to hide the growing deformity. Cicero once observed that it had been long before he had taken seriously, or dreaded as an enemy of the state, the man who could spend so much time and thought over his personal appearance. In his latter days, it was remarked, nothing pleased him so much, of all the honours which were heaped upon him, as the grant of the laurel crown, which served to hide the disappearance of his once abundant locks. But Cæsar was much more than an exquisite. It is doubtful whether his recklessness in money affairs or his promiscuous amours were the more displeasing to those of his contemporaries who still loved the old Roman virtues. Of all the rakes of Rome, he was by far the most notorious. His admirers who plead that "his life was perhaps lax according to our notions, but within the bounds set up by the age in which he lived," are grossly understating his reputation. He was, so to speak, the inevitable co-respondent in every fashionable divorce; no household was sacred to him; the elder Curio called him in one of his orations, "omnium mulierum virum." When we look at the list of the ladies whose names are linked with his in the pages of Suetonius, we can only wonder at the state of society in Rome which permitted him to survive unscathed to middle age. The marvel is that he did not end in some dark corner, with a dagger between his ribs, long before he attained the age of thirty. The Romans did not fight duels, but they understood the use of the assassin for the righting of domestic scandals. It is strange that none of the injured husbands named by our historians took advantage of the fact that bravos were to be hired on moderate terms in every court of the Suburra. But Cæsar lived on, and his reputation seems to have been a source of peculiar pride to his satellites. When he entered Rome in triumph, his veterans sang behind him a lewd song with the burden—

"Urbani, servate uxores ! Calvum moechum adducimus !"

These were certainly odd beginnings for a saviour of society. Unfortunately the end was even as the commencement; there were scandals in Gaul, and even Cleopatra had a successor in the last years of the old dictator's life—Eunoe, the wife of Bogud the Moor. It is grotesque to have to remember that in spite of his own career he was the author of the famous dictum that "Cæsar's wife must be above suspicion."

If there was any other point of Cæsar's character even more strongly marked than his licentiousness, it was his power of getting through money—especially other people's money. There was only one thing in which he was economical, his eating and drinking, for he was free from the very common Roman vice of gluttony.[1] But on everything else his expenditure was reckless. He did not, like Crassus, merely spend money on politics with the definite aim of getting on in the world. Much of his waste was on mere personal luxury; furniture, plate, gems, jewellery, pictures, slaves of distinguished appearance or accomplishments, he never could resist. He once (but this was in his later days) gave a lady friend a pearl which he had bought for 6,000,000 sesterces—£60,000 of our money. As an example of his recklessness, we are told that long before he had got to the front in politics, and while he was still overwhelmed with debts, he built himself a villa at Aricia at great cost. When it was finished, he found that there was something about its architecture that he did not like, and had it pulled down to the very foundation stone.

But it was, after all, on politics that Cæsar threw away the greater part of his money. He had worked through all his private fortune before he had reached the age of twenty-four. When he entered on his quaestorship he was already 1300 talents in debt, and it was not till more than ten years after that he was in a position to begin to pay off what he owed. By that time he had exhausted other lenders, and was depending on the inexhaustible purse of Crassus alone. The millionaire had picked him out from among all the other young demagogues of Rome, and had been so much struck with his ready ability and boundless self-confidence, that he was prepared, in return for political services, to finance him to any extent. The

---

[1] Cato, as Suetonius tells us, remarked that "he was the only one of the enemies of the constitution who came sober to the work of destruction." Fulvius Flaccus, Marius, Saturninus, Sulla, Catiline, had all loved the cup over well.

greater part of the money which Cæsar ran through was lavished on the most useless and extravagant bribes to the multitude. He was determined to surpass all who had ever lived before him in self-advertisement. When he held the aedileship, three hundred and twenty pairs of gladiators died for the amusement of the mob. He spent countless sums in theatrical exhibitions, processions, and entertainments of the public at free dinners, which cast into the shade even Crassus's great open-air banquets of B.C. 70. The more useless and extravagant was his outlay, the better the urban multitude was pleased. After this, one begins to understand the freaks of Caligula and other descendants of the Cæsarian family. But the wild extravagance caught the popular eye, and was much more admired than the magnificent porticos which he built to the Capitol, or the great *Basilica Julia* which he erected for the improvement of the sittings of the law courts.

The art of self-advertisement, in short, Cæsar possessed to the highest degree. Even when he had the misfortune to lose near relatives, their funerals served him as a means for providing the people with a splendid show. When his aged aunt Julia, the widow of Marius, died, he took the opportunity of startling the assembled multitude by parading before them the long forbidden effigy of the old lady's deceased husband, to the joy of all Democrats. A fragment of Cæsar's funeral oration over Julia has been preserved by Suetonius; it is very characteristic, as showing that the affectionate nephew knew how to speak one word for his respected aunt and two for himself. " On the mother's side," he said, " Julia descended from the ancient kings, on the father's from the immortal gods themselves. For her mother and my grandmother, Marcia, descended from Ancus Marcius, the fourth king of Rome; while we of the Julian house trace back our origin to Venus herself.

In our family, therefore, we combine the divine right of kings, who are the greatest among men, and the worship of the gods, to whose power even kings must bow." What could be more flattering to the sovereign people than to see a gentleman of such illustrious descent courting their approval? The mob, it is said, "loves a lord." How much more must it love a suitor who was, as he carefully pointed out to them, not merely of noble, but of divine descent! Another funeral oration of this same sort was made by Cæsar over his second wife, Cornelia. In earlier days, we are told, only ancient matrons were honoured with a public funeral and a laudation from the rostra. He first broke through the custom, by celebrating the show for a spouse who had not yet passed her prime. "This contributed," says Plutarch, "to fix him in the affections of the people, who sympathised with him, and considered him as a man of feeling, and one who had his social duties at heart." They must have been disappointed when he divorced instead of burying his third wife, Pompeia, after the scandal concerning the mysteries of the *Bona Dea*.

Cæsar, then, was, from his earliest entrance into politics, working for the definite end of achieving greatness, but what sort of greatness he can hardly himself have realised. Certainly we may be excused from holding, with Mommsen, that he had recognised within his breast the promptings of a kingly heart, and was determined to be a king. That development belongs to a much later date. Yet there can be no doubt that his aim was always to get to the front. Every one knows how he wept when he looked upon the statue of Alexander the Great, and muttered that the Macedonian had conquered the whole East before reaching the age at which he himself had merely obtained the quaestorship. It was a few years later that passing, on his journey to Spain, through a miserable village in

CÆSAR AS DEMAGOGUE

the Alps, he exclaimed to his travelling companions that he would rather be the first man there than the second man in Rome.

But it seems clear that Cæsar in his early days was set on reaching political greatness rather by the dusty and dirty path through the Forum, than by the road through the battlefield, by which he was ultimately destined to come to the front. He was determined to be the first man in Rome, but till he discovered, late in life, that he chanced to be a military genius, he intended to rise by the aid of the reeking multitude of the Suburra. The Democratic party had hitherto been led by a dynasty of failures; he would provide it with a chief who had none of the weak points of his predecessors: he would be a Gracchus who should be neither austere nor impracticable; a Drusus destitute of priggishness; a Glaucia whose jokes should always be in good taste; a Saturninus whose riots should always be interesting, so as not to end in boring the public opinion of the streets by mere commonplace repetitions of club-law and arson. All this he became: yet he felt, when he had achieved this particular form of greatness, that there was still something wanting. It was unsatisfactory to remember that all his largesses had to come out of the pocket of Crassus, and that he might at any moment be given some dirty job by the stolid millionaire and be unable to refuse it. Still more tiresome must it have been to realise, as Cæsar did realise without a doubt, that an end might be put to all his games on the day when Pompey should be provoked to throw his sword into the balance. None knew better the powerlessness of a mob against an army; one of the most striking recollections of his boyhood must have been that of the bloody day when Sulla's legions cleared the gangs of Sulpicius Rufus out of the streets, and came, first of all

Roman soldiers, armed and triumphant to the Forum and the Capitol. There must have been a moment, its date we cannot dare to fix, when Cæsar finally came to the conclusion that the domination which he had achieved in the streets would avail him nothing if ever swords were drawn. When once he had realised the fact, his mind must have been turned to the only possible alternative. Had he within himself the makings of a great general? That he had a soldier's courage and readiness he had proved at Mytilene in B.C. 79, and in Asia in B.C. 74. That he could assert a personal ascendency over his followers he knew well, from his experiences during ten years of mob-management. But a man may be a good fighter and an inspiring leader, and yet lack the main qualities of generalship. Cæsar, like other young Romans of his class, had undoubtedly studied the theory of the art of war from the popular Greek manuals then in vogue. But so had many an incapable Optimate who had disgraced himself on the battlefield: it yet remained to be seen whether he possessed real military ability. This could only be learnt by making the experiment. The first occasion on which Cæsar had the opportunity of trying his hand at the game of war upon a considerable scale was when he went to Spain as propraetor in B.C. 61. This governorship was the turning-point in his whole career: his contemporaries supposed that it was important to him merely because it gave him the chance of paying off the enormous debts which hung round his neck like a mill-stone, and had made him the tool of Crassus. This no doubt had some weight in Cæsar's eyes: it is certain that by some wonderful *tour de force* he wrung vast sums out of Spain without earning a specially bad name for rapacity. But a Roman governor of those days had to emulate the exploits of Verres and Antonius if he wished to shock the public opinion of his contemporaries. There can be no doubt that Cæsar must have shorn the Spaniards close, to raise the money that paid off his debts; but, probably (as the Irish wit wrote of Lord Carteret), "he had a more genteel manner of binding their chains than most of his predecessors." A considerable part of the sum, too, was secured by the selling as slaves of his numerous prisoners of war, an obvious method of money-making on which the successful commander could always rely.

But the financial importance of Cæsar's Spanish governorship was nothing in comparison with its military importance. For the first time he found himself at the head of a considerable army—he took over two legions and raised a third—and able to deal with it as he pleased. Nor were enemies wanting; never, since the Spanish provinces had been formed, had border warfare ceased on their north-western frontiers. The Galæci and Cantabrians still maintained their freedom in their hills, and many of the northern Lusitanians were practically independent, though nominally included within the borders of the empire. Even if Cæsar had not been wishing to try his fortune as a soldier, he would have been compelled to chastise these fierce hillmen for their perpetual raids into the more settled districts. But he was only too eager to discover his own possibilities in the military sphere. He carried out a long and difficult campaign in the valleys of the Lower Douro, the Mondego, and the Minho with complete success, showing an untiring watchfulness and a wary skill that must have surprised his soldiery, who knew him only as the hero of the Roman streets. It must have been in this Galician and Lusitanian campaign of B.C. 61 that Cæsar came to know himself, and to recognise that he was capable of the highest things in the field. It must have been a stirring moment, for it changed the whole of the outlook of his life. He need no longer make it his loftiest aim to be the king of the Suburra and the hero and model of the young rakes of Rome. He might now aspire to beat Pompey on his own lines. If he could obtain a great military province and raise a large army, he might hope to achieve a more splendid reputation than that of the conqueror of the Pirates and of Mithradates. There would be no need to shed futile tears again before the statue of Alexander the Great; he might, after all, make up for the years lost in demagogy and in evil living. At forty-one years of age it is still not too late to start on the soldier's trade, though there is hardly another case in history, save Oliver Cromwell, of a general who discovered his avocation when so far advanced in middle life. Endowed with a splendid physique, which had not been ruined even by the twenty ill-spent years of his Roman career, Cæsar was still wiry, alert, and untiring. Probably the one virtue of his youth, his contempt for the delights of the cup and the platter, now stood him in good stead. He could march and starve with the sturdiest of his own legionaries. There seemed to be no danger that his body would fail him, and his mind was at its best. The readiness and ingenuity which he had always displayed in the tactics of the Forum were easily transferred to the tactics of the field. The power of inspiring confidence, which had enabled him to discipline even the demoralised city mob, served him still better with the simple soldiery. Indeed it must have been a comparatively easy task to manage the conscripts of the Spanish or the Cisalpine province after managing the unruly and untrustworthy denizens of the Roman slums.

We cannot doubt that Cæsar returned to Rome in B.C. 60 with one desire before his eyes, that of obtaining first the consulate, and then, as proconsul, a military province of the first class—the Gauls for choice, since there he would both remain comparatively near to Italy, and also have a splendid field for operations and a great recruiting ground. It was fortunate for him that the change in his outlook on life, which had resulted from his Spanish campaign, was not apparent to his contemporaries. To Pompey and Crassus, no less than to Cicero and Cato, he was still the rakish demagogue of the past twenty years. Had Crassus guessed that his late debtor, the manager for many a day of his hirelings, was aspiring to climb to greatness over the pile of his money-bags—had Pompey known that the man who offered to deliver him from the insults of the Senate, was intending to supersede him in the position of Rome's greatest general, there would have been no First Triumvirate. But the change in Cæsar's character and designs was hidden from them: they allied themselves, as they supposed, with a mob-manager of genius, who undertook to clear the streets for them and to work the machinery of the Comitia. There was little in Cæsar's conduct in B.C. 60–59 to make them suspect that they were giving themselves a master, when they acquiesced in the bargain. He was to secure them what they desired, and they, in return, were to concede to him the consulship and the Gallic Provinces.

The combination of Cæsar's management and Crassus's money carried all before it, and the consulate was duly secured to the Democratic candidate. In older days it would have been a serious drawback that he failed to carry the election of L. Lucceius, the obscure person who ran with him, and that he was saddled with Bibulus, the most obstinate of Optimates, as his colleague. But in Cæsar's year of office it did not matter much whether he had a colleague or not. His consulship was a sort of carnival of illegality and mob law, which made a fitting close to the whole of his demagogic career. He violated every rule of the constitution with a cheerful nonchalance that surprised even his own lieutenants. He openly displayed armed men in the Comitia; he not only drove away the partisans of the Senatorial party by force—that was now the ordinary rule in domestic politics—but arrested and hurried off in custody every one who dared to speak against his proposals—even the respectable Cato himself. His crowning act of illegality took place at the passing of his Agrarian Law; when Bibulus put up three tribunes to veto it, Cæsar quietly disregarded them, and proceeded with his business. The Optimate consul sprang to his feet, and began declaiming to the people that the whole proceedings were null and void, and that his colleague was violating the most fundamental laws of the constitution. Cæsar had him seized by his lictors, bundled him off the rostra, and told the attendants to see that no harm happened to him, and to turn him loose in some quiet street. Cato and the three dissentient tribunes were treated in the same unceremonious fashion. Then Cæsar bade the proceedings go on, and passed his law! If ever *majestas*, the open and deliberate commission of high treason, took place at Rome, this was the occasion. A magistrate had disregarded the veto of his own colleague and of three tribunes, and had finally laid violent hands on their sacrosanct persons and expelled them from the Assembly. The Optimates wondered that the sky did not fall then and there. But nothing happened, and Cæsar declared his bill to be law, and carried out its provisions. Bibulus formally summoned the Senate next day, narrated the indignities that he had suffered, and called upon the Fathers to support him in open resistance, and to declare all his colleague's doings invalid. He was met with a mournful silence: the days of Nasica and Opimius were over; no one offered to arm his clients and go forth to save the state. The veterans of Pompey and the mob of Cæsar seemed too formidable.

So Bibulus shut himself up in his house, and contented himself with posting a daily placard, to the effect that he was "observing the heavens," and that it was therefore impossible that any legal meeting of the Comitia could take place. By the letter of the law he was undoubtedly right, and every bill that passed during the remainder of the year B.C. 59 was null and void. But what was to be done if the bills were not only carried but obeyed? The wits of Rome called the time "the consulship of Julius and of Cæsar," in derision of the unfortunate Bibulus. It would have been more correct to call it not a consulship at all, but a fine specimen of a tyranny.

Cæsar meanwhile went on in his reckless career, passing bills good, bad, and indifferent. Some of them were excellent administrative measures; others—such as the ratification of Pompey's Asiatic *acta*—were eminently proper and justifiable. Others again were shameless bribes to the mob or the Equites. The one which struck contemporary opinion as the most objectionable was that which made a plebeian of Publius Clodius. That detestable young man had given Cæsar good cause of offence by the scandal at the mysteries of the *Bona Dea*, and had forced him (not without reason) to divorce his wife. But the consul bore him no grudge; indeed he seems to have regarded him with a sort of parental affection, as the destined successor who was about to repeat his own early career of political riot and private debauchery. Clodius wished to become a plebeian, in order to qualify for the tribunate. Cæsar indulged him, and proposed himself the *lex curiata* by which the adoption of the young man into a plebeian family was managed. The ceremony was carried out in an irregular, not to say a farcical, fashion. No sanction was procured from the *Pontifices*, the legal notice of three *nundinae* before the meeting of the Curies was not given. The adopter who undertook to make

Clodius his son was a lad of nineteen, one P. Fonteius, who was far younger than Clodius, and unmarried. Yet he was made to profess his want of issue, and the necessity of his adopting a son to continue his race! (As a matter of fact he married not long after, and had many children.) Cæsar carried through the scandalous show, and left Clodius behind him as his agent for the due maintenance of mob law and anarchy during his absence in Gaul.

Early in B.C. 58, the moment that his turbulent consulship was over, Cæsar hurried off to take over charge of the Gallic provinces and their legions. He had secured himself no mere annual governorship, but a long term of five years of command. Such had been the purport of the Vatinian Law, which was drafted on the same lines as the Gabinian and Manilian Laws that had been passed for Pompey's benefit nearly ten years before. Clearly Cæsar thought that five years would be required to enable him to make his name and to frame his army. What he was to do when his term ran out, we may doubt whether he had yet determined. His Spanish command had been a great experiment—his Gaulish one would be an even greater. As yet he cannot have framed any other intention than that of being the greatest man in Rome. Of what sort his predominance was to be, he had probably formed no fixed plan. All would depend on how affairs went in the land of the Celts.

That Cæsar went to Gaul with a fixed intention of carrying the boundaries of the empire to the Rhine and the Ocean there is no reason to doubt. The existing frontier of the Transalpine province was drawn in an illogical and haphazard fashion; beyond it lay tribes in various ill-defined relations of vassalship and amity to Rome. Ever since the Cimbric campaign of Marius, the province had been needing, and always failing to obtain, the hand of a master. But even if Cæsar had arrived with the most pacific intentions, he would have been forced to fight before his governorship was six months old. There were troubles brewing on the eastern frontier of Gaul which were already becoming dangerous, not only to the independent tribes, but to the Transalpine dominions of Rome. The Suevian king Ariovistus with a miscellaneous horde of migratory Germans, compacted from many races, had crossed the Rhine, as the Cimbri had crossed it fifty years before, and was threatening to overrun all Central Gaul. At the same moment the warlike Helvetii were deserting their narrow and mountainous home in Switzerland, with the object of conquering for themselves a more spacious and fertile abode in the valley of the Rhone. No proconsul, however slack and indolent, could have avoided interference in both these movements; to Cæsar they were an absolute godsend, as they provided him with the best possible reasons for enlarging his army and engaging in active hostilities the very moment that he reached his province.

The Gaul and German were enemies well known to the Roman soldier. In marching against them Cæsar had none of the disadvantages which Crassus had suffered when he went forth to meet the unknown tactics of the Parthians. The Gaul, indeed, was one of the most familiar foes of the state; the bands whom Cæsar fought in B.C. 58–51 were precisely similar to those with whom Camillus or Marcellus had contended two or three centuries before. Their gallant but unstable hordes, "more than men at the first onslaught, less than women after a severe repulse," were precisely the sort of troops against whom the steady and untiring legion was most effective. The only really dangerous part of their hosts was the cavalry, formed of the chiefs and their sworn henchmen, who were far superior to any mounted troops of whom Cæsar could dispose when first he went to Gaul. To withstand them he had to enlist "friendlies" of their own nationality, and Spanish mercenaries: a little later Germans also, for the latter were found to be superior to the Gauls themselves in the cavalry arm. As to the tribal levies of infantry, they were difficult to check at their first rush, but when it was spent the individual swordsman with his immense claymore and big shield was not fit to cope, either in a single-handed fencing match or in a large body, with the well-trained legionary. The rank and file understood this as well as Cæsar himself, and their knowledge of the fact was no mean help to their general.

With the Germans it was at first otherwise. The Roman army remembered Arausio quite as well as it remembered Vercellæ, and had an exaggerated respect for the "giants" of the northern forests, and their indomitable pluck. At his first encounter with Ariovistus, Cæsar had many anxious moments. There was a doubt whether the legions could be trusted to do their best: their general acknowledges that when he marched against the German many of his officers showed signs of malingering, and the rank and file began to make their wills—as if they were going forward to certain death. It required a wonderful mixture of tact and firmness on the part of Cæsar to induce his troops to make their first attack on Ariovistus. But when the feat was accomplished the legionary discovered that the Teuton was, if bigger and fiercer, yet even more undisciplined and clumsy than the Celt, and far worse armed. The German tribes, even a century later, had hardly got to the stage of wearing armour or forming an orderly battle array.

Yet both Gaul and German were enemies not to be

despised, and it was no ordinary general who could have set out with a light heart for the deliberate purpose of attacking them in order to win a great military reputation at their expense. Nothing but an ever-pressing, unconquerable ambition could have driven Cæsar to the taking up of such a formidable task.

To give a detailed account of the eight marvellous campaigns, which laid Gaul at the feet of the great proconsul, does not fall within the scope of our task. We are concerned with the character of Cæsar as man and as general, rather than with the annals of his battles and sieges. In the main we must draw our conception of his work in Gaul from his own *Commentaries;* what information we get from other sources is comparatively unimportant. The book was published with a political object—probably it was written in haste during the year B.C. 50 as a vindication and advertisement of the author's doings before the eyes of the Roman public. Yet it compares favourably with most works issued with such a purpose: it is reticent and business-like; there is little self-laudation; the greatness of the author's achievements is not dinned into the reader's ears, but allowed to speak for itself. Moreover, it is difficult to detect in the *Commentaries* any very serious tampering with facts. They give, of course, Cæsar's own view of his wars, but they seem as little marred by a desire to hide reverses or to exaggerate successes as those of any other commander who has ever written the narrative of his own campaigns. The general result of the war speaks for itself. It is sufficient to look at the Roman boundary in B.C. 58 and to compare it with that of B.C. 50, in order to see that the main result of Cæsar's activity was much what he claimed. If minor checks are sometimes glozed over, the final triumph was indubitably complete. It can have been no ordinary conqueror who not merely subdued

Gaul, but left it behind him so thoroughly tamed that, during the subsequent Civil War, the once turbulent tribes made no serious attempt to rise, and to rid themselves of the wholly inadequate garrison which had been left to hold them down.

There were many things which combined to make the conquest of Gaul a less formidable undertaking than it appeared at the first glance. If numerous and warlike, the Celtic tribes were fickle and faction-ridden. A real national sentiment existed, but there were other sentiments which were stronger. Wherever Cæsar went, he found communities which were ready to join him in suppressing their neighbours, either because of ancestral feuds, or because of the self-interest of the moment. Gaul, in the first century before Christ, was much like the Highlands of Scotland in the seventeenth or eighteenth century after Christ. It sufficed that one clan should espouse one rival cause, and its neighbour out of ancient jealousy would take up the other. A power intervening from outside would be certain of support from all the enemies of the dominant tribe or chief of the moment. It has been truly said that Cæsar subdued Gaul by the arms of Gauls, just as Clive or Wellesley subdued India by the arms of Indians. In each case the conqueror had a strong nucleus of national troops in his host, but they would not have sufficed for his task if they had not been supported by thousands of local auxiliaries. Moreover, in each case powerful native states backed the invader. The Aedui and the Remi stood to Cæsar in Gaul much as the Nawabs of Oude and the Carnatic stood to the British in India. Nor was it merely inter-tribal feuds that made the foreigner's work easy. The factions within the several communities were almost as fiercely opposed, and as disloyal to the common weal, as the states in general were disloyal to the national cause of Gaul. A great

THE STATE OF GAUL

proportion of the clans were torn to pieces by feuds between some predominant chief who aimed at regal power, and the rest of the local oligarchy. If the would-be tyrant was a nationalist, the lesser chiefs called in Cæsar to help them—if the oligarchs were nationalists, it was their ambitious rival who made the appeal.

Hence came the futility of the resistance of the Gauls to the great proconsul. They were always betraying each other, the individual sacrificing the tribe, the tribe the nation. So much we gather from Cæsar's own works: to the numerous instances which he gives there must have been many more to be added, of which we have no knowledge. Every one of Cæsar's victories, military or diplomatic, was probably aided by local feuds and jealousies, which an intelligent Gallic witness could easily have explained, but which are omitted in the pages of the *Commentaries*, whose author could only give the situation as it appeared to himself, not as it appeared to his foes. This is the reason why Vercingetorix, a man of real genius, failed to hold together the patriotic confederacy which he had taken such pains to build up. An appeal to Gallic national feeling might rouse the tribes for a moment, but after a few months particularism resumed its sway. Each one of the confederates suspected the rest of doing less than their share, and then, in sulky resentment, resolved not to be exploited for the benefit of the neighbouring states.

It is certain, moreover, that the Gauls, even when they came together in the largest force, cannot have put in line the enormous armies of which the *Commentaries* speak. It is always hard to calculate with accuracy the numbers of a tribal *levée-en-masse*. No doubt Cæsar often doubled or trebled the real figures of the hosts that were opposed to him. The ancients had an even smaller power of estimating or realising large numbers than the men of the present age. If we note the tendency among generals of to-day to swell the figures of savage hordes with whom they have had to deal, we need not doubt that Cæsar was liable to the same failing. Every commander in such wars states his own resources at a minimum, and sees those of the foe through a magnifying glass. No doubt the 200,000 swords of the Belgic army at the battle on the Aisne in B.C. 57, and the 250,000 men whom Vercassivelaunus is said to have led to the relief of Alesia are wild and reckless estimates. Yet probably they represent the numbers which the Gauls believed that they had raised, and which the Romans believed that they had faced. There is no reason to think that Cæsar invented them, or added extra thousands to the figures which were reported to him. The hordes were enormous; there was no certain method of counting them. The conqueror cannot be much blamed for reproducing the current estimate. Nor can we expect him to point out another fact which was certainly a great advantage to him. Of the wild masses which formed the Gallic tribal levies, only a certain proportion were really formidable fighting men. The horse was excellent: the chiefs and their bands of sworn henchmen and "debtors" were gallant and desperate foes. But the main body of a *levée-en-masse* must have consisted of half-armed husbandmen, like the English *fyrd* at Hastings. When the pugnacious and well-armed nobility and their retainers had been killed off in the forefront of the battle, there must have been little power to resist among the ill-equipped horde which formed the bulk of the tribal host.

All this we state to explain Cæsar's triumphs, not to diminish them. If these antecedent advantages had not existed, his task would have been impossible, considering the very modest resources that were at his disposition.

CÆSAR'S CRUELTY IN GAUL

Even when all is conceded, the achievement remains marvellous. It was an intellectual and diplomatic triumph quite as much as a mere series of successful campaigns; for it required even something more than a soldier of genius to carry the business through. Cæsar fought with his brains, utilising the unrivalled knowledge of human weakness and vanity which he had acquired during twenty years of political intrigue at Rome, no less than his military skill. He discovered how to turn to account all the personal and tribal rivalries and jealousies of the Gauls. He knew how to buy and how to retain allies and auxiliaries. He could be a powerful and a liberal friend; but he was also an awe-inspiring enemy. For nothing is more striking in all his career than the way in which this affable and easy-going conqueror had recourse to massacre on the most vast and ruthless scale when he desired to strike terror into his adversaries. The reader of the *Commentaries* shudders at the callous fashion in which their author narrates his deeds of bloodshed, done not from any feeling of honest resentment but out of cold-blooded policy. The Veneti had placed in bonds (not murdered or tortured) some Roman officers whom Cæsar had sent into their territory. For this offence, when they had been attacked and conquered, their whole Senate was put to death, and the rest of the tribe sold as slaves. This was not the worst; there are cases where Cæsar puts it on record that his army slew not only the fighting men of a conquered enemy, but the aged, the women, the infants, every living soul.[1] On other occasions he mutilated many thousands of prisoners by cutting off their right hands.[2] Of the case of the Usipetes and Tencteri, whose fate moved horror and compassion even among Romans,

[1] As at Avaricum in B.C. 52.
[2] As with the garrison of Uxellodunum in B.C. 51.

we have already had occasion to speak, while dealing with the life of Cato. Nothing can give a more sinister effect than Cæsar's own confession, that he received their ambassadors, who came to explain and apologise for a breach of truce, put them in confinement, and then marched without giving further notice against the unfortunate Germans, whom he surprised unarmed, and cut to pieces—to the number of 430,000 souls, according to the account in the *Commentaries*. But the most repulsive of all Cæsar's acts of ruthlessness was one which has no parallel for long-delayed and deliberate cruelty, even in the dismal annals of the Later Republic. When the gallant rebel Vercingetorix freely surrendered himself at Alesia to save the lives of his comrades, Cæsar would have done nothing strange or improper if he had ordered him to be put to death on the spot. The Arvernian himself expected no less. But for the conqueror to commit him to prison for *six years*, and then to bring him out at his triumph, parade him through the streets of Rome, and duly execute him in the Tullianum, shows a mixture of callousness and vanity for which no words of reproof are sufficiently hard.

After this, Cæsar's admirers persist in telling us that he was naturally clement;[1] they point to the fact that during the Civil War he very rarely put to death one of his captives,[2] and show that he pardoned some of his most irritating opponents when they fell into his hands. Remembering his awful doings in Gaul, we are driven to believe that his clemency was but a policy or a pose.

---

[1] Twice in the *Commentaries* he gives himself handsome testimonials for his clemency.

[2] But the cases of Lucius Cæsar and others may be remembered. It is suspicious that in so many cases Cæsar's soldiers are said to have put to death important prisoners, *e.g.* Faustus Sulla and Afranius, without their master's leave, and contrary to his intention

Sulla had tried the method of Proscriptions, and it had been a failure. Warned by his experience, Cæsar may have made up his mind to adopt the opposite policy in its most complete form. The Ides of March bear witness that this experiment also had its disadvantages. Augustus reverted to the methods of Sulla, but had the art to throw most of the odium on his colleague, Mark Antony.

In the actual details of Cæsar's strategy and tactics in Gaul there is much that is interesting; at first sight they seem to involve some curious puzzles and contradictions. On the one hand he was, of all the great generals whom the world has seen, the one who made the greatest use of the spade. In a single campaign he would throw up more field entrenchments than Napoleon or Hannibal constructed in the whole of their military careers. This tendency is usually the mark of a cautious commander, and has for the most part gone along with slow movements, small risks, and a preference for the defensive. But this same Cæsar, who on some occasions stockaded himself up to the eyes, and fortified every inch of ground that he covered, blossomed out at other times into the most reckless ventures. He would fly across the land with marches of almost incredible rapidity, risk undertakings that combined the maximum of danger with the minimum of profit, and stake his whole career on the most audacious strokes, all in the style of Charles XII. of Sweden. There is, however, no real incongruity in his actions. It has only to be remembered that his final object was not so much the conquest of Gaul, as the building up for himself of an unrivalled military reputation and a devoted army. His methods differed according to the necessities of the moment, political as well as military, and he was not the slave of any one system of tactics. One does not associate him with any particular order of battle, as we associate Alexander with the advance in *échelon* with the cavalry leading, or Frederic the Great with his famous "oblique order," or Napoleon with the intense artillery preparation followed by a blow with heavy columns at one critical point of the adversaries' line. Cæsar was the least monotonous in his tactics of all the great generals whom the world has seen. There is probably in this a trace of the fact that he was essentially an amateur of genius, who had taken to war late in life, and not a soldier steeped from his youth upwards in the study of the drill-book and the manœuvres of the barrack yard. He worked by the inspiration of the moment, rather than by the aid of the maxims of experience and the traditions of Roman military art.

But, speaking generally, we may say that before he had thoroughly come to know the exact strength and value of his enemy, and when no stake of vital importance was in question, Cæsar was usually cautious. In B.C. 58, while he was still new to his legions, and while Gaul and German were still known to him by repute only, he used the spade with untiring energy, and risked as little as he possibly could. His first military act in Gaul was to fortify lines of enormous length against the Helvetii. When he first met Ariovistus he would not stir far from his camp, and entrenched every point that he seized. It was much the same when he made his earliest acquaintance with the Belgæ on the Aisne. He checkmated them by his impregnable position, and held them at bay till they dispersed. In the campaign about Alesia, in a similar way, he executed field-works of enormous length and magnitude, making ditch and palisade serve in place of the numbers that were insufficient, because he had not really the force required to perform the double operation of holding Vercingetorix blockaded and of keeping back the army of relief. But even the Alesian circumvallation and contravallation seem small things compared with the interminable lines which Cæsar erected along the hills above Dyrrhachium during the campaign of B.C. 48.

When, however, Cæsar was driven into a corner, or when he was forced to choose between compromising his reputation and career by a retreat and running a grave risk, he repeatedly staked everything on a single blow. There often arises a moment in war when a commander has to decide between a movement which will be ruinous if it fails, but decisive of the whole campaign if it succeeds, and another which is safe but indecisive. A general who is fighting merely to defend a frontier, or to hold an enemy in check, naturally chooses the latter course. But Cæsar, who was aiming at establishing a reputation and winning a dominant position among his fellow-countrymen, often chose to accept the risk; a thoroughly unsuccessful campaign, even if accompanied with no crushing defeat, would have lowered his prestige so much that his career would have been blighted. He preferred rather to hazard everything on a bold stroke: if he had failed, he would probably have chosen not to survive the day. But fortune was ever his friend, and the possible disaster never came, though it was often deserved. Cæsar did not talk of his "star" (though his friends invented one for him after his death), but he had more reason to be grateful for unearned pieces of luck than any other great general in the world's history. He might well have seen his career wrecked when he was surprised by the Nervii on the Sambre, or when he was beset by overwhelming numbers on his march to Samarobriva in B.C. 54, or when the lines of Alesia were all but pierced by the army of Vercassivelaunus. Still nearer was the risk at Dyrrhachium, when, before the arrival of his reinforcements, he seemed doomed to inevitable destruction. At Alexandria the peril was quite as great, and far more gratuitously incurred: indeed the whole Egyptian expedition was reckless almost beyond the bounds of sanity. But fortune never failed Cæsar on the battlefield. It seemed that he could not perish by the sword: the dagger was his appointed doom.

In B.C. 50 Gaul lay completely prostrate before the victor's feet. For the first time he could turn his complete attention to Roman politics, without the fear of being distracted by some dangerous rebellion within his province. This was the greatest of all Cæsar's strokes of luck, for the breach with Pompey and the Senate was clearly at hand, and every man of whom he could dispose would be wanted on the Rubicon. It passes our conception to guess what might have happened if Vercingetorix had but delayed his great rising for two years, and the general revolt of the Gauls had occurred in B.C. 50 instead of in B.C. 52. The declaration of open war by the Optimate party might have reached Cæsar at the moment of some check, like that which he suffered before Gergovia, or in the midst of a long protracted siege like that of Alesia. He could never have concentrated his army to march on Italy: it would have been completely tied up in the difficult Gallic operations. Apparently the whole course of the world's history would have been changed if the Arvernian chief had been a little more dilatory in his organisation of the great national league.

But as things actually went, Cæsar was as well prepared for the struggle as he could ever hope to be when the final crisis came. His adversaries had even been good enough to supply him with a plausible *casus belli*, and to refuse with contumely the many specious proposals for a pacification which he made to them. That he had ever seriously intended that these proposals should be accepted it is hard to believe. In return for a mere permission to stand in his absence for the consulship of B.C. 48, he had offered to give up the Transalpine province and eight of his legions. If the Optimates had accepted the terms, he must either have found some excuse for drawing back from his plighted word, or have been ruined by keeping it. The only possible deduction seems to be that he was well aware that his enemies would refuse every offer, however moderate, which he might make to them. His proposals, therefore, were only intended to influence public opinion, and to cause Cato, Pompey, and their friends to appear in the character of the foes of a reasonable peace. This was the actual result of the negotiations: he was able to pose as a well-meaning citizen, driven into war against his will, and to claim that the passage of the Rubicon was a mere act of self-defence. His ingenious pleas will not stand examination—least of all his solemn complaint that the Optimates had violated the constitution by disregarding the vetos of his friends, the tribunes Antony and Cassius. To any one who remembers how Cæsar himself had treated tribunes and their vetos during his consulship in B.C. 59, it must appear ludicrous that he should urge this particular grievance against his adversaries.

We have already, when dealing with the life of Pompey, explained the meaning of Cæsar's short and brilliant Italian campaign. He had seen that at this particular moment rapidity was the one chance of success. Without waiting even for his own main body to come up, he had charged down into Italy with headlong speed, and struck his blow before the enemy could mobilise. Not only was he himself in his happiest vein, but fortune was even more propitious than usual, and his adversaries played into his hands. The folly of Domitius wrecked the last chance of the Optimates, and in the short nine weeks between December 16, B.C. 50, and February 20, B.C. 49, he had cleared the enemy out of the whole peninsula. He had seized Rome, whose possession conferred a false air of legality on its master, and at the same time he had occupied the whole recruiting ground where Pompey had intended to raise those legions which were "to start from the earth when he stamped his foot."

Yet this was but the first act of the drama. Cæsar's position was most precarious: there was a widespread impression that his first success would be followed by massacres, in the style of those by which Marius and Sulla had celebrated their capture of Rome. No one had forgotten that Cæsar's name had once been linked with that of Catiline. To cast a glance around the circle of his lieutenants was anything but reassuring. Assembled around him were all the notorious profligates and bankrupts of the day, Mark Antony and Curio, Cælius and Dolabella, Vatinius and the rest. They were a sinister crowd: Cicero called them the νεκυία, the troop of vampires. That any conqueror with such a past as Cæsar, surrounded by such a gang of reprobates, could be intending less than wholesale murder and confiscation seemed hardly possible. It took a long time to convince the Romans that they were not to expect "red ruin and the breaking up of laws," and meanwhile public opinion would have welcomed the return of the respectable Pompey, even though his Optimate friends were certain to make a clean sweep of the Cæsarians when they came back victorious.

It was necessary to strike a second blow, as hard as the first had been, if Cæsar was to retain what he had won. If he lingered at Rome the seven Pompeian legions from Spain would soon be heard of in the valley of the Po, and Pompey himself, the moment that he had collected a respectable army in Epirus, might descend from his ships on some unexpected point of the Italian seaboard. Cæsar had but two advantages—the central position, and the fact that he had a veteran army already mobilised, while his foes were but drawing their levies together. More than most generals he appreciated the value of time. His one chance was to beat his adversaries in detail before they could combine,—even before they could get into communication and settle on a common plan of campaign. It was certain that Pompey could not be ready for many months; on the other hand, the army in Spain was fit to move at once, but was commanded by men whose measure Cæsar had taken long before—commonplace soldiers without a stroke of genius. Hence came the dictator's determination to make a dash at Spain in the spring, with the hope of destroying, or at least of defeating and disabling, Afranius and Petreius, before Pompey could assemble an army in Epirus with which a general of his cautious character would dare to assault Italy.

It was a most hazardous plan, for if Pompey had but risen to the occasion and cast off his methodical ways, he would have found Rome and Italy weakly garrisoned against an attack. But fortune was, as usual, in Cæsar's camp. Afranius and Petreius advanced almost to the foot of the Pyrenees to meet him, and allowed themselves to be out-manœvured, beaten, and taken prisoners at Ilerda (July 2, 49). The Pompeian army of Spain was almost annihilated: only in remote corners of the Iberian peninsula did resistance linger on. Completely freed from the fear of an attack upon his rear by the Pompeians of the West, Cæsar could hurry back to Italy to face the Optimate army in Epirus, which was at last growing formidable in numbers, and beginning to acquire a certain military value. It mattered little to him that, while he was victorious at Ilerda, his lieutenant Curio had lost his life and his army while executing a daring but unlucky attack on the Pompeians in Africa.

The Spanish business had been hazardous, for all

might have gone wrong for Cæsar if only his opponents
had refused to fight him, and had adopted guerilla tactics
after the fashion of Sertorius. Had they refused battle,
and withdrawn into the mountains with their forces
intact, Cæsar would have been left in a quandary. If he
pursued them and was drawn into a long campaign, Italy
might well have been lost behind his back. If, on the
other hand, he had refused to commit himself to operations in the interior of Spain, and had gone back to Italy
with his reserves, he could not have spared an army
sufficient to hold back the Pompeian generals. They would
have driven in any covering force that he might leave
behind, and have once more begun to threaten his rear.
But they fought and were annihilated. Again Cæsar had
been granted the one stroke of fortune that could save
him.

Yet he had to hurry from risk to risk. If there had
been dangerous possibilities in Spain, those which followed
in Epirus were still more threatening. Some of the
dangers were of his own making; nothing can excuse the
recklessness with which he flung his troops across the sea
before he had transports enough to carry them all at one
voyage. It was, no doubt, an advantage to be able to cross
the straits before Pompey's admirals, who fancied that
all armies must necessarily go into winter quarters in
November, had begun to suspect him of any such intention. But the compensating disadvantage of being
obliged to leave behind nearly half his army for want of
shipping was greater. The second division could not
follow him, when the Optimate fleet proceeded to
blockade Brundisium. Cæsar had to maintain himself in Epirus, with seven weak legions and a handful
of cavalry, for nearly three months. By land the
superior forces of Pompey held him in check. On the
side of the sea he was watched by the squadron which

cut his communication with Italy. It was a miracle that he was not destroyed; it required all his good luck to aid his consummate generalship. Once he thought that even his luck had failed him; this was on the occasion when he made his celebrated attempt to run across to Italy in a small open boat, in order to hurry up his reserves at any risk and at all costs. He got out to sea, but his sailors could not face the storm, in spite of his well-known adjuration to them to "fear nothing, for they carried Cæsar and his fortunes." The vessel was beaten back to shore, and the great general had to stave off apparently inevitable disaster for some weeks more, till, in the middle of February, Antony at last succeeded in eluding the Pompeian fleet, and came over to Epirus. How nearly the squadron of the future triumvir came to disaster we have told in an earlier chapter. But after suffering the extreme of peril he reached Epirus and joined his master. Even then the game was not won. There followed the long and well-contested struggle at the lines in front of Dyrrhachium, the most wonderful piece of spade-work in the wars of the ancient world. Modern history has nothing to compare to it except the long contest in 1864–65 between Grant and Lee, in their interminable entrenchments around Richmond and Petersburg, which stretched out to even greater length than those of Cæsar and Pompey. But the struggle in Epirus differed in one extraordinary point from the struggle in Virginia; here it was the general with the smaller veteran army who tried to enclose his opponent by running field-works round his flanks and reducing him to starvation. Even Cæsar could not carry out such an astonishing plan. He failed with heavy loss, and Pompey broke loose, and seemed for a moment victorious. It was perhaps the greatest of all Cæsar's military achievements that he succeeded in drawing off from his shattered lines without a fatal disaster. But the moment must have been a bitter one to him; it was his first defeat on a large scale, and it was hard to see how it could be retrieved. He had no base on which to retreat, he had no large reinforcements to expect, he was still cut off from Italy by the Pompeian fleet. The sudden march into Thessaly with which he ended the campaign round Dyrrhachium must have been the council of despair. If Pompey failed to follow him into the interior, and chose instead to ship himself over into undefended Italy, the game was lost. Cæsar had no fleet in which to follow his rival, and it would have profited him little to take Thessalonica or to ravage Greece.

But once more fortune came to the aid of the great adventurer. Pompey refused to make the bold stroke and to sail for Italy; he followed his enemy across the mountains and offered him battle at Pharsalus. Ruined by the misbehaviour of his numerous cavalry, with which he had hoped to ride down the Gallic legions, he saw his army break and fly, and rode off the field a ruined man.

Pharsalus made Cæsar master of the world. The game was at last in his hands, and he had but to hunt down the scattered remnants of the Pompeian party, who maintained a hopeless resistance in the remoter provinces. That the Civil War lingered on for another three years was due not so much to the truly Roman obstinacy of the surviving Optimates, as to Cæsar's inexplicable divagation to Egypt. There was no need to chase the forlorn little band which followed Pompey down to the mouth of the Nile; but if the enterprise were taken in hand, it was foolhardy to set out with but one single legion. The East might have been safely neglected for the present; the real objective for the Cæsarian host was Africa, the one region where the enemy had still a considerable force under arms. If the victor of Pharsalus had started at once to deal with Scipio and King Juba, he might easily have finished the war ere the year B.C. 48 was out. Five months of the summer and autumn were still before him, and the news of Pompey's hopeless disaster had struck terror into his foes. But Cæsar chose to go off to Egypt, where he was busy for eight precious months on a trifling and unnecessary task, which became difficult and dangerous merely because he essayed it with wholly inadequate resources. If he had taken three legions instead of one to Alexandria, there would have been no Egyptian war. The whole episode is unworthy of Cæsar; the conqueror of Gaul should not have placed himself in the position to be besieged for months by a Levantine rabble, and saved by an Oriental condottiere like Mithradates of Pergamus. Still less should he have lapsed into his silly and undignified entanglement with Cleopatra. It was his Alexandrian dangers and dalliance which allowed his adversaries in the west and south to recover their spirits and rally their armies. If he had sailed for Africa in August, B.C. 48, Thapsus would have been fought eighteen months sooner, and Munda would never have been fought at all. For southern Spain only slipped out of Cæsar's hands after Pharsalus had been won; and if Africa had been reduced in the autumn of B.C. 48, the two sons of Pompey would never have had their chance of recovering Baetica, and rallying all the last desperate adherents of their father's cause for one final stand in the west. Cæsar owed it entirely to his own carelessness that he was nearly "beaten by boys" at Munda, where (as he had to confess) "for the first time in his life he was forced to fight, not for victory, but for his bare life." In short, it must be owned that during the latter years of the Civil War, Cæsar as tactician was as great as ever, but Cæsar as political strategist was reckless and overweening. He seems to have grown so confident in his own skill and luck that he did not take the trouble to use common precautions, to turn all his strength to account, or to take his enemies seriously. Indeed, after Dyrrhachium and Pharsalus, all should have been child's-play to him; if it was not, the fault lay with himself.

But at last, after Munda, his "crowning mercy," as Cromwell would have called it, Cæsar found no more enemies to subdue, and made his final return to Rome. He set out for the city in July, B.C. 45; he was only destined to survive till the Ides of March, B.C. 44. Of Cæsar as soldier we have said enough: it only remains to consider him as the master of the world and the founder of the Imperial system. What are we to make of the few months of supreme power, during which he was at last settled down in the city,[1] and laying the foundation for a permanent settlement of the Roman world?

Suetonius and Plutarch have preserved for us a large number of details concerning his civil activity in these months. One thing is undoubted. It was pure autocracy, and no mere modification of the republican constitution, that he intended to introduce. Unlike Sulla, whose career was in so many ways the antitype of his own, Cæsar had fought and conquered not for his party but for himself. There was, in fact, no longer a Democratic party—the very name of party implies the existence of a body of persons who agree to act together for some common political end. But the Cæsarians were nothing of this sort, they were simply the hired servants of the dictator, who humbly carried out his orders without any attempt to criticise or to understand them. The one man of the faction who showed a spirit of his own perished miserably. This was the headstrong Cælius Rufus, who against his employer's orders raised an old Democratic cry—*novae tabulae*, the

[1] He had also been in Rome during the winter of 47-6, before Munda.

abolition of debts—and tried to carry out some of the anarchic designs which had been dear to Catiline. Cæsar was absent from Rome himself, but his agents saw to the suppression of Cælius. He was deposed from his praetorship, whereupon he fled into the south of Italy, and raised bands of slaves and debtors in the true Catilinarian style, enlisting as his lieutenant the old Optimate bravo, Milo. The rebellion proved a fiasco, and the rebels were destroyed by a regiment of Gallic horse. Those who had joined Cæsar in the mere hope of plunder and proscriptions were thus warned that it was their master's programme, not their own, that was to be carried out. Those, on the other hand, who remained faithful to him, were rewarded by huge gifts of money and estates, sufficient to pay off all their debts; but they were not indulged with the *novae tabulae*, which would have frightened the Equestrian Order and all the capitalists whom the dictator was anxious to conciliate. However disappointed they may have been at seeing that they were to be the well-paid hirelings of their leader, and not his colleagues or councillors, the Cæsarian gang had to accept the position.

A vast amount of praise has been bestowed upon Cæsar for introducing good and firm government into Italy, when it had been expected that his triumph would be followed by plunder and proscriptions. But it is only a savage, or a man who has injuries to avenge, who would deliberately choose to slay those whom he might safely spare, or to destroy riches which he might safely utilise. Cæsar was not in the position of Marius or Sulla; he had not been hunted round Italy by his foes like the former, nor did he return to find Rome red with the blood of his friends like the latter. He had taken the city almost before a blow had been struck in the Civil War, and had no tangible injuries to avenge; the hustling of his tribunes and his own outlawing would hardly have been made a convincing excuse for a general massacre. Indeed, the leading Optimates had evacuated Rome, and it would have been on men of small importance, or on "moderates," like Cicero, that a proscription must have fallen. Again, a general confiscation of property would have thrown Rome and Italy into chaos and bankruptcy. But Cæsar wished to have as much money at his disposal as possible, for the equipment of the great armies that he was raising. Clearly, from the most selfish point of view, it was wiser for him not to throw the financial world into a crisis, and thereby to make enemies of all the capitalists who had not retired in the company of Pompey. There is no need to praise the magnanimity of one who acts from enlightened self-interest, and this would appear to have been the case with Cæsar. So is it also with his good government, both in Italy and in the provinces. When once he had established his domination, it was to his advantage that he should rule over a wealthy and a contented rather than over a poor and disloyal empire.

There is this difference between the rule of an autocrat and that of an oligarchy, that in the first case the ruler's individual gain is best secured by the prosperity of his subjects, while in the second the personal interest of each member of the oligarchy may lead him to "feather his nest" to the grave detriment of the state, because his legitimate share of the profits of empire is comparatively a small one. It was in Rome in Cæsar's day much as it was in France in the day of Bonaparte. The "Directory" whom the Corsican superseded were infinitely worse rulers than he, because their personal interest did not, like his, coincide with the interest of the majority of the French people. The change was undoubtedly beneficial to the country at large, yet we do not therefore regard Bonaparte as entitled to an enthusiastic moral approval. Any despot who is not a lunatic will adopt the same programme, so far as he is able.

This being understood, we may grant that the practical benefits conferred by Cæsar alike on the City and the Empire were enormous. If he had done nothing more than put an end to the turbulence of the Roman streets, by the institution of his *præfectus urbi* backed by armed cohorts, it would have been a considerable boon. It was something that he cut down the number of the recipients of the corn-dole—though since he had posed as a Democrat he could not abolish it altogether. Still better was it to persuade as many of the citizens as possible to go forth to transmarine colonies. But any successful despot must have taken all these measures: to keep an armed force in the capital, to endeavour to distract the energies of the multitude into colonisation, were devices as old as Periander and Dionysius. As to the settlements inside the peninsula, which Cæsar planned out for his veterans, they do not seem to have been much more successful than the earlier attempts of the Democrats. Agriculture in Italy, south of the Rubicon, was ruined beyond redemption. As to the legislation concerning debt and "luxury" which the dictator introduced, we cannot take it very seriously: it was a case of "Satan rebuking Sin." His own licentious extravagance in his youth, and the astounding loads of indebtedness which he had contracted, prevented him from attacking the problem with any moral weight. "No man can be made good by Act of Parliament," still less by the rescript of an autocrat. A moral reformation in the governing classes of the state was the only possible road to reform, and a Cæsar was not the man to start such a movement. Bad as was the general tone of the Roman aristocracy in the first century B.C., it was to be worse in the first century A.D. Servility to the omnipotent Emperor was added to the other vices which they had previously displayed. In short, the Cæsarian laws were palliatives for the moment; they had no ameliorating force for the future.

In the Provinces there can be no doubt that the new monarchy was far more effective and benevolent than in the City. The fact that the governors were made responsible to a wary autocrat, instead of to corrupt law-courts and a feeble Senate, improved the lot of the subjects of Rome to an incalculable extent. It was to Cæsar's interest that the provincials should be wealthy and contented, and therefore the oppresive governor and the swindling *publicanus* had to be kept in check and punished. The dictator did not himself live long enough to set the centralised system in proper working, but the mere fact that he had established a monarchy made the improvement inevitable. The reforms of Augustus were but the necessary corollary of his great-uncle's triumph. It was the same with the internal organisation of the empire: Cæsar wished to rule willing rather than disloyal subjects: hence came his endeavours to encourage municipal patriotism, to open a Roman career to prominent provincials (he even made senators of many Gauls and Spaniards), to develop new towns, and to strengthen old ones by his numerous colonies.

All, and more than all, that he had planned was carried out by Augustus, and the first century of the empire was undoubtedly a period of material prosperity in the Mediterranean lands such as had never been known in the days of the Republican *régime*. But it must be remembered that it was purely material—Cæsar could give no moral impulse to the world. The empire was a time of lost ideals, because its founder was himself a man who had lived down, or had never possessed, any governing enthusiasm, save that of personal ambition. Nations, like men, need an aim and an ideal to keep them sound. The mere enjoyment of good administrative government is wholly inadequate to create or preserve real moral energy. And it is hard to see what the Roman of the empire which Cæsar created had to live for. Religion could not help him; indeed it barely existed. Cæsar himself was a sceptic; his great-nephew—equally irreligious at heart—served out to his subjects the archaistic revival of old ceremonial worship, and the hollow cult of *Divus Julius*. In neither of them was there the least breath of reality. The only moral force that existed for the subjects of the empire was the Stoic philosophy, which influenced but a few choice spirits, and at the best was but a counsel of despair—to keep the soul free and unpolluted if the body was doomed to servitude and misery. It was a philosophy for the individual, not for the state; its ground-idea was that the times were evil, and that the good man could do no more than preserve his own self-respect. In an empire which pretended to have restored the Golden Age, the holding of such views was almost treasonable in itself.

Where neither religion nor philosophy can serve to maintain a healthy spirit and a moral basis for society, a vigorous national patriotism has sometimes served as a substitute. But the empire destroyed patriotism; it was cosmopolitan in its tendencies, and swamped the narrow but very real devotion to the city, which had been the main source of the strength of the earlier republic. Patriotism needs stress and adversity to develop its best features. It almost presupposes that the state has dangerous enemies, and aspirations that have yet to be fulfilled. But under the empire the Romans absorbed all their old neighbours and foes; Syrian and Spaniard, Briton and Numidian, were all made Romans of a sort. There was no peril from the external barbarian for two hundred years. The Parthian Empire was slowly dwindling in strength; the Germans had not yet learnt to combine; they might perhaps check an invading army, but they could be no serious danger to the state. In short, there was no adequate object against which the patriotic impulse could be directed, and it gradually dwindled away into a vague and unfruitful pride. When external matters at last became serious, in the third century after Christ, there is no trace whatever of any sense of national duty among the heterogeneous "Romans" of the day. The bureaucracy, which the empire had bred, and the professional army, had to face the storm from the North without any support from the indifferent masses. What more could they have hoped, when the individual citizen was debarred from politics, and invited to entrust all his cares to the divine autocrat who had superseded the Senate and People?

Cæsar, in short, put an end to urban sedition and provincial misgovernment. But he and his great-nephew gave the world, instead of its old anarchy, a period of mere soulless material prosperity. If the Barbarians had never resumed the attack from without, if Christianity had never arisen to give new ideals from within, the Roman Empire would have gradually sunk into a self-satisfied stationary civilisation of the Chinese type. Whether it be considered as a despotism or as a bureaucracy, it was a magnificent failure. Already by the end of the second century, before the German attack grew dangerous, it had lapsed into moral and physical impotence. On the civil side it was over-governed and over-taxed; on the military side it had developed a denationalised army, which had begun to sell the diadem to the highest bidder. It is hardly necessary to recall the fact that between the death of Commodus and the accession of Diocletian—a period of no more than ninety years—some thirty emperors (not

THE PROBLEMS OF MONARCHY

to speak of unrecognised usurpers and "tyrants") came to violent ends at the hands of their own soldiery. The first Cæsar "had taken the sword"—a clear majority of his successors "perished by the sword."

What Julius himself intended to make of the empire we can but guess. He was cut off before he had made his intentions clear. His plans, we cannot doubt, were still in the process of development when he was cut off by the hands of Brutus and Cassius. He had enjoyed less than a year of complete sovereignty, and was still in the stage of trying experiments. Probably he designed to take the name of king: probably he intended to make his power hereditary, for he had adopted his great-nephew Octavian, and had begun to train him as his heir and successor. He was dealing with Senate and People in the true vein of the autocrat; to the one he was issuing undisguised commands, the other he was beginning to ignore as a factor in the constitution. Probably his heir had read his intentions, and we may interpret the plan of Julius by its execution under Augustus. The dictator was always an opportunist who watched the times with a wary eye; he had withdrawn his first tentative grasp at the diadem, and was still wearing the *imperator's* laurel wreath when he perished. But there can be little doubt that his purpose was deferred and not renounced. He had still far to go when the daggers of the conspirators intervened, and restored for a short space the anarchy which they called liberty. Yet if his work was not complete, he had at least done so much that the Republic could never be restored. He had worked out to its logical end the movement which Tiberius Gracchus had begun, which Marius had continued, which Sulla had vainly striven to stem, and which Pompey had unwittingly furthered. The problem of sovereignty had been solved; neither Senate nor People could rule the empire, and the inevitable autocrat had taken over the powers which they had abused. Whither autocracy would lead neither he nor any of his contemporaries could have foreseen. A new chapter in the world's history had been begun, but no more than its opening lines had been written when the great dictator perished on the fatal Ides of March.

INDEX

N.B.—*Romans are indexed under the name by which they are best known, e.g. C. Julius Cæsar under Cæsar, but Gn. Pompeius Magnus under Pompey.*

ABGARUS, his treacherous advice to Crassus, 197
Achillas, murders Pompey, 287
Aedui, allied to Cæsar, 316
Æmilianus, P. Cornelius, put to death by Pompey, 242
Afranius, L., defeated by Cæsar in Spain, 327
Africa, province of, annexed, 5; colonial scheme of C. Gracchus in, 61, 75; of Saturninus in, 99; conquered by Pompey, 240; conquered by Cæsar, 230, 331
Ager Publicus, the, its history, 25–26; *see* Agrarian Laws
Agrarian Laws, of Ti. Gracchus, 27–31; renewed by C. Gracchus, 60; of Saturninus, 100; of Drusus, 105; of Rullus, 180–181; of Cæsar, 335
Agriculture, decline of Italian, 15–20, 90–91; *see* Agrarian Laws
Ahenobarbus, L. Domitius stands for the consulship, 222; captured by Cæsar at Corfinium, 282
Alesia, siege of, by Cæsar, 322
Alexandria, Cæsar at, 331
Antistius, C., praetor, saves the life of Pompey, 238; murdered, 240
Antonius, M., orator, slain by Marius, 128
Antonius, C. (Hybrida), prosecuted by Cæsar, 295
Antonius, M. Creticus, foiled by the Pirates, 249

Antonius, M. (the Triumvir), assists Cæsar, 326, 329
Antullius, Q., murdered by the Democrats, 79–80
Aquae Sextiae, battle of, 97
Aquilius, M', Governor of Asia, 64
Arausio, victory of the Cimbri at 96
Archelaus, defeated by Sulla, 131 134
Ariovistus, defeated by Cæsar, 314
Armenia, Pompey subdues, 257
Asia, province of, 6; annexed by Rome, 37; the tithe-farming system introduced in, 67; revolts to Mithradates, 68; reorganised by Sulla, 136; his arrangements in, 155; the tithe-system restored by Pompey and Crassus, 175
Ateius, P., his opposition to Crassus, 195
Athens, captured by Sulla, 130–131
Attalus III., bequeaths his kingdom to Rome, 37
Augustus (C. Julius Cæsar Octavianus), designated as his heir by Cæsar, 331; his administrative system, 336
Avaricum, massacre at, 319
Aventine, Mt., battle on the, 83–84

BELGÆ, Cæsar's campaign against the, 318, 322

Bestia, L. Calpurnius, his misconduct in Africa, 93
Bibulus, M. Calpurnius, colleague of Cæsar in the consulship, oppressed by him, 217, 310; heads Pompey's fleet, 227-228
Blossius, C., the tutor of Ti. Gracchus, 24, 45
Bocchus, king of Numidia, surrenders Jugurtha to Sulla, 120-121
Brundisium, Sulla at, 140; besieged by Cæsar, 282
Brutus, L. Junius Damasippus, massacres the Optimates, 142; defeated and slain by Sulla, 144
Brutus, M. Junius, defeated and executed by Pompey, 242
Byzantium, Cato at, 218-219

CÆLIUS, M. Rufus, slain for opposing Cæsar, 333
Caepio, Q. Servilius, defeated at Arausio, 96
Cæsar, C. Julius, his early life, 292-295; his political début, 295; seized by Pirates, 296; aids in passing the Gabinian Law, 250; his connection with Catiline, 299; aids Metellus Nepos, 212; his governorship in Spain, 306-307; forms the First Triumvirate, 309; his first consulship, 310-311; his Gallic campaigns, 315-322; at the Conference of Lucca, 273; his breach with Pompey, 278-279; commences the Civil War, 280; his Italian campaign, 281-282; his first Spanish campaign, 327; his Epirot campaign, 284; his Egyptian campaign, 331; his African campaign, 331; his settlement of the empire, 335-337; personal characteristics of, 288-291
Cæsar, L. Julius, enfranchises the Italians, 111; murdered by the Democrats, 128
Campus Martius, Lepidus defeated in, 164
Caninius L. Gallus, aids Pompey, 271

Capua, projected colony of C. Gracchus at, 61; of Drusus at, 105
Carbo, C. Papirius, democratic leader, 52
Carbo, Gn. Papirius, aids Cinna, 140; resists Sulla, 142; his massacres, 142; driven out of Italy, 145; executed by Pompey, 240
Carrhae, Crassus defeated at, 197-200
Carrinas, C., defeated by Pompey, 239; defeated and slain by Sulla, 144
Carthage, colony at, founded by C. Gracchus, 61
Catilina, L. Sergius, his connection with Crassus, 181-183; and with Cæsar, 299
Cato, M. Porcius, his character and position, 203-205; anecdotes of his youth, 206-207; his military services, 208; reforms the treasury, 209; aids Cicero, 210; opposes Metellus Nepos, 211-212; aids Bibulus against Cæsar, 217; sent to Cyprus by Clodius, 218; heads the extreme Optimates, 221; his proposal to impeach Cæsar, 223; encourages Pompey to resist Cæsar, 226; his part in the campaign in Epirus, 227; retires to Africa, 229; his suicide at Utica, 231-232
Catulus, Q. Lutatius, defeats the Cimbri, 121; massacred by Marius, 128
Catulus, Q. Lutatius, junior, a prominent Optimate, 162; defeats Lepidus, 164
Censorship, the, Sulla's dealings with, 153; restored by Crassus and Pompey, 176
Chaeronea, Sulla's victory at, 131-132
Cicero, M. Tullius, supports the Manilian Law, 255; opposes Catiline, 183; his attitude toward Crassus, 185; his futile attempts to conciliate Pompey

188; quarrels with Cato, 215; banished by Clodius, 192; his return, 193; his adventure at Corcyra, 228–229
Cilicia, the Pirates of, 8; Sulla's rule in, 121–122; Pompey's conquests in, 253, 258
Cimbri, their victories over the Romans, 95–96; campaign of Marius against, 97–98
Cinna, L. Cornelius, heads the Democratic party, 127; his massacres, 128; his futile legislation, 138; murdered by his soldiers, 140
Claudius, Appius, father-in-law of Ti. Gracchus, 14; a member of the Land Commission, 36
Claudius, P. Pulcher, *see* Clodius
Cleopatra, Cæsar's relations with, 292
Clodius, P. Pulcher, supported by Crassus, 192; drives Cicero into exile, 193; sends Cato to Cyprus, 218; assails and thwarts Pompey, 268, 272; his murder, 277
Colline Gate, battle of the, 143–144
Corcyra, Cato at, 228
Corn-dole, the, instituted by C. Gracchus, 59; increased by Saturninus, 99; and by Drusus, 106; abolished by Sulla, 155; restored in B.C. 70, 176
Corfinium, capture of, by Cæsar, 282
Cornelia (mother of the Gracchi), 14, 58
Cotta, C. Aurelius, uncle of Cæsar, 175, 297
Crassus, L. Licinius, orator, murdered by the Marians, 128
Crassus, M. Licinius, the Triumvir, escapes from the massacres of Marius, 166; joins Sulla, 167; his military exploits, 144; ostracized by Sulla for corruption, 168; his methods of money-making, 169–170; commands against Spartacus, 172; allies himself with Pompey to obtain the consulship, 173; laws carried by them, 175–176; intrigues of during Pompey's absence, 179–182; his relations with Catiline, 182; estranges Cicero from Pompey, 188; forms the First Triumvirate, 190; persecutes Cicero, 193; endeavours to induce Cæsar to desert Pompey, 273; obtains a second consulship, 194; goes to the East, 195; defeated and slain by the Parthians at Carrhae, 199–201

Crassus, P. Licinius, reconciles his father to Cicero, 193; slain at Carrhae, 199
Curio, C. Scribonius, partisan of Cæsar, 326; slain in Africa, 327
Cyprus, annexed by Rome, 218; doings of Cato in, 219

DARDANUS, treaty of, between Sulla and Mithradates, 136
Delos, sacked by the fleet of Mithradates, 129
Delphi, plundered by Sulla, 130
Drusus, M. Livius, opposes and outbids C. Gracchus, 73–74
Drusus, M. Livius, junior, his schemes of reform, 104–105; introduces and carries laws, 107; is thwarted by the Senate, 107; murdered, 108
Dyrrhachium, campaign of Cæsar and Pompey round, 227, 284, 329

EGYPT, the Democrats endeavour to annex it, 180; Pompey offers to go to, 269–270; murder of Pompey in, 287; campaign of Cæsar in, 331
Equester Ordo, the, its early history, 63–64; privileges bestowed on it by C. Gracchus, 65; its misuse of them, 67, 91; attacked by Drusus, 104; Sulla legislates against it, 154–155; its privileges restored by Pompey and Crassus, 175
Etruria, depopulation of, 15; campaigns of Sulla in, 143; of Lepidus in, 164

FANNIUS, C., consul, opposes C. Gracchus, 72

344 INDEX

Favonius, M., friend of Cato, 225
Fimbria, C. Flavius, murders L. Flaccus, 133; invades Asia, 135; slain by his troops, 136
Flaccus, M. Fulvius, endeavours to enfranchise the Italians, 53; his campaign in Gaul, 53; aids C. Gracchus, 70; takes arms, 81; slain by the Optimates, 84
Flaccus, L. Valerius, opposes Sulla, 133; his debt-laws, 138; murdered by Fimbria, 133
Fonteius, P., adopts Clodius, 312
Freedmen, measures of Sulpicius in favour of, 113; dealings of Sulla with, 149
Fregellae, revolt and destruction of, 53

GABINIUS, A., his law to send Pompey against the Pirates, 251–253
Gallæci, campaign of Cæsar against 307
Gaul, conquests of M. Flaccus in, 53; campaign of Marius in, 97; character of its population, 315–317; conquered by Cæsar, 315–322
Glaucia, C. Servilius, demagogue, his career and death, 99–103
Gracchus, Caius Sempronius, his early career, 53–54; obtains the tribunate, 55; his attack on Popilius and Octavius, 57–58; institutes the Corn-dole, 59; his legislature concerning the *Equester Ordo*, 63–65; the Asiatic tithe-farming, 67; concerning roads, 62; his colonial schemes, 69; his desire to enfranchise the Italians, 70–71; opposed by Drusus, 72–73; his schemes frustrated, 74–75; takes arms against the Senate, 81; slain, 85
Gracchus, Tiberius Sempronius, his character and early career, 11–13; his doings in Spain, 14–15; his views on the Agrarian question, 16–19; introduces his Agrarian Law, 27; opposed by Octavius, 31–33; deposes him, 35: carries

his law, 36; its results, 37–38, 49; his popularity decays, 40; he fails to be re-elected tribune, 43; the Optimates take arms against him, 47; his murder, 48
Granius, Q., put to death by Sulla, 161
Greece, campaigns of Sulla in, 130–135

HELVETII, campaign of Cæsar against, 313
Hortensius, Q., his strange marriage, 221

ILERDA, Cæsar's victory at, 327
Isauria, subdued by Pompey, 253; his colonies in, 237
Italian franchise question, the, 69–71; raised by Ti. Gracchus, 41; pressed by Fulvius Flaccus, 53; by C. Gracchus, 71; by Livius Drusus, 107–108; causes the Social War, 109–110; partly settled by the Julian Law, 111; completely settled by the Plautio-Papirian Law, 111; dealings of Sulpicius with the, 113

JERUSALEM, taken by Pompey, 259; its temple plundered by Crassus, 196
Juba, king of Numidia, opposes Cæsar, 331
Judicia, see Jury-Courts.
Jugurtha, his war with Rome, 92–95; his capture by Sulla, 121
Julia, wife of Marius, her funeral, 303
Julia, daughter of C. J. Cæsar, married to Pompey, 266; her death, 278
Junonia (Carthage), colony of, 61
Jury-courts, taken from the Senators and given to the Knights, 64–65; abuses of the, 91; dealings of Drusus with, 105–106; multiplied and restored to the Senators by Sulla, 155; legislation of Pompey and Crassus on, 175

KNIGHTS, *see Equester Ordo*.

INDEX 345

Lælius, C., his views on the Agrarian question, 26
Latins, receives the citizenship, 111
Lentulus, P. Cornelius, friend of Catiline, 176; executed, 210
Lepidus, M. Æmilius, made consul by Pompey's aid, 241; his rebellion and death, 164-165
Lucca, the conference at, 271-273
Luceria, Pompey at, 281-282
Lucullus, L. Licinius, his campaigns against Mithradates, 165; his final failure, 249; opposes the demands of Pompey, 214, 263
Lusitania, Cæsar's campaign in, 307

Macedonia, annexed by the Romans, 5
Mallius, Gn. Maximus, defeated at Arausio, 96
Mamilius, C. Limetanus, impeaches Optimate leaders, 93
Mancinus, C. Hostilius, defeated by the Numantines, 14-15
Manilius, C., carries the law giving Pompey the Eastern command, 254-255
Marius, C., obtains the recall of Metellus, 94; his demagogic arts, 93-94; conquers Numidia, 95; defeats the Cimbri, 97; his intrigues with Saturninus, 98-99; his failure in politics, 103; commands in the Social War, 110; allies himself with Sulpicius, 114; expelled by Sulla, 125; reconquers Rome, 127; his massacres, 128; his death, 128
Marius C., junior, defeated at Sacriportus, 142; death of at Praeneste, 144
Memmius, C., murdered by Saturninus, 101
Merula, L. Cornelius, murdered by the Democrats, 294
Mesopotamia, invaded by Crassus, 196-198
Messius, C., his law in favour of Pompey, 269
Metellus, Q. Caecilius, his campaign in Numidia, 93-94

Metellus, Q. Caecilius Nepos, his strife with Cato, 211-213
Metellus, Q. Caecilius Pius, aids Sulla, 126, 141; his campaigns in Spain, 243, 245
Milo, T. Annius, murders Clodius, 277; slain, 333
Minucius L. Thermus, assists Cato, 213
Mithradates, king of Pontus, conquers Asia from the Romans, 112, 123; conquers Greece, 129; his armies defeated by Sulla, 130-134; makes peace with Sulla, 136; his later wars, 165; his struggle with Lucullus, 249; beaten by Pompey, 257; his death, 259
Mithradates of Pergamus, aids Cæsar, 321
Mummius, Q., aids Ti. Gracchus, 36, 44
Munda, Cæsar's victory at, 331
Muraena, L. Licinius, defended by Cicero, 210; protects Cato, 213
Mytilene, siege of, 295

Nasica, P. Cornelius Scipio, slays Ti. Gracchus, 48-49
Nola, siege of, by Sulla, 115, 123
Nonius, Q., murdered by Saturninus, 101
Norbanus, C., defeated by Sulla, 140-141
Numantia, Ti. Gracchus at, 14-15
Numidia, wars of Metellus and Marius in, 93-94; wars of Cæsar in, 331

Octavianus, C. Julius Cæsar, designated heir by Cæsar, 339
Octavius, Cn., opposes the Democrats, 127; murdered by the Democrats, 128
Octavius, M., opposes Ti. Gracchus, 31; deposed by him, 34; attacked by C. Gracchus, 58
Octavius, M., admiral of Pompey, 228
Ofella, Q. Lucretius, put to death by Sulla, 156
Opimius, L., takes Fregellae, 53;

z

opposes C. Gracchus, 78; puts down the Gracchan insurgents, 83

Orchomenus, battle of, 134

PARTHIANS, Sulla's relation with, 122; Pompey's relation with, 257; attacked by Crassus, 196; defeat him, 198-200

Pelusium, murder of Pompey at, 287

Pergamus, kingdom of, annexed by Rome, 37

Perpenna, M., aids Lepidus, 165; murders Sertorius, 246; put to death by Pompey, 246

Petreius, M., sent to Spain by Pompey, 276; defeated by Cæsar at Ilerda, 327

Pharnaces, deposes his father Mithradates, 260

Philippus L. Marcius, opposes the laws of Drusus, 107; his epigram on Pompey, 243

Piræus, siege of, by Sulla, 130-131

Pirates, their daring during the last century of the Republic, 7; allied to Mithradates and to Spartacus, 249; capture Julius Cæsar, 296-297; suppressed by Pompey, 252-253

Pompeius Q. Rufus, aids Sulla, 124; murdered, 127

Pompeius, Gn. Strabo, his equivocal policy in the Civil War, 237; his death, 238

Pompeius, Gn. Magnus, his early life, 237-238; joins Sulla, 239; conquers Africa, 240; supports Lepidus, 241; his campaign in Cisalpine Gaul, 242; sent to Spain, 243; his war with Sertorius, 245-246; his consulship with Crassus, 174, 248; suppresses the Pirates, 252-253; sent against Mithradates, 254-255; conquers the East, 257; his return to Rome, 187, 261; thwarted by the Optimates, 263; joins the First Triumvirate, 264; his struggle with Clodius, 267; reforms the corn supply, 269; at the conference of Lucca, 273; his second consulship, 274; his estrangement from Cæsar, 276-278; allies himself to the Optimates, 279; driven from Italy by Cæsar, 282; his last campaign in Epirus, 284; defeated at Pharsalus, 285; murdered, 287

Pontius Telesinus, C., Samnite general, slain at the Colline Gate, 143-144

Popilius, C. Laenas, banished by C. Gracchus, 57

Præfectus Urbi, office of, instituted by Cæsar, 335

Praeneste, taken by Sulla, 144

Proscription, the Sullan, 145-146

Ptolemy, Auletes, restored by Gabinius, 271

Quaestiones Perpetuae, see Jury Courts

Quinctius, T., Democratic Leader, 250

RABIRIUS, C. Postumus, prosecuted by Cæsar, 177

Remi, the, aid Cæsar, 316

Rhodians, the, aid Sulla, 130

Roscius, S. Otho, his legislation, 175; opposes the Gabinian Law, 252

Rubicon, Cæsar crosses the, 281

Rufus, see Cælius, Sulpicius, Rutilius

Rullus, P. Servilius, his Agrarian Law, 180-181

Rutilius, Lupus P., commands against the Italians, 109

Rutilius, P. Rufus, his unjust condemnation, 66, 105

SAMNITES, join the Italian revolt, 111; their long resistance, 122; allied to the Democrats, 127; defeated and subdued by Sulla, 145

Sardinia, 5; C. Gracchus in, 54

Satureius, P., murders Ti. Gracchus, 48

Saturninus, L. Appuleius, quarrels

INDEX 347

with the Senate, 98; his alliance with Marius, 99; his political schemes, 199-100; his violence, 101; heads an insurrection, 102; slain, 103
Scævola, Q. Mucius, murdered by Democrats, 142
Scipio Nasica, P., *see* Nasica
Scipio, Q. Metellus, commands against Cæsar in Africa, 229-230
Septimuleius, L., sells the head of C. Gracchus, 86
Sertorius, Q., Marian leader, 163; maintains the war in Spain, 165; his campaigns against Metellus and Pompey, 244-245; murdered by Perpenna, 246
Servile War, the, 165-172; terminated by Crassus, 173
Sibylline books, the, consulted, 271
Silo, Q. Pompædius, his meeting with Cato, 206
Social War, causes of the, 107-108; its character, 109-110; ended by the Plautio-Papirian law, 111
Soli (Pompeiopolis), restored by Pompey, 253
Spain, Roman government in, 5, 8-9; Ti. Gracchus in, 14-15; campaign of Sertorius in, 165, 244-246; governorship of Cæsar in, 306-307; campaign of Cæsar in, 327, 331
Spartacus, his rising, 165-172; slain by Crassus, 173
Statilius, P., friend of Cato, 231
Stoics, the, under the Empire, 337
Sulla, Faustus Cornelius, put to death by the Cæsarians, 320
Sulla, L. Cornelius, his early life, 116-118; serves in Numidia and captures Jugurtha, 120-121; governor of Cilicia, 121-122; fights in the Social War, 122; appointed to command in the East, 123; deposed by Sulpicius, 123; marches on Rome, 124; captures the city, 125; sails for the East, 127; his victorious campaign in Greece, 129-134; forces Mithradates to make peace, 136· his return to Italy, 140;
his campaign against the Democrats, 141-145; his Proscription, 146; reforms the constitution, 147-155; retires from public life, 156; his death, 160-161
Sulpicius, P. Rufus, leads the Democratic party, 113; his schemes, 114; deposes Sulla, 115; attacked and slain by Sulla, 125
Sura, P. Bruttius, resists Mithradates, 129
Syria, ceded by Tigranes to Rome, 257; organised as a province by Pompey, 259

TARENTUM, C. Gracchus founds a colony at, 61
Tarquinius, L., informs against Crassus, 185
Taxiles, defeated by Sulla, 131
Tencteri, massacred by Cæsar, 223, 319-320
Teutons, allied with Cimbri invade Gaul, 96; exterminated by Marius, 97
Thapsus, Cæsar's victory at, 230
Theodotus of Chios, plots the murder of Pompey, 287
Tigranes, king of Armenia, submits to Pompey, 257
Tigranes, junior (son of last), released by Clodius, 268
Tilphossium, Mt., Sulla's victory at, 130
Trebellius, L., endeavours to resist the Gabinian Law, 252
Tribuni Aerarii, placed among the Jurors, 175
Tribuni Plebis, their powers, 28; use of their power by Ti. Gracchus, 29; and by C. Gracchus, 68; Sulla cuts down their authority, 149-150; restored to their former status by Pompey and Crassus, 175
Triumvirate, the First, formed, 190, 264

USIPETES, the, massacred by Cæsar, 223, 319-320

INDEX

Utica, death of Cato at, 230-231
Uxellodunum, atrocities of Cæsar at, 319

VALERIA, wife of Sulla, 160
Varius, Q., persecutes the followers of Drusus, 109
Vatinius, P., passes law giving Cæsar the command in Gaul, 312; aids Cæsar in the Civil War, 326

Veneti, atrocities of Cæsar among the, 319
Vercassivelaunus, opposes Cæsar, 318, 323
Vercellae, victory of Marius at, 97
Vercingetorix, his rebellion, 317; put to death by Cæsar, 320
Volaterrae, siege of, 145

ZIELA, defeat of Triarius at, 249

THE END